MICROBES AND MORALS

ALSO BY THEODOR ROSEBURY

Experimental Air-Borne Infection

Peace or Pestilence

Microorganisms Indigenous to Man

Life on Man

MICROBES AND MORALS

THE STRANGE STORY OF
VENEREAL DISEASE

THEODOR ROSEBURY

The Viking Press / New York

First published in 1971 by The Viking Press, Inc.
625 Madison Avenue, New York, N.Y. 10022

Published simultaneously in Canada by
The Macmillan Company of Canada Limited

SBN 670-47398-7
Library of Congress catalog card number: 72-119781

Printed in U.S.A. by Vail-Ballou Press, Inc.

Acknowledgments: BANTAM BOOKS, INC.: From *The Complete Works of François Villon*, edited and translated by Anthony Bonner. Copyright © 1960 by Bantam Books, Inc. THE CLARENDON PRESS: From *An Alabama Student and Other Biographical Essays* by William Osler, 1908. Reprinted by permission of the Clarendon Press, Oxford. CROWN PUBLISHERS, INC.: From *The Complete Works of Francois Villon*. Translated, with an introduction and notes by J. U. Nicolson. Copyright 1928 by Covici, Friede, Inc., Copyright © renewed 1956 by Crown Publishers, Inc. Used by permission of Crown Publishers, Inc. DOVER PUBLICATIONS, INC.: From *Source Book of Medical History* by Logan Clendening. W. W. NORTON & CO., INC.: From *An American Doctor's Odyssey* by Dr. Victor G. Heiser. Copyright 1936 by Dr. Victor Heiser. Copyright renewed 1963 by Dr. Victor Heiser. Quotations reprinted with the permission of the publisher, W. W. Norton & Company, Inc. G. P. PUTNAM'S SONS: From *Hieronymus Fracastorius* translated by Wilmer Cave Wright. Copyright by Wilmer Cave Wright. Reprinted by permission of G. P. Putnam's Sons.

To lovers of all ages,
especially young ones

. . . the small pox has gone out of late;
Perhaps it may be follow'd by the great.

'Tis said the great came from America;
    Perhaps it may set out on its return,—
The population there so spreads, they say
    'Tis grown high time to thin it in its turn,
With war, or plague, or famine, any way,
    So that civilization they may learn;
And which in ravage the more loathsome evil is—
Their real lues, or our pseudo-syphilis?

—B Y R O N (1818)

AUTHOR'S NOTE

This book is mainly for ordinary people rather than for
specialists or scholars; but I hope both groups will
read it. For the sake of the ordinary people I have
avoided cluttering the text with superscripts and footnotes. For the specialists and scholars I have supplied
notes and a bibliography. The notes include additional details and some statistical material which may
be as important as anything else in the book. They
are keyed forward to page numbers in the text, and,
where necessary, backward to the bibliography, so
that the reader who likes superscripts can easily put
them in himself. A preliminary glance at the back of
the book will show how this has been arranged.

ACKNOWLEDGMENTS

I am alone responsible for putting this book together, for all opinions expressed in it that are not directly attributed to somebody else (sometimes only in the back of the book), and for any errors of fact that may have got by me. But I owe thanks to many people: to Dr. William J. Brown and his group at the VD Branch of the U.S. Public Health Service at its National Center for Disease Control in Atlanta, Georgia; to Dr. T. Guthe, chief medical officer for VD and Treponematoses (a word that will be explained) of the Division of Communicable Diseases of the World Health Organization in Geneva; to Dr. R. R. Willcox, consultant venereologist at St. Mary's Hospital, London; to Dr. Pierre Collart and his colleagues at the Fournier Institute in Paris; and to the uncounted researchers who sent me reprints of their work, a selection of which appears in my bibliography. Also to Mr. A. Dickson Wright, a London doctor who let me have an unpublished manuscript on "Venereal disease among the great"; to Academician Ivan Malek, director of the Institute of Microbiology, Czechoslovak Academy of Science in Prague for sending me extensive statistics on VD in his country; and to Dr. Willis P. Butler for information about Cuba. Also to Mr. Henrik Beer, secretary-general of the League of

Red Cross Societies in Geneva, for some notes on North Vietnam; and to Dr. Julius Goldberg especially for the chance to talk of our common interest in an uncommon problem. Also to Dr. Francis Biquard for finding and sending me a copy of *Les Avariés* (from Paris). Also, among others, who I hope will forgive me for not mentioning them, to Dr. Walter Necker and Dena Epstein of the University of Chicago Libraries for numerous favors; to Harold Freeman, Wendy Posner, and Jessie Sheridan for assistance; and, of course, to Amy, my wife, who is not used to being thanked by me but mustn't be left out, for reading the manuscript as principal representative of the nontechnical public for whom I have written this book.

Contents

Part III ❧ FACTS AND FIGURES

Part IV ❧ CONTROL:
PAST, PRESENT, FUTURE

Introduction

SUBJECTS UNPLEASANT, TERRIBLE, OR REVOLTING are often written about pleasantly, engagingly, for thrills, even comically; venereal disease is not an absolute exception, but it is pretty close. The commonest of such subjects, of course, is murder, a favorite theme over the span from Genesis to your nearest paperback book rack. Terrible disease as a literary subject is only relatively less fashionable. Bubonic plague probably tops this category, from the introduction to Boccaccio's *Decameron*, and *The Journal of the Plague Year* by the author of *Robinson Crusoe*, down to Albert Camus in our own time. Hans Zinsser's *Rats, Lice, and History*, which is mainly about typhus fever, is a perennial best seller. As a literary motif, venereal disease has claimed the attention mainly of playwrights, among whom we can number no less than Shakespeare, Ibsen, and Tennessee Williams; but of what they wrote that relates to VD I suspect most people will remember only *Ghosts*. Even so, what there is in the literature of VD tends to accentuate ugliness. This is true not only of fiction but of nonfiction as well, most of which —apart from technical works—is likely to be cautionary, moralistic, or just plain dull. I hope to fill this gap.

I assume that the trouble with VD as the subject of a book

lies less with readers than with writers—less, that is, with people generally (especially young people) than with those who
know enough to write such a book (who tend to be somewhat
older). Venereal disease is important and getting more so.
Gonorrhea leads the list of diseases in the number of cases currently reported to the U.S. Public Health Service, and syphilis
has recently moved up from fourth to third on the same list and
is even more serious; the trend of both today is to increase. I am
under the impression that young people have not learned much
from the efforts of their elders to inform them on VD, and that
they are thirsty to know more, but prefer not to be fed the information as though it were a dose of castor oil. I don't think
they want it sugar-coated, diluted, or expurgated, either. Ideally
it would come from an expert contemporary, if there were such,
as from boy to boy or girl to girl. Dr. Eugene Schoenfeld has
approached this ideal. He included VD among medical topics
in his column in the Berkeley Barb and other underground newspapers, and collected some of his stuff in the book *Dear Doctor
HIPpocrates* (New York: Grove Press, 1968). But his book
touches VD only lightly; there is a lot more to be said. I admire
his tone; and although mine can't hope to be anything like his, it
is my intention to talk straight, which is to say, neither up nor
down.

VD as the theme of a book ought to have all the terror and
fascination of murder and bubonic plague and more, because it
is inescapably tied to sex. Sex is now and perhaps has always
been the most engrossing of all subjects. It seems extraordinary
that VD has been so unpopular among writers, and it is going
to be part of our job to try to find out why this is so. But it
isn't only writers. VD is also peculiarly unpopular among
doctors, a fact of obvious importance which, I suspect, is part
of the same pattern. The subject is considered dirty, perhaps
the dirtiest subject of them all. The argument is that sex itself
is dirty, and VD is dirty in its own right; the combination is
just about untouchable, a little like somebody else's snotty

handkerchief, but in fact like nothing in the world. I don't agree
with this dirty-subject business. I have to take the point of view
into account and it will keep coming up; but let it be understood
from the start that I think sex is natural and good while disease is unnatural and bad. Venereal disease is bad like other
disease, but especially because it corrupts sex.

VD has been unpopular as a *literary* subject and among
practicing doctors, and has generally been dealt with poorly
or downright disgracefully by writers who have tried to explain
it to general readers. Just the same VD, especially syphilis,
has exercised a certain fascination over medical historians and
medical writers as well as scientists. The result is a vast literature, in which technical, medical, and historical items more than
make up for the deficiency of literary ones. I intend to include
all these aspects of the subject in my book.

The word "morals" in my title is meant to refer broadly to
all the aspects of my subject that are *not* medical or technical,
especially as they touch on relevant matters of human behavior
ramifying out of the core subject of sex. Under "microbes" I
include the many technical aspects of VD, some of which are
only remotely related to germs. Much of this whole subject is
easily within reach of the general reader. Some of it is more difficult in its original form. Part of the effort I promised, not to
talk either up or down, calls for handling the technical material
so as to make it accessible without skimping on essential detail.
The rest of the promise implies an intention to offer information,
ideas, and opinions, including some ideas and opinions of my
own (labeled as such) without any claim to or pretense of superior wisdom. VD is an unsolved problem and needs to be
approached with a certain humility.

This is not a big book as books go, but VD is a big subject. If
it appears that I have not included enough, you will find more
in the Notes at the back of the book, which among other things
refer to the Bibliography that follows.

PART I

CONTAGION

I

Some Background, and a Look Ahead

DISEASE IS PROBABLY as ancient as the life it affects. Man's parasites are likely to have evolved with him, and some of his diseases must have been present thousands of years before the historical record begins. We think bacteria may be the most ancient of living things. Viruses are so similar to such integral parts of the cell as its genes that they, too, must have been around from the earliest appearance of life on the earth, something like two billion years ago. But epidemics, including venereal diseases, are likely to have started later, arising by accidents of some sort, or growing out of drastic or sudden events which upset the balance of nature. Epidemics of infectious disease start when the infection is introduced into a group—a herd or a population—that has had no previous experience with it and therefore has no immunity against it.

Different living species in association tend to become adapted to one another; and although mutual damage is inherent in the arrangement, it does not explode under stable conditions. The small things that live on larger ones, which we call parasites, and the large things that eat smaller or weaker ones, which we call predators, usually avoid eliminating their food supply. The host learns to protect himself against the parasite and the prey

learns to hide from the predator or to fight back. The host develops antibodies against the parasite, which in turn builds up
its own defenses together with its capacity to nourish itself at
the host's expense. Adaptation leads to stable mutuality or to
destruction of one species or the other, sometimes of both. The
predator improves his claws, teeth, venom, or other weapons;
and the prey evolves by selection of varieties which blend best
with the environment or which sense the foe and fly. Loss of either species may lead to trouble for the other: starvation from
loss of prey or overpopulation from loss of predator; both are
forms of ecological disease.

Today a kind of instability or ecological imbalance resulting
from man's wholesale meddling with the earth is becoming a
matter for widespread concern, but only the magnitude of the
problem is new. Ages before glaciation led to the extinction of
dinosaurs, when the first amphibians began to emerge from the
water to test life with lungs, they must have run into new perils.
No doubt many such efforts at progress met with failure and
death. When one at last succeeded it could only have been because the new enemies were not virulent enough to exterminate
the venturesome pioneers. The new enemies must have included
microbes and viruses; and the microbes and viruses that
counted, I think, must have shared properties within a narrow
range; they needed to be similar enough to the ones already
parasitic on the pioneers to get and keep a foothold there, and
yet different enough to set up a disturbance.

As we have come to understand the germs that produce disease today, we have recognized a rule that is sometimes lost
sight of. Every disease-producing microbe or virus is either
closely related to a stable parasite or has another host in which
it is itself a stable parasite. (There are exceptions that do not invalidate the rule: a few disease-producing microbes are not parasites at all.) To put the rule in other words, disease-producing
parasites are likely to be cousins of "normal" parasites (the ones

that make up what I have called "life on man" *) either in the host they make sick or in another host. It is through the relatives of the spirochete of syphilis that we can begin to trace the origins of the disease. The coccus of gonorrhea ("gonococcus") has cousins that live harmlessly in our mouths and throats.

There may be a lesson here for those fear-ridden people who are ready to believe that a microbe from outer space could cause an epidemic in man. Nobody has had any experience with microbes from outer space (if there are such), and so we tend to be guarded about the possibility of such a disaster: it is undeniable that we don't really know. But the possibility is so remote as to be a little foolish. The probability that a space microbe would fall within the range of adaptability to man, or to any other living thing on earth from which it might pass to man, may be just barely enough to justify the cost of decontaminating space probes; but it's not worth more than this short paragraph, the purpose of which is to tell you to forget it.

The question of the origin of venereal diseases has two aspects: when? and how? When? is history; how? is biology. Both have their subtleties and their pitfalls. Gonorrhea and syphilis have both been dealt with historically, but only syphilis, so far as I know, has stimulated the question, how?—and that only relatively recently. It is pretty much agreed that VD as such is very ancient, but there is disagreement as to whether syphilis itself is more than a few centuries old. The commonest view in medical circles is that syphilis began—in Europe—at the end of the fifteenth century, and may have been brought there by Columbus's sailors returning from the New World. The other theory is that it goes back to prehistory, to the beginnings of urban life. The two views can't be reconciled. We can have one or the other—or neither—but not both. The details ramify into all sorts of byways that will be worth exploring—later.

"Venereal disease" means, mainly, syphilis and gonorrhea. But

* See the first note on page 331.

we had better be more precise. Some experts use the adjective "venereal" (pertaining to Venus, goddess of love) broadly to include any disease that *can be* transmitted by sexual contact, which means contact between the genital organs, either of one sex with the other, as in heterosexual intercourse, or between two members of the same sex, or of the genitals of one person with any moist surface of another. "Can be" makes the category large, so that it includes diseases like genital herpes ("fever blisters") or scabies (itch mites) or "crabs" (crab lice), as well as several others. Since these diseases are *not necessarily* transmitted by sexual contact, and since traditionally they are not under the peculiar dark cloud that hangs over the idea of VD, giving them this name may bring forth much unnecessary anguish. Some public health people today would like to give up the whole idea of "venereal" as a disease category; but established practice makes that harder to do than to say. Anyway, it looks to me and many others like an attempt to solve a problem by running away from it.

In fact the name "VD" is useful; and the widest practice today is to limit the category to diseases that are *hardly ever transmitted except by sexual contact*. I'm sorry about that "hardly ever": it means that the edges of the territory covered by the definition are a little blurred. If we follow this rule, we have two more diseases to deal with besides syphilis and gonorrhea, plus a third that seems to be up for more or less honorable discharge from the club. Total, then, four plus a doubtful one. But the two you know about are much more important than the others. Details will come later.

If we eliminate from the area covered by the word "venereal" all diseases that are not particular about the way they are transmitted, we are still left with a mixed bag, different one from another in many ways, but yet having features in common that are worth looking at. The common features tend to be those which limit the microbes to spread by sexual contact. They tell us why the diseases are peculiarly venereal, and maybe they will help us understand other things about them.

As microbes go, those of venereal diseases in the strict sense have a certain weakness, and if you can imagine such a thing, they are fastidious! Compared with other microbes, which survive and multiply in many different environments, these VD microbes grow, in nature, only in man. Outside of his tissues they not only fail to grow but are very quickly killed. Again, the diseases they produce in man have a common feature—maybe only one: at some stage in their course, usually early, the microbes are concentrated on sexual (and other moist) surfaces, and at this stage there is either no pain at all, or anyway the afflicted person is not too sick for sexual activity. The microbes' delicacy, their inability to survive outside human tissues, prevents them from being transmitted from one person to another by any sort of *indirect* means—through air or water (or on toilet seats). Their inability to infect other animals in nature prevents them from being spread by animals or insects. For practical purposes, under the cultural conditions we know best, the only way left for them to maintain themselves, which requires that they find themselves a fresh host every so often, is sexual contact. So they are distinctively sexual, or venereal, diseases; and however much they differ among themselves in all other respects, they are linked together by all the physical, social, cultural, and emotional oddities of human sexual behavior.

In other respects the venereal diseases differ widely. Briefly, and only to help us get started, gonorrhea, the commonest of the lot, usually starts as an acute infection of the urethra or the vagina. Untreated, it tends to become chronic and to spread especially to the Fallopian tubes, the joints, and the heart. There is a nonvenereal form that affects the eyes of babies as they are born and leads to blindness, a calamity easily prevented by routine treatment of babies' eyes at birth. The gonococcus is a member of a common class of parasitic bacteria. Magnified a little more than a thousand times it looks like a partly deflated balloon a little smaller than the head of a pin, punched in on one side. Usually they are found as pairs with the punched-in sides together.

Syphilis is less common than gonorrhea but generally much more serious. Ordinarily it starts as a single painless sore (chancre) on the penis or vulva or within the vagina, and leads to a succession of other symptoms thereafter, so varied that syphilis may mimic almost all other diseases. A chancre is sometimes found on the lips, and may come from a kiss, but more often from mouth-genital contact. Doctors and dentists have been known to have a chancre of a fingertip from touching an active sore with an ungloved hand. In other words, syphilis can also be nonvenereal, which is why I had to say "hardly ever" a little while back.

The microbe of syphilis is a moving corkscrew-shaped (helical) thing called a spirochete. Under the same magnification we used for the gonococcus it looks about half an inch long, but so thin, even when magnified a thousand times or more, as to be nearly invisible without special microscopic methods. There is a "normal" spirochete in everybody's mouth that looks almost the same.

The rarer venereal diseases include chancroid, with a sore different from the chancre of syphilis, caused by a tiny stick-shaped microbe—a bacillus, again a member of a common class of bacilli; and lymphogranuloma (usually "lymphogranuloma venereum" or LGV), with genital sores and swelling of adjacent lymph nodes, caused by a tiny microbe which used to be classified as a virus. The final member of the group is granuloma inguinale, with genital sores and often involving anus and rectum as well. This one is caused by another sort of bacillus. Recent evidence that this bacillus may be found normally in the intestinal tract is enough to start proceedings to expel the disease from the exclusive VD club.

Although the lesser venereal diseases are not to be disparaged, especially in the presence of somebody who has one of them, it is fair to say that the public health problem of VD is almost entirely confined to gonorrhea and syphilis. We will be mainly occupied with these two diseases. But we will not neglect the others; and, in fact, it will be necessary to speak of still other diseases, including those we have excluded from the VD category.

❧ 2 ❧

A Few Old Ideas and the Beginnings of Gonorrhea

W E HAVE MADE great advances in the control of infectious diseases, but they didn't really get started until the late nineteenth century. Even so it is obvious that venereal diseases were left out; they have not been brought under control even today. It is part of our job to try to understand how they came to be left out. We will see that the venereal nature of the diseases itself, their entanglement with all the ramifications of sex, is part of the story, but only part of it. Our unwillingness or inability to deal openly with matters of sex has made the VD problem more difficult than many other disease problems. To understand this we must go back into the history of the whole question. Fundamental to this inquiry is the idea of contagion as it was understood—or misunderstood—in early times.

Modern disease control could develop only as an application of a theory, the germ theory, which we owe largely to Louis Pasteur and Robert Koch and their followers. As a result of their work the idea of "causes" of disease became real where before it had been abstract, natural where it had been supernatural or fantastic, and gained a compelling force it never had before their time. They demonstrated that particular kinds of microbes, which breed true like larger living things, were undoubtedly responsible for particular diseases. The discovery that diphtheria could be cured with an antitoxin made from the blood of horses which had been carefully treated with the poison of the specific bacillus of diphtheria, and that anthrax could be dramatically prevented by previous treatment of animals with modified anthrax microbes themselves, showed too clearly for further denial that there were specific causes of disease.

These discoveries abolished the persistently lingering doubts about contagion. Disease could indeed be transferred from one person to another, and the significance of some earlier observations began to fall into a pattern which before could always be disputed. The suggestion by the elder Oliver Wendell Holmes in 1843 that childbed fever was carried on the hands of doctors had been greeted—by the doctors—with scorn. Four years later, Ignaz Semmelweiss, in Vienna, demonstrated that this same disease could be prevented if the doctors washed their hands before attending a woman in labor. For fear of childbed fever women had rightly preferred the cleaner midwives to doctors reeking of the autopsy room. But Semmelweiss's pains achieved little more than to put him in an insane asylum. Pasteur braved the ire of doctors of the French Academy by drawing a string of beads on the blackboard—a chain of streptococci —and calling them the cause of the childbed fever of Holmes and Semmelweiss; and his facts proved inescapable. The developing germ theory also validated the conclusion of John Snow, offered back in 1855, that the Broad Street pump in London had been the source of a cholera epidemic. Another Englishman, William Budd, was shown to be justified in his opinion, first put forward in 1856, that typhoid fever was carried by feces into drinking water, or on the hands to food. But contagion had been disputed well into the second half of the nineteenth century!

Before the microscope, and experiments with microbes and with animals, put the idea of contagion beyond dispute, it always seemed possible to find evidence on both sides of the question. In 1679, for instance, when bubonic plague struck Vienna and people were falling dead in the streets, a lot of people took the idea of contagion seriously enough to impel them to escape from the city if they could. One who couldn't was the ballad singer and bagpipe player Max Augustin, who made his living in the cafés. Johannes Nohl tells the story at the end of his book, *The Black Death*. One evening Max found himself without customers in the empty taproom of the Red Dragon café, and vented his feelings about the sad state of business in the song that has come down to us, "Ach, du lieber Augustin," the words of which bear witness to the event. He then drowned his grief in drink and, staggering into the street, fell into a drunken stupor. Carried by plague bearers with a load of corpses, he spent the night in an open common grave; and awakening in the morning with no more ill effects than fright and a hangover, he was helped out of the grave by the bearers when they arrived with more bodies. He lived on until 1705. Nobody knew until the turn of the nineteenth century that bubonic plague is carried by the rat flea, from rats to man and then from man to man. The flea takes leave of either rat or man as the dying body begins to cool. By the time Max Augustin came into involuntary contact with the dead their fleas had departed in search of the warmth of the living. His survival unscathed could not have appeared to his contemporaries as anything but a miracle.

In fact, the earlier ideas of contagion were almost always freighted with the miraculous, the mysterious, or the supernatural. They go back to the Babylonians and Egyptians of 1500 B.C. or earlier, to the Israelites of the Old Testament, possibly even before that to the emperor Hoang Ty of China—the legendary "Yellow Emperor," who is said to have lived in the third millennium B.C.; but modern scholars suggest that his era may have been as much as a millennium more recent.

One of the earliest written explanations of epidemic disease was made in terms not of contagion but of divine wrath. It appears in I Samuel 5, the plague among the Philistines, who had stolen the ark of the God of Israel:

> 6   But the hand of the Lord was heavy upon them of Ashdod, and he destroyed them, and smote them with emerods. . . .
>
> 9   And it was so, that . . . the hand of the Lord was against the city with a very great destruction: and he smote the men of the city, both small and great, and they had emerods in their secret parts.

This epidemic is generally thought to have been bubonic plague, and "emerods" is usually interpreted to mean the buboes or swellings in the groin from which the disease takes its name. Under certain conditions bubonic plague develops into the even deadlier pneumonic form, which starts as a disease of the lungs and has no buboes. The epidemic of the Israelites of Beth She-mesh, which closely followed the other one and presumably de-veloped out of it, has been suggested as the first recorded out-break of this form of plague. The description says nothing of emerods (I Samuel 6):

> 19   And he smote the men of Beth-shemesh, because they had looked into the ark of the Lord, even he smote of the people fifty thousand and threescore and ten men: and the people lamented, because the Lord had smitten many of the people with a great slaughter.

The Bible also contains more direct references to contagion it-self, relating mainly to what is called leprosy but may some-times have actually been venereal disease. Indeed, disease trans-mission by sexual intercourse is rather clearly implied, together with some of the earliest ideas of hygiene, but still associated with the notion of divine punishment. We will want to examine these matters in detail, but it will be better to do so in a later chapter (Chapter 9). Here let us recognize only that the ancient Jews had some pretty shrewd ideas about the spread of disease by contact, even though their "causes" were always supernat-ural.

These early ideas were all but lost in the Greek and Roman period. Hippocrates, the great Greek physician of the Golden

Age, makes no clear reference in his writings to anything resembling the modern view of contagion. His contemporary, the historian Thucydides, on the other hand, may have been the first to set down a clear description of an epidemic, the one that raged in Athens in 430 B.C. After casually suggesting that

> it first attacked the population in Piraeus—which was the occasion of their saying that the Peloponnesians had poisoned the reservoirs, there being as yet no wells there,

Thucydides proceeds to say of the plague:

> All speculation as to its origin and its causes, if causes can be found adequate to produce so great a disturbance, I leave to other writers, whether lay or professional; for myself, I shall simply set down its nature, and explain the symptoms by which perhaps it may be recognized by the student, if it should ever break out again. This I can the better do, as I had the disease myself, and watched its operation in the case of others.

For many centuries thereafter, down to the time of Boccaccio, ideas of contagion were more often expressed by poets and literary people than by medical writers. Such expressions go back to Homer, and are found among the Romans in Livy, Lucretius, Virgil, and others. When causes are suggested, they are nearly always supernatural or fantastic. In the *Iliad*, for instance, epidemic disease was produced in the army before Troy by the god Apollo, and relieved only by the supplication of Chryses. Yet here and there a distinctly modern sort of idea turns up. We saw Thucydides suggesting that the plague of Athens may have begun from poisoned reservoirs. Dion Cassius thought that a plague in the reign of Commodus, toward the end of the second century A.D., was caused by people hired to dip small needles into a pestilent poison and jab the populace with them.

Hippocrates suggested that bad air was a cause of disease, and variants of this notion persisted in several forms for many centuries. Even in its original form traces of this idea still prevail, apart from the modern phenomenon of widespread air pollution. The word "malaria" originated out of the old Hippocratic conception. Mixed in with bad air as causes of disease were floods and earthquakes, and events outside of the earth—astrological phenomena; epidemic disease continued to be ascribed to things of this sort well into the sixteenth century. Meanwhile the biblical conception of epidemic disease resulting from divine wrath (or, at times, the machinations of devils) never disappeared. Boccaccio, in the classic description of bubonic plague with which he introduces his *Decameron* (*ca.* 1353), suggested as causes a combination of the operation of heavenly bodies and God's punishment for human iniquity.

Nevertheless, like the Viennese of Max Augustin's much later time, Boccaccio knew enough to have his young people escape from the human contact of plague in the city. Many people must have imagined that something real, although invisible and mysterious, passed from one person to another to convey disease. Such ideas were written down by the first century B.C., when Marcus Terentius Varro, a friend of Cicero, attributed disease to invisible animalcules which get into the body through the mouth and nose. About a hundred years later Lucius Columella suggested that "envenomed pests" may rise out of mud and fermented dirt to cause disease. But for the most part such ideas were dismissed as fanciful (which of course they were), just as John Astruc, the French doctor whose work we will examine more closely, could label a similar notion utter nonsense as late as the mid-eighteenth century (see Figures 3 and 4, and the note at the back of the book).

What all this adds up to is that through these long centuries, until a germ theory could emerge from experimentally verified fact, notions of contagion could never really take form. There were shrewd guesses that turned out much later to be right, but they were intermingled with fantasy and mysticism, and nobody could really know what was going on. One writer, the poet-physician Fracastor (Girolamo Fracastoro), came closer to the truth in the early sixteenth century than anyone before him or for many centuries afterward. We will hear more of Fracastor, and

3. From the manuscript Rules and Ordinances of the Stews, that were by public Authority allowed to be kept at London, in the Borough of Southwark, and are supposed to have been drawn up about the Year 1430. one of which Articles begins thus, *Of those who keep Women having a wicked Infirmity*, and orders under a severe Penalty, *that no Stew-holder keep noo Woman wythin his hous that hath any Sycknesse of brenning.*

His later Authorities are taken, 1. from the *Supplication of Beggars*, a Book presented by one Simon Fish, a zealous Promoter of the Reformation in England and a bitter Enemy of the Roman-Catholicks, to Henry VIII. in which speaking of the Priests he says, *These be they that corrupt the whole Generation of Mankind in your Realm, that catch the Pockes of one Woman, and bear them to another; that be burnt with one woman, and bear it to another.*

2. From a Book published in 1546 by Andrew Boord, Doctor of Physick, and a Romish Priest, entituled the *Breviary of Health*, where one of the Chapters begins thus, *The 19th Chapiter doth shew of burning of an Harlotte*; and then he adds, *that if a man be burnt with an Harlot, and do meddle with another Woman within a Day, he shall burn the Woman that he shall meddle withal.*

3. From an Epistle placed before Stephen Gardiner's Oration *de verâ obedientiâ* printed at Rouen in 1553. by Michael Wood, in which mention is made of the *burning*.

4. From a manuscript Work of John Bale, which Mr. Becket had in his Custody, wherein Bale speaking of Dr. Weston (who was Dean of Windsor in 1556, but deprived by Cardinal Pool for Adultery) says as follows; *at this Day is lecherous Weston, who is more practised in the Art of Brech-Burning, than all the Whores of the Stews.* And again, speaking of the same Person he says, *He not long ago brent a beggar in St. Botolph's Parish.*

5. From a treatise of William Bulleyn, Dr. of Physic, called the *Bulwark of Defence, &c.* printed in 1562, wherein he treats of *the burning of Harlots.*

Here indeed we have several Authorities, but few or none of them valid, for they all stand upon an unsure Foundation. For not to mention, that these Testimonies are chiefly drawn from unpublished Records, or such Books as are hard to be met with, so that we cannot either examine them as we ought, or take such a View of them as to be certain of their Age or the Faithfulness of the Quotations made from them; omitting, I say, these Circumstances, that I may not seem to cavil as distrusting my Cause, and granting that Mr. Becket has been exact in his Relations, which is a large Concession, I do still deny the Consequence he has drawn from them, that this *burning* in Dispute was the same Disease with a *Venereal Gonorrhœa*, or that a *Venereal Gonarrhœa* contracted by unclean Coition was formerly signified by the name of *burning*. But to explain myself more fully, it will be requisite to enlarge a little upon this Subject.

These Authorities explained.

I. Then, the Leprosy of the Arabians, which was formerly a common Disease in England, as well as in other Parts of Europe, was capable of being communicated, not only by living in the same House, but even by visiting a leprous Person, insomuch that all Lepers were by several very severe Edicts separated from the rest of Mankind, and prohibited all manner of Conversation with them.

II. And

Figures 1–4. Facsimiles of pages 52–53 and 126–127 of the 1754 edition of John Astruc's *A Treatise of Venereal Diseases.*

Figure 1.

II. And therefore, in caſe any laſcivious Perſon had carnal Knowledge of a leprous Woman, as no Contact can be cloſer than that, the Leproſy could not fail of being thereby communicated, by an almoſt immediate Infection. And that it was this way communicated, we have the unanimous Teſtimony of almoſt all the phyſical Writers upon this Subject; as of Foreſtus, *Obſervat. Chirurgic. Lib.* 4. *Obſ.* 8. Palmarius, *De Elephantiaſi, Cap.* 2. Paræus, *Op. Lib.* 20. *Cap.* 8. Fernelius, *De partium morbis & ſymptomatis, Lib.* 6. *Cap.* 19. Valeſcus de Tarantâ, *Philon.* 7. *Cap.* 39. Gordon's *Lilii partic.* 1. *Cap.* 22. where he relates, *That a certain Counteſs ill of the Leproſy came to Montpelier, and was at laſt under his Care; and that a certain Batchelor of Phyſic waited on her, lay with her and got her with Child, and became perfectly leprous*; ſimilar to which you have a Story told by Philip Schopffius, *Lib. de Leprâ*, of a Carpenter, who caught the Leproſy by lying with a leprous Woman.

The Leproſy might be communicated by Coition.

III. But if through good Fortune the Caſe did not prove quite ſo bad, yet the private Parts, at leaſt, of ſuch Perſons as had to do with leprous Women, or ſuch, as though ſound themſelves had lately converſed with leprous Men, were for the moſt part affected with an Inflammation, Eryſipelas, herpetick or miliary Exulcerations, cuticular Eruptions, *&c.* whence aroſe a *Dyſuria*, in the language of that time called *ardor*, *arſura*, *incendium*, *calefactio*; in *Engliſh Brenning*.

At leaſt the private Parts might be ſeized with a burning.

IV. In Confirmation whereof we have ſeveral ſufficient Eye-Witneſſes to produce. As

1. Theodoric *, a celebrated Phyſician in the Year 1290, who in his *Chirurg. Lib.* 6. *Cap.* 55. ſays, that whoever converſes with a Woman, who has lain with a Leper, will catch the Diſtemper.

2. The Author of a manuſcript Treatiſe of Surgery, called *Rogerina*, by ſome thought to be Roger Bacon's, but in the Opinion of the very learned Dr. Friend, *Hiſt. of Phyſick, Part* 3. more likely to have been writ by Roger of Parma, in which, as we learn from Dr. Freind, *ibid.* we have an Account of the Diſorders which follow from Coition with a Woman, who had lately converſed with a Leper.

3. Gilbert, an Engliſhman, who in *Compend. Medicin. tam morborum univerſalium quàm particularium* gives the ſame Deſcription we find in the *Rogerina*.

4. Bartholomew, commonly named Glanville, whoſe *Breviarium Medicinæ*, extant in Manuſcript, agrees ſo well with the *Compendium* of Gilbert, that it may ſeem to be the ſame Work. In this Breviary, *Lib.* 2. *Cap.* 4. according to Dr. Freind, there is the ſame account almoſt Word for Word concerning *the Danger of lying with a Woman who has lately had to do with a leprous Perſon*, as in the *Compendium* of Gilbert.

5. John of Gaddeſden, an Engliſh Phyſician, who in *Pract. Medicinæ ſeu Roſâ Anglicâ* has a diſtinct Chapter *De infectione ex concubitu cum leproſo vel Leproſa*, where he ſays, " That he who lyes with a Woman, who has had to do with a

* Theodoric, whoſe Book *De Chirurgia* is ſtill extant, was a Phyſician of Catalonia, and when he grew old became a Dominican. Although he was of the ſame Name with the other Theodoric, the Dominican, who was an Italian, and at laſt created Biſhop of Cervia, yet he was of quite a different Country and Profeſſion, whatever the Mob of Scribblers may alledge. Concerning which conſult Father Echard, *De Scriptoribus Ordinis Prædicatorum.*

Leper,

Figure 2.

their sharp Teeth; the Poison of Scorpions, the Tarantula, &c. in the Humour which is reposited in the little Bags situate at the Tail, or in hooked Teeth, as in so many proper Vehicles.

They are mistaken, who fancy the Venereal Disease to be produced by a Swarm of little Animalcula.

There are some however, whom I forbear now to spend Time in confuting, such as [a] Augustus Hauptman and [b] Christian Langius, who think that the Venereal Poison is nothing else but a numerous Shoal of little nimble, brisk *Animalcula*, of a very prolifick Nature, which when once admitted, encrease, and multiply in Abundance; which lead frequent Colonies to different Parts of the Body; and inflame, erode, and exulcerate the Parts they fix on, by vellicating, stinging and biting them; in short, which, without any Regard had to the particular Quality of any Humour, occasion all the Symptoms that occur in the Venereal Disease. But as these are mere visionary Imaginations, unsupported by any Authority, they do not require any Argument to invalidate them. Nor is it necessary that any Pains should be taken to overthrow, what is built upon no Foundation. It is enough that we apply here what was said by [c] Tully upon a like Occasion, " That there " is nothing more unbecoming, not to say a *Physician*, but even any Person, " than to object that to his Adversary, which in Case it is denied, he can " bring nothing to prove it."

Besides, if it was once admitted, that the Venereal Disease could be produc'd by *Animalcula* swimming in the Blood, one might with equal Reason alledge the same Thing, not only of the Plague, as [d] Athanasius Kircher, the Jesuit formerly, and [e] John Saguens, a Minim, lately have done, but also in the Small-pox, *Hydrophobia*, Itch, Tetters, and other contagious Diseases, and indeed of all Distempers whatsoever; and thus the whole Theory of Medicine would fall to the Ground, as nothing could be said to prove the Venereal Disease depending upon *Animalcula*, which might not be urged to prove that all other Diseases were derived from the like *Animalcula*, though of a different Species, than which nothing can be more absurd.

The Story of a certain Quack, who maintained that all Diseases arose from *Animalcula* swimming in the Blood.

I remember that these foolish Notions were impudently propagated at Paris in 1727, by a certain Quack, whose Name was Boile, with a Cunning indeed, as might at first View surprize, but with such an unfortunate Success, as ought to make others afraid of engaging in a like Attempt. The Story is neither long, nor foreign to our Purpose, and therefore may the more easily be excused. He maintained that all Diseases were produced by *Animalcula* in the Blood, and different Diseases by different *Animalcula*; that there were other Animals, which were capital Enemies to these noxious *Animalcula*; by which they were capable of being pursued and destroyed, as Hares by Hounds, or Pigeons by Hawks; that he was well acquainted with the several Kinds of pestiferous *Animalcula*, from whence these different Diseases sprung,

[a] In his preliminary Epistle to a Treatise soon to be published, *De Vivâ Mortis imagine sacratâ*, Anno 1650.
[b] In the *Preface prefixed* to Kircher's *Scrutinium Pestis*, published by Langius *at Leipsic*, Anno 1659.
[c] *Philipp.* 2.
[d] In his *Scrutinium Physico-Medicum Pestis.*
[e] In his *Systema Physicum.*

Figure 3.

as alfo with their feveral Enemies, by Means of which the Sick might be reliev-ed, and likewife with the feveral Medicines, which moft abounded with thefe auxiliary Animals; and therefore that he knew perfectly how to cure all Dif-eafes, by the fafeft, fhorteft, and moft effectual Method.

To make good what he had advanced, he had a Microfcope at hand, by which he pretended, that he could prove to the naked Eye the Truth of his Pro-pofition. This Microfcope was very large, and did not confift of one ftreight Tube after the ufual Manner, but of five Tubes, obliquely joined by alter-nate Bendings at given Angles. For thus he faid the Image of the Objects was more enlarged, not only by the Refraction of the Rays through the Glaffes interpofed as in the common Microfcopes, but alfo by their Reflection from certain *Specula*, which were placed within at each Angle; by a like Ar-tifice with that, which Sir Ifaac Newton not long fince ufed in making of Te-lefcopes, which though fhort, could by Means of Reflexion joined with Re-fraction, be of more Service in aftronomical Obfervations, than could be ex-pected from longer Telefcopes.

To the Extremity of the Tube in this Microfcope, the fartheft from the Eye, he fitted plain Glaffes, or fuch as were a little Concave, containing a few Drops of Serum of the Blood lately taken from the Veins of any fick Perfon; and then turning his Inftrument, in Order to fix his Glaffes in their proper Places, there immediately prefented itfelf to the Eyes of the Spec-tators a large Shoal of fmall Animals, fwimming very brifkly in a clear fluid Humour, which as he faid were of different Shapes according to the different Nature of the Difeafe. After thefe had been fufficiently ftared at, taking off the fame Glaffes from the Microfcope, he let fall into the Serum a few Drops of another Liquor, containing, as he faid, the Animals, which would purfue and deftroy the other, and then fitting them again to his Inftrument, on a fudden the Scene was changed, and nothing was now to be feen, as if the former *Animalcula*, being deftroyed by the latter, had at once difappeared.

'Tis by no Means furprizing, that fuch Tricks as thefe fhould for fome Time impofe upon Abundance of People; but at laft after a diligent Enquiry it was found, that the four laft Tubes of this Microfcope did in no Refpect contribute to Vifion, but were only formed to carry on the Deceit; that the Glaffes containing the Serum, or any other Liquor, which were with fo much Form adapted to the Extremity of the laft Tube, were defigned only to promote the Cheat, as neither the Liquor they contained, nor the *Animalcula*, if there were any in them, could come under the View; that the firft Tube only was the In-ftrument of Vifion, and the Microfcope confifted in that alone, in the Extremity whereof were certain private Glaffes, artfully containing fome Liquid replete with Animals, of which there are known to be many Sorts; and whilft the Im-poftor feem'd to be putting his other Tubes in Order, his Way was to place his private Glaffes in the Focus of this Tube, or remove them thence, as he faw Occafion, and by that Means expofe the *Animalcula*, which were in his Liquors, to the Spectator's View, or take them away, as he thought fit.

Thefe were the Arts of a very crafty and impudent Impoftor, who had the Affurance to carry on this Fraud in this enlightened Age, when Learning and Phyfic are in fo flourifhing a Condition, and at Paris too, where fo many learned Men refide. What Reward he expected from his Impofture indeed I

know

Figure 4.

we will see that even he could do little more than guess what contagion might be, and that his sagacity could be appreciated only in the hindsight of modern science.

What is true of contagion in general is also true of venereal disease as one form of the whole process. As I have mentioned, there are suggestions in the Old Testament and in other ancient writings of disease associated with sexual intercourse, as well as descriptions which seem to fit one or more forms of VD. Similar suggestions and descriptions turn up in the subsequent pages of history. The record is muddled and always debatable not only because of confusion regarding contagion but also because diagnosis from ancient descriptions of symptoms is a tricky business at best. What makes the whole account even trickier is the widely accepted idea that syphilis did not exist in the Old World before the end of the fifteenth century, from which it would follow that any evidence of VD before that time would be thought of as something else, usually gonorrhea.

The late J. D. Thayer, an expert on gonorrhea, who emphasizes some of these uncertainties, tells us of suggestive references to gonorrhea in ancient Egyptian prescriptions, in early Chinese and Japanese sources, and in Biblical and Vedic writings. E. G. Crabtree gives the following as a presumed translation or paraphrase of a description from the work of the legendary Chinese emperor Hoang Ty, of whom I spoke before:

> Among the external diseases is one that is different from all others, the symptoms of which are easy to recognize: They are (1) affections of the urethra and vagina at the same time as the bladder. (2) Drainage of corrupt materials white or red by the urethra or vagina.

Descriptions suggestive of gonorrhea are also found on an ancient Assyrian tablet, which speaks of thick or cloudy urine, and in Hippocrates, who mentions "strangury" or stricture (blockage) of the urethra, both of which are symptoms of the disease. Victor Robinson, in his history of medicine, tells us that the Arabian physicians during the Dark Ages in Europe were

familiar with gonorrhea, and says that one of them, Rhazes
(850–923 A.D.)

> was so sagacious in this field that he may be considered a genito-
> urinary specialist. He gave a detailed description of strictures, and if
> they produced any degree of retention of urine . . . he at once in-
> troduced a catheter. . . . It seems that a gonorrheic was as safe in
> his hands as in our own.

(Robinson's book is dated 1931, before sulfa drugs or penicillin.)
He also says this:

> In treating gonorrhea, Avicenna [980–1037 A.D.] was probably
> the first to use catheters made of the skin of various animals, and
> he mentions intravesical [into the bladder] injections by means of
> a silver syringe. That he advised a louse to be inserted into the
> meatus [the opening of the urethra] of persons suffering from
> retention of urine, is simply additional evidence of the easy capac-
> ity of the Arabians to mix absurdities with their rational procedures.

Avicenna's louse frequently reappears in the later literature of
gonorrhea, sometimes transformed into a bug or a flea.

Thayer also speaks of William of Saliceto, a thirteenth-cen-
tury physician, who knew of gonorrhea and seemed aware of its
venereal nature. William attributed the disease to impurities re-
tained under the male prepuce after exposure to an "unclean"
woman, and suggested prevention by washing. The word "unclean" might have meant several different things, including leprosy, or merely menstruation.

There are several other references during this period to what
is usually regarded as gonorrhea, but I find them ambiguous
and prefer to hold them and speak of them later. Worth including here, however, as perhaps typical of the lot, is the mention
by Astruc, of whom I spoke a few paragraphs back, of a "venereal gonorrhea" known in England in the fourteenth century
under such names as *ardor, arsura,* or *incendium,* or by the
more anglicized names of *brenning* or *burning.* We will see that
Astruc mentioned these matters only to discount them, since he

was convinced that no true venereal disease existed at that time. As part of the reasoning which brought him to this conclusion, he thought of gonorrhea as no more than a symptom of syphilis, an idea attributed initially to Paracelsus in the early sixteenth century. In the facsimiles of pages 52 and 53 of Astruc's treatise shown in Figures 1 and 2 you will see that the two meanings of "brenning"—as a symptom, and to be consumed by fire (which might have applied metaphorically to syphilis as well as to gonorrhea)—seem to be mixed up so that it is hard to tell which is meant. Even more significant is Astruc's idea, which he introduces near the bottom of his page 52 (Figure 1), that descriptions of disease acquired by sexual contact which were dated before the late fifteenth century applied not to venereal disease as Astruc defined it but to *leprosy*. We shall see that the good doctor was in error on this point.

𝇏 3 𝇏

Syphilis: Enter Columbus

THE DISEASE we can now clearly identify as syphilis is thought by many people to have come to the notice of physicians for the first time in the late fifteenth century. We have nothing for that period like today's statistics, but there is plenty of evidence that the disease did suddenly emerge into great prominence then, and that many doctors thought it was new. Moreover, there is something of a consensus today that syphilis was much more severe then than it has ever been since. We have Zinsser offering this authoritative opinion in his book, *Rats, Lice, and History*:

> There is little doubt that when syphilis first appeared in epidemic form, at the beginning of the sixteenth century, it was a far more virulent, acute, and fatal condition than it is now.

These words were written in 1935 by one of the greatest bacteriologists in the United States. He goes on to discuss the belief that the disease was introduced into Europe by Columbus's sailors returning from Hispaniola, and on the basis of the information then available, Zinsser comes to the conclusion that it was probably so, leaving the door open, however, as a true scientist would, so that he could get back through in case of need. Moreover, Zinsser accepts the statement of Fracastor (he says, "We

cannot question the accuracy of his observations") that in as
brief a period as "twenty years or so" (the words are Fracastor's) syphilis had become much less severe, less florid, less painful, than it had been when it first appeared. Here, in fact, we
have a basic piece of evidence for the Columbus story: not only
that the story suited the time of the first admitted outbreak, but
especially this marked rapid decline in severity, which suggested development of immunity to a disease which had been
entirely unknown when it was first introduced. But it is odd that
immunity developed so far and no further, particularly when we
see, as we will much later on, what a peculiar thing immunity to
syphilis is, anyway.

Let it be noted that if the Columbian origin of syphilis were
to be established, we would still be faced with its existence in
America before that time, so that its true origin, on a worldwide
basis, would still be a problem. We have here something like
the "discovery" of America itself. The American Indian, who to
my knowledge has never been consulted on this syphilis story,
or given a chance to answer the charge against him, is just starting to argue the other question, telling us that he knew of the
existence of what we call "America" long before we did.

The matter of coincidence is abundantly but not quite convincingly documented. Under the name of "evil pocks" (*pösen
plattern,* or *bösen Blattern*) syphilis was mentioned in print on
August 7, 1495, in the Edict of the Holy Roman Emperor Maxi-
milian, who looked on it as something "which had never occurred before nor been heard of within the memory of man,"
and labeled it a punishment sent by God *for blasphemy.* It is
certainly remarkable that between 1495 and 1498 there were at
least nine separate tracts published on the disease in Germany,
Italy, Spain, and Austria. The Spaniard Torrella of Valencia described seventeen cases he had treated in the papal court in the
two months of September and October, 1497. Yet it seems extraordinary that the first to give evidence that syphilis came to
Europe in Columbus's sailors in 1494 should have been a certain

Ruy Dias de Isla, in a book said to have been written (and presumably passed around) between 1510 and 1520, but not published until 1539—from sixteen to forty-five years after the alleged fact! Dias de Isla recalled that, practicing in Barcelona, he had been visited by many of Columbus's sailors who were suffering from a dreadful unknown scourge. Another writer, the historian Gonzalo Hernandez de Oviedo y Valdez, lent his support to this observation of de Isla. But Oviedo wrote in 1525. His father is said to have been with Columbus on the second voyage; in 1494 Oviedo had been all of sixteen years old! Oviedo seems to be responsible for a detail that has since become a set part of the account: that the disease first appeared in epidemic form among Spanish mercenaries, some of whom had been Columbus's sailors, in the French army of Charles VIII at the siege of Naples in December, 1494.

In 1530 Fracastor published his famous poem, *Syphilis sive Morbus Gallicus* ("Syphilis or the French Disease"), in which he wove an avowedly fanciful tale of a shepherd in Hispaniola who had been smitten with the disease for being disrespectful to the gods. Sixteen years later Fracastor, who was a physician as well as a poet, published his serious medical work, *Contagion,* in which he describes syphilis in great and convincing detail. But observe some additional curious circumstances. It is in *Contagion* that Fracastor presents the modern idea of transmission of many diseases by "seeds" or "germs"—which, of course, he had never seen; and he had no doubt that the "French disease" was *often* transmitted by sexual intercourse. He goes on to say that

some have believed that this contagion was carried to us from the New World which was discovered by the Spanish voyages, for there this malady is extremely prevalent. In proof of this, they point to the fact that this disease first appeared among us in Italy at the very time when the voyage had been made and trading had been carried on with the people of that country. For this reason, too, they say, it was first observed among the Spaniards. Accordingly, they think that in all cases this malady depends on a contagion transmitted by one person to another. But, as a matter of fact, although the majority of those who have contracted this disease have done so through contagion, nevertheless it has been observed that countless others have been infected without any contagion per se. *Moreover, it would have been impossible that this contagion, which per se is slow to act and is not easily received, should have traversed so much of the world after having been first conveyed to the Spanish by a single fleet of ships.* For it is well known that at the same time, or nearly the same, it was observed in Spain, France, Italy, Germany, and almost all Scythia [South Russia; the italics have been added].

These are the words of a contemporary of Oviedo's for whom later medical historians have shown the utmost respect. Fracastor makes the further point that syphilis had been predicted by astrologers some years before it arrived; he tells us that the sudden appearance of a new and unusual disease had happened before, and predicts that it would happen again. He takes refuge in the idea that such diseases arise "from their own peculiar causes," by which he implies astrological and consequent atmospheric effects. Fracastor, for all that he is deservedly thought of as having given us the modern idea of contagion, was obviously no flaming radical. He had not broken entirely with the old ideas. What is more, he seems to have been misled by a correct observation, that late syphilis, of which he evidently saw a good deal, is not contagious, even though its clinical signs may be those of horrible sores and disfigurement. Today we speak of "early" syphilis, which is infectious, and "late" syphilis, which is not. It is true, then, that the second is "not easily received."

I have emphasized part of the quotation for this reason: Fracastor was right, even if his reasons were imperfect. Early syphilis is "received" easily enough, although it does indeed tend to be "slow to act." It is spread from one person to another during sexual contact. One person may give it to many, but to only one at a time. In this respect syphilis differs as an epidemic disease from those which spread through a common medium such as air, water, or food, or by insects, which may be present in multitudes. Influenza, cholera, or yellow fever may appear as explosive epidemics, with hundreds or thousands of victims stricken virtually at once. Such diseases could have spread as syphilis is supposed to have spread when it was first noticed. Syphilis would have moved more slowly. And whereas explosive epidemic diseases are likely to emerge as full-blown illness in a few days, syphilis would take weeks, so that its progress would be the more retarded.

This doubt, recognized by Fracastor, that syphilis could have been spread by a few people on Columbus's ships who might have been infected, has been emphasized more recently by one of several scholars who have rejected the whole Columbian theory—E. H. Hudson, whom we will talk about later.

Except for scholars like Hudson, who have become interested in this question as a matter of history, most venereologists and nearly all textbook writers have either dismissed the subject as unimportant, or have gone along with the Columbus story either without questioning it, or with minor scientific reservations like those of Zinsser. I used to do as they did when I was busy teaching this and other aspects of bacteriology, and working with the spirochete and other microbes. But the new look at VD that is called for by the collapse of our recent efforts to control it means a new look at the whole subject, including the Columbus story. The fact is that it has always been easy, and tempting, to amuse medical students with stories like this, as a way of stimulating their interest in the subject. Venereal disease has always been good for a few belly laughs in the lecture room, and I have done my share to provoke them.

It was a relatively recent experience that made me reflect and reconsider. During the 1950s, when penicillin was working miracles, medicine in general, and bacteriology in particular, reset their sights and began concentrating on chemistry and physics. Whatever unfinished business remained in the control of infectious disease was left largely to public health people; and VD was among the first problems to be written off in the medical schools. It isn't quite accurate to say that the subject became

unfashionable: we will see later that it was really never anything else; but what there had been of it tended to disappear. So
much so that by the early 1960s, when VD was staging an em-
barrassing comeback, the appalling discovery was made that
young doctors and medical students knew practically nothing
about it.

In the recent experience I spoke of, an earnest young physician from a local U.S. Public Health Service VD unit was attempting one Saturday morning to introduce the practical subject to a large audience of medical students, interns, and
residents, with a sprinkling of older people, including me. The
speaker was knowledgeable and skillful. He tried hard *not* to be
funny; but to the two hundred or so young men and women
who heard him nearly every word he said exploded like a dirty
joke, provoking belly laughs and the kind of infectious giggling
adolescent girls go in for when they know secretly more than
they are expected to know. I found the audience response of-
fensive. The laughter of doctors in the face of disease is cruel;
something is wrong when it happens.

Medical students traditionally find the Columbus story funny.
That is not a reason for discarding the story, but it prompts me
the more to ask: is it true?

We could establish the probability of the Columbian origin of
syphilis by showing first, that there is no evidence that syphilis
existed in the Old World before 1494, and secondly, that it did
exist at the time in America. Conversely, we could lay the ghost
of the story with good evidence that syphilis was known in Europe before Columbus's time. This would be enough without reference to the New World; but the argument would gain strength
if it appeared that there was no syphilis in Hispaniola when Columbus and his crew were there.

This enterprise will be forwarded if we go back and pick up
the main thread of our story by taking a closer look at Fracastor's two works. The Columbus story will often be visible in the
wings as Fracastor moves to center stage.

❧ 4 ❧

Syphilis or the French Disease, by Fracastor

F RACASTOR, in 1530, used the name "syphilis" both for the shepherd in his poem who first got the disease as a result of blasphemy, and as the name of the disease itself. The thought of "carnal sin" does not seem to have entered his mind. Fracastor's own synonym for "syphilis" was "the French disease" (*morbus gallicus*). The name "syphilis" did not come into use for a long time. Daniel Turner revived it in 1717; but it was not generally used until about 1850, or more than three centuries after Fracastor's poem.

In his later work on contagion Fracastor has this to say:

In Italy [the disease] broke out about the time when the French under King Charles took possession of the Kingdom of Naples about ten years before 1500 [*sic*], and from them it was called the French Sickness. The French retort the scandal of the name against us [Fracastor was a Veronese] by calling it the Italian Sickness, while the Spanish call it Patursa, and the Germans sometimes call it the Sickness of Maevius, sometimes French Sickness. Some have invented a new word for it and call it Pudendagra, because it begins with the pudenda, on the analogy of Mentagra [=rough chin, interpreted today usually as sycosis, a fungus disease; but see below]. . . . In my poem I have called this disease Syphilis.

One of the stories that has always brought a laugh from medical sophomores in the lecture room is the way different regions blamed the disease on others by naming it for them. Today the basis of the joke is obviously sexual, but originally it was not, since the disease was thought to be a punishment for blasphemy. Yet its sexual basis began to be clear by the late Renaissance, and perhaps sex and blasphemy were equally satisfactory foundations for an implied insult. Let us see how Astruc, who looked into this business of names with a good deal of care, tells the story:

> . . . the *Neapolitans,* and the rest of the *Italians* called it the *French* Disease, *Mal Francese,* alledging it was imported into *Italy* by the *French* when they attacked the Kingdom of *Naples* in the year 1494; while the *French,* on the contrary, called it the *Neapolitan* or *Italian* Disease, *Mal de Naples,* because it was first catched by them in the Kingdom of *Naples* during the abovementioned Expedition: the *Germans* too call it *Frantzozen,* or *Frantzozischen Pocken,* that is, *The French Disease,* or *The French Pox;* and the *English* likewise call it by the same Name, because it was propagated in those different nations by the French . . . it was called by the *Flemish* and *Dutch Spaanse Pocken;* by the *Portuguese, The Castilian Disease,* by the *East-Indians* and *Japonese* [*sic*], *The Disease of the Portuguese* . . . by the *Persians, The Disease of the Turks;* by the *Polanders,* the *Disease of the Germans;* and last of all, by the *Russians, The Disease of the Polanders.* . . .

One can usually get another rise out of the students by quoting, after some of the foregoing, the remark attributed to the contemporary soldier, Pierre Terrard de Bayard, that syphilis is best called *le mal de celui qui l'a*—"the disease of him who has it."

The somewhat wordy Astruc has more on the matter of names. The Spaniards, he says, also called syphilis *Las Bubas, Buvas, Buas* or *Boas;* the Tuscans called it *Il malo delle Bolle,* the Lombardians *Lo malo de la Brosule*—all signifying "pustules." Among the French it was also called *La Verole* or *La Vairole* (pox), and it came to be called great pox as compared with small pox, which is still technically *variola.* Astruc also

mentions the German name, the disease of St. Mevius, and its
attribution by Valentians, Catalans, and Aragonese to St. Sementius, as well as by others to Job, to St. Regius, St. Evagrius,
and St. Roche. And he notes the names Pudendagra, Mentula-
gra, and Mentagra, there being a possibly symbolic pre-Freudian
association of chin to penis. Astruc gives John Fernelius (probably Jean Fernel, 1497–1558) credit for coining the term "venereal disease," and adopts it "to prevent national Hatreds increasing from such foolish Reflections." Astruc included many
diseases under this term in a complex loosely thought of as a
single disease. The name in Latin, in which Astruc wrote originally, was *lues veneris* or *lues venereum*. The word "lues"
merely means "disease" (or sickness, or pestilence); today it has
become, without a modifier, a doctor's nickname for syphilis.

Sir William Osler has left us a famous essay on Fracastor's
poem. He says:

> To appreciate the rapid popularity of the poem, it is to be re-
> membered that in the early part of the sixteenth century syphilis
> was regarded as a mysterious epidemic, hitherto unknown, which
> had struck terror into all hearts by the rapidity of its spread, the
> ravages it made, and the apparent helplessness of the physicians to
> cure it.
>
> The poem is an exposition of Fracastor's views on the origin,
> symptomatology, and cure of the new disease which had seized as-
> tonished Europe. He accepts the usual statement that it first ap-
> peared in the French army before Naples about 1495.

> To Naples first it came
> From France, and justly took from France his name,
> Companion of the War.

> He discussed the American origin, the popular one of the day:

> Say, Goddess, to what cause we shall at last
> Assign this plague, unknown to ages past;
> If from the western climes 'twas wafted o'er,
> When daring Spaniards left their native shore;
> Resolv'd beyond th' Atlantick to descry
> Conjectured worlds, or in the search to dye.

More probable it is, he thinks, that the malign influence of the planets, particularly the conjunction of Mars and Saturn, had brought about conditions favourable for the outbreak of the plague which had existed for ages but slumbered at intervals.

> Long since he scatter'd his infernal flame,
> And always being had, though not a name.

Osler calls Fracastor's description of the disease in the poem "very complete," and offers his opinion, which is that of possibly the greatest doctor of all time, that "there is no difficulty in recognizing the disease." He points out in passing that "Fracastor, with a majority of the writers of that date, thought the disease had very often an extra-genital origin." And he goes on to consider the details of treatment given in the poem, including exercise, diet ("Avoid fish . . ." and "wine as a rule is to be avoided"), and mercury:

> The greater part, and with success more sure,
> By mercury perform the happy cure;
> A wondrous virtue in that mineral lies.

Some of the practices that were later alluded to by Shakespeare are given in Fracastor's directions, as transmitted by Osler:

> Full directions for inunction [of mercury] are given. The "lard of swine" is used for a vehicle, mixed with larch gum and turpentine. The whole body is to be smeared except the head and breast, and then the patient is to sweat profusely under thick bed-clothing. The course is to be repeated for ten days until
>
> > The mass of humours, not dissolved within
> > To purge themselves by spittle shall begin.
>
> Victorious health is now at hand, and all that remains is to take a bath with rosemary and lavender, vervain and yarrow, to wash all the dregs away.

Then comes an account of the seemingly greater therapeutic virtues of guaiac, a matter on which Fracastor agrees in remarkable detail with his contemporary writer on syphilis, Ulrich von Hutten, particularly in the last injunction, to "house" the patient [for thirty days] . . . so that no fresh air can reach him, to restrict the diet to "just so much food as can bare life preserve."

Osler gives Fracastor's story of the origin of the disease in these words:

There is told the story of the discovery of the New World by Columbus, and the joy of the sailors in its wonders. Unhappily they shot some beautiful birds, beloved of the Sun-God, and a prophesy of dire ills was uttered by one of the birds which escaped:

Nor end your sufferings here; a strange disease,
And most obscene, shall on your bodies seize.

By chance, before they left the natives held a great festival to the Sun-God, but grief was on all faces—"all languished with the same obscene disease"; but the priest in snowy robes displayed the boughs of healing guaiacum with which he purged the tainted ground. This the native prince assured the Spanish General was the disease the holy bird had predicted would attack his men, and he told the story of the origin of the plague, and the discovery of guaiacum as a cure.

A shepherd once (distrust not ancient fame)
Possest these downs, and Syphilus was his name.

He kept the flocks of King Alcithous, and one year the drought was so extreme that the cattle perished for want of water. So incensed was Syphilus that he blasphemed the Sun-God in good set terms and decided from henceforth to offer no sacrifices to him, but to worship King Alcithous. The shepherd won all the people to his way, and the king was overjoyed and proclaimed himself "in Earth's low sphere to be the only and sufficient deity." But the Sun-God, enraged, darted forth infection on air, earth, and streams, and Syphilus became the first victim of the new disease.

He first wore buboes dreadful to the sight,
First felt strange pains and sleepless past the night;
From him the malady received its name.

Becoming a general pestilence, the Sun-God was appealed to [and after proper sacrifices had been made] . . . guaiacum was given as a cure for the disease. The afflicted sailors learned of the natives

how to prepare the remedy, and not forgetful of their country's
good, freighted their largest ships with the rich wood.

> Iberian coasts, you first were happy made
> With this rich plant, and wonder'd at its aid;
> Known now to France and neighboring Germany,
> Cold Scythian coasts, and temp'rate Italy,
> To Europe's bounds all bless the vital tree.

In a prose translation of Fracastor's poem by another doctor,
Solomon C. Martin, the disease is said to have "attacked all
Europe in one day, and spread itself over a part of Africa and of
Asia . . ."; and later:

> This subject though poetical in form, takes on at times a serious in-
> terest, under a frivolous guise. . . .

Fracastor's ideas of venereal contagion evidently developed
and changed somewhat after he wrote the poem; but even so he
does not seem to have thought of blaming the disease on the
women of Hispaniola. An idea repeated in *Contagion* is given as
follows in Martin's translation of the poem:

> Was [syphilis] imported among us from those new worlds which
> were discovered by the brave mariners of Spain . . . ?
> No, it is not in this manner that the disease has developed itself.
> Incontestable testimony proves that it is not of a strange or foreign
> origin and that it was not necessary to cross the ocean to arrive in
> our midst.
> Among the first victims who were attacked in our climate, I
> could mention a number of patients who were spontaneously at-
> tacked, without having exposed themselves to the least chance of
> contagion. Besides, how would it be possible to attribute to a con-
> tagious influence a disease which attacked so many people in such
> a short time?

Another curious idea appears in this translation of the poem,
to be noted but not taken too seriously or quibbled over:

> Is it true that it [syphilis] was born weak and obscure, to increase
> its force a hundredfold later on as it extended its ravages and in-
> vaded, little by little, the entire universe?

To which the poet attempts an answer a little later in words
translated thus:

> All diseases do not have a common or identical origin. The ones,
> the majority even, have an easy development which accounts for
> their habitual frequency; but others are of a different sort to deliver
> and succeed but slowly to constitute themselves, after having long
> fought against the infinite difficulties which destiny opposed to
> their birth. Of this number is the French Disease which, for a long
> time wrapped up in the darkness of the nothing, has suddenly freed
> itself from its bindings, after many centuries of waiting, to finally
> rise in the light and make an irruption among us.

We will come to see that Fracastor worked out some of the ob-
scurity of his thinking by the time he wrote *Contagion*, but
never quite overcame it.

Fracastor wrote this poem during the dawn of modern science, when it seemed entirely appropriate to mix the serious
with the frivolous. He used a fashionable literary form to embel-
lish a pleasant story with echoes of Ovid and Virgil. It was art
as well as science, deliberate imaginative fiction as well as fact.
The remarkable phrase quoted earlier, "incontestable testimony
proves that it is not of a strange or foreign origin," may have
been Fracastor's way of warning us that he didn't mean his
story of Hispaniola to be taken seriously.

Astruc cites one Alexander Benedict of Verona as having asserted in 1496 that "the French Disease [was] a NEW plague
. . . contracted by lying together. . . ." Astruc also quotes Paracelsus, writing around the time of Fracastor's poem or a little
later, as saying this:

> That the French Disease derived its origin from the Coition of a lep-
> rous Frenchman with an Impudent whore, who had venereal Bu-
> boes, and after that infected every one that lay with her; and thus
> from the Leprosy and venereal Bubo, *proceeds he*, the French Dis-
> ease arising, infected the whole World with its Contagion, in the
> same manner as from a Coition of a Horse and Ass the Race of
> Mules is produced.

In introducing the idea that VD came from leprosy I am also anticipating something to be developed in a later chapter: this notion was anything but new. What seems significant for the moment is that the idea of a venereal source of the allegedly new disease *had no essential connection with the story of its Columbian origin.*

There was a great deal of syphilis in the late fifteenth and early sixteenth centuries. It attracted a lot of attention in medical circles and elsewhere. There was a lot of speculation as to where it came from, how it arose. At the time, ideas of contagion were beginning to crystallize out of a mixture of observed fact, coincidence, and astrological and other mystical notions. Venereal transmission was one of the suggestions put forward. The idea that the disease came to Europe with Columbus's sailors, or with Indians on one of his boats, was another notion, based mainly on coincidence and later supported by the clinical hindsight of de Isla and in part by the fantasy of poet-physician Fracastor. I wonder if that great Veronese wouldn't be astonished if he could see today how his pretty story had acquired the authority of history by repetition and embellishment!

❧ 5 ❧

More Fracastor:
Contagion

W E HAVE LOOKED at Fracastor's poem of syphilis and tried to
place its poetry and its mixture of fact and fantasy in the
context of its time. Modern science was very young then, and
ideas of disease were just starting to shed the mysticism of the
Dark Ages and take on elements of their present form. Fracastor
was one of the great pioneers in developing the new ideas. His
poem is cherished for its beauty and as testimony to the versatil-
ity of the Renaissance man; but his fame as a pioneer in medicine rests more securely on his later serious prose work on contagion, dated 1546. There is an excellent English translation by
Mrs. Wilmer Cave Wright, published in 1930, which also gives
the Latin original and much scholarly embellishment. The book
is well worth a chapter in this one, particularly two of Fracastor's several topics: something of his general idea of contagion,
the main theme; and his discussion of syphilis itself, which Osler
thought by far the best part of the book.

Fracastor begins with an attempt to reconcile his idea of contagion with the still prevailing Pythagorean notion that the essence of matter is found in four primary qualities, the contrasting pairs hot and cold, wet and dry, which united to form the
four elements earth, water, air, and fire. Out of these, in various

proportions, all matter was formed. Contagion implies *infection,* but obviously this word could not mean to him what it now means to us. Infection, he assures us, is conveyed by "imperceptible particles," upon which the contagion acts. In this respect infection differs from fire, in which "the whole thing is destroyed primarily as a whole." A few pages later these imperceptible particles become *"germs of contagion" (seminaria contagium);* and then Fracastor adds the further important property of contagion, that it entails *a precisely similar infection of one thing by another.* So here are the great modern ideas of microbes and of specificity—each kind of microbe being responsible for a different disease. But the new idea seems to struggle to free itself from old Greek dogma. Contagion still

> seems to be a certain passive affection of elements in combination. But . . . such combinations can be corrupted and destroyed in two ways, either by the advent of a contrary element, owing to which the combination cannot retain its form, or secondly by the dissolution of the combination, as happens when things have putrefied . . .

so that we see an idea being born with remnants of what later, like an afterbirth, will be discarded. Most scholars have stressed such elements of prophecy in Fracastor as his recognition of the relationship of putrefaction to contagion (both, as we know now, being due to microbes); but it is plain that he had not entirely discarded the myths of the past.

And now he comes to distinguish three types of contagion, of which the basic type spreads by direct contact only; the second uses the *additional* means of "fomes" or, as they have since come to be called, "fomites"; while the third, in addition to both of these, can also infect "at a distance." The notion of "fomites" seems to have been original with Fracastor, and much has been made of it down to the very recent past. Fracastor defines it thus:

> By fomes I mean clothing, wooden objects, and things of that sort, which though not themselves corrupted, can, nevertheless, preserve

the original germs of the contagion and infect by means of these. . . .

which sounds like a modern idea, and is, in fact, preserved today as true, but within much narrower limits than prevailed even fifty years or so ago, when, as older people may remember, we used to fumigate the bedroom with sulfur dioxide or formaldehyde after the child recovered (or died) from diphtheria, scarlet fever, or smallpox. That the practice has been largely abandoned is owing to our recognition that *indirect contact* is much less important in the transmission of infectious disease than we used to think.

Fracastor emphasizes his idea that each of the three types of contagion adds something in turn so that the third still includes the first:

> These different contagions seem to obey a certain law; for those which carry contagion to a distant object infect both by direct contact and by fomes; those that are contagious by means of fomes are equally so by direct contact; not all of them are contagious at a distance, but all are contagious by direct contact.

It would seem that it ought to be so, and it seems somehow illogical that it isn't. Fracastor was not fully emancipated from the belief of the scholastics of a few centuries earlier that all truth could be divined by proper logical thought. It was one of the major contributions of the new science that the sequence of logical arguments needed support at strategic points by observed facts verified by trial and experiment.

But Fracastor is very shrewd. He gives us as an example of contagion by contact "that which occurs in fruits, as when grape infects grape, or apple infects apple. . . . Since the first fruit . . . has putrefied, we must suppose that the second has contracted a precisely similar putrefaction." And then he proceeds to offer us a rather nonsensical definition of putrefaction, "a sort of dissolution of a combination due to evaporation of the innate warmth and moisture," because he was impatient and couldn't wait for Pasteur and his more perfected germ theory. But it is in connection with this type of contagion, and his discussion of fruits, that he spells out his idea of germs, again with more as well as less than he needed,

> those imperceptible particles, which are hot and sharp when they evaporate, but are moist in combination.

In connection with the discussion of fomites we find Fracastor using the word *virus* (given thus in the original Latin) as denoting the germ of contagion in general. We also find him struggling with the problem of contagion at a distance, trying magnificently to avoid recourse to what he speaks of as "occult properties"; he insists that "the active principles are only substances and qualities" and so takes an important step toward the material explanation of popular superstitions. But the very word "qualities" leaves him in difficulties, against which he labors with sound instincts but little success. Among his qualities is "luminousness" which he calls "spiritual." Yet the principle of contagion is to him "a body that can be carried"; the germs or particles have certain properties; and if his attempts to describe them are a bit off the mark, he is nevertheless unswerving in the effort to keep them natural, not supernatural. If they are "broken up by very cold water" (which they are not), "the germs of all contagions are consumed by fire," which is true. And he reasons with wonderful inspiration from his own word "germ" or "seed":

> One method of penetration is by propagation and, so to speak, progeny. For the original germs which have adhered to the neighboring humors with which they are analogous, generate and propagate other germs precisely like themselves, and these in turn propagate others, until the whole mass and bulk of humors is infected by them.

The "humors" come from the Hippocratic doctrine, allied with that of the four elements, that the body is composed of four liquids or humors: blood (fire), phlegm (cold, or water), black bile (melancholy, or earth), and yellow bile (anger, or air). This scheme persisted into the seventeenth century and still remains in metaphor. The word "humor" is still used for body fluids, either directly as in the "aqueous humor" of the eye, or as in "humoral" pertaining to body fluids as opposed to "cellular."

Fracastor went as far in developing the modern idea of contagion as shrewd observation and logic could take him, without the advantages of knowledge that came only centuries later through improved instruments and the experimental method; and he continued accordingly to mix what we now recognize as fact with portions of fanciful nonsense. He could say this, for instance, as though with a straight face:

> when you see in the sky that several of the stars called planets are assembling into one quarter (as it often happens, for instance, that several planets are in the north or south and are entering into conjunction reciprocally), then be sure that in that quarter important changes will take place on the earth. First there will be very great humidity due to masses of vapor rising and water, soon followed by severe droughts, when the vapors are at length consumed by the scorching heat about the earth and in the atmosphere. These phenomena usually bring putrefactions also. If the conjunction of several of these stars occurs under the influence of the greater stars which are called "fixed," then you may predict that some remarkable contagion is portended.

Fracastor's first chapter on syphilis is lucidly descriptive. He has obviously seen a lot of it. He does not mention the primary sore or chancre, but he emphasizes the venereal nature of the disease. He says that

> [in the majority of cases] it was contracted by contagion . . . but only when two bodies [were] in close contact. . . . Now this happened in sexual intercourse especially, and it was by this means that the great majority of persons were infected. However, some cases were observed of infants who, by sucking milk from a mother or nurse who was infected, were themselves infected in a precisely similar way. . . .

Fomites are seldom or never involved, "nor did it propagate it-self to a distant object." There was a latent period of a month or more—as much as four months—but the context suggests not the incubation period as we now know it, between contact and the appearance of the chancre, but rather a symptom-free inter-val before the appearance of generalized syphilis, in which early and late symptoms as we now know them seem to be merged:

> The patient's mind was dominated by a sort of sadness, his body by lassitude, and his face became pale. At last, in the majority of cases, small ulcers began to appear on the sexual organs. . . . [This] kind that appears in syphilis was intractable and would not depart, but when subdued in one part of the body it would germinate in an-other place. . . . Next, the skin broke out with incrusted pustules, in some cases beginning with the scalp. . . . When they first ap-peared, the pustules were small, but they soon grew little by little till they were the size of the cup of an acorn, which in fact they re-sembled. . . . Many very different varieties of these were observed . . . [there is additional vivid detail here]. In [some] cases . . . the patients suffered from pernicious catarrh which eroded the pal-ate or the uvula, or the pharynx and tonsils. In some cases the lips or nose or eyes were eaten away, or in others the whole of the sex-ual organs. Moreover, many patients suffered from the great de-formity of gummata. . . . These were often as large as an egg. . . . Violent pains attacked the muscles, often at the same time as the pustules. . . . These pains were persistent, tormented the sufferer chiefly at night, and were the most cruel of all the symptoms. . . .

This is severe secondary syphilis, with pustules and pain, com-bined with late symptoms including eroding, destructive "gum-mata." Fracastor goes on to say that he used the past tense in the preceding passage because the disease

> seems to have changed its character since those earliest periods of its appearance. . . . Within the last twenty years or so, fewer pus-tules began to appear, but more gummata, whereas the contrary had been the case in the earlier years. Moreover, whenever the pustules did appear, they were drier, and the accompanying pains (if any) were, in every case, more acute. Moreover, . . . within about the last six years of the present generation . . . pustules are

now observed in very few cases, and hardly any pains, or much less severe, but many gummata. Also, to the general amazement, the hair falls out from the head and the other hairy parts to such an extent that it makes men look ridiculous; for some go about in public without a beard, some without eyebrows, others with heads totally bald. This mishap was at first supposed to be due to medicines, especially to quicksilver. But later, with greater knowledge, all are now aware that it is the result of a change in the form of the disease; moreover, and this is still more serious, it is observed that the teeth in many cases now become loose, or in some cases even fall out.

We know today that baldness is a characteristic feature of severe secondary syphilis; but loosening and loss of teeth are due to the use, or abuse, of mercury.

Fracastor suggests that syphilis had become less severe over a period of twenty years, or even, as he says, in six. I must confess to some nagging doubt on this point. I don't know that anyone has had the temerity to make this suggestion before. But the fact is that severe and florid syphilis was common down to the advent at least of the arsenical drugs in 1910, and "malignant" syphilis is still being reported today. Such malignant syphilis was probably never common, even during the "great epidemic" of that early time. There is good reason to believe that many cases at the height of the epidemic were mild. Finally, some of the worst manifestations of late syphilis as we know it today— affecting the heart and blood vessels and in particular the brain and spinal cord—although they must have been seen in the epidemic period, were not recognized then as due to syphilis. The fact is that if syphilis was a horrible disease at that time, there is no good reason to use a milder adjective for it today.

As he proceeds to take up the "causes" of syphilis in his next chapter, Fracastor is in trouble from the beginning. He has a compulsion to explain every observed fact and can't help appealing for support to astrological or other fanciful nonsense. Logic itself leaves him; he forgets his own conclusion that the disease came mainly from sexual intercourse; he now dwells

heavily on two points, that the disease was new, and that, being
new, it must have been due to some uncommon atmospheric or
analogous phenomenon:

> Whatever may be the cause and principle that produced this conta-
> gion, it must be one of those that seldom happen; seeing that this
> disposition of the air which gave birth to this contagion, so seldom
> seen, is among those which seldom happen . . .

and he goes on in this curiously repetitive vein at length, almost
as though he were trying to convince himself: the three heavenly bodies of "highest rank," Saturn, Jupiter and Mars, had "in
our time" been in a conjunction that seldom occurs, "and when
it does, it always brings in its train great events" for certain reasons duly elaborated. Hispaniola seems to be forgotten, even apart
from its women, who had never been thought of. Yet underneath
the attempts to explain, for instance, that intervals without
symptoms in syphilis are due to "the coldness and density" of its
germs, so that "it would creep on sluggishly, but presently
would eat its way out and attack the solid parts of the body
also," we find more of the careful descriptions of symptoms on
which Fracastor's fame rests. As though unaware of any contra-
diction, he says:

> First small ulcers appeared on the sexual organs, because it was in
> that locality and mainly from sexual intercourse that the contagion
> had its origin and beginning.

He is evidently speaking again here of *secondary* syphilis, in
which there may be pustules anywhere, for he says a sentence or
two later that these pustules "very often invaded the hairy scalp
first," and he notes the presence of pain, tending to be more violent when the pustules were fewer.

There is a reversion now to the lessening in the severity of the
disease. My doubts on this point are bolstered by Fracastor's
compulsion to explain everything with fanciful embroidery. In
fairness let me separate the grain from the chaff, substituting ellipses for obvious absurdities:

> In the course of years . . . there has come about a certain altera-
> tion in this disease. . . . The contagions of the earliest period . . .
> were observed to be more foul and of fatter substance, and caused
> more pustules and fewer pains. But the contagions of the following
> years . . . caused fewer pustules but more pains. . . . Further-
> more, in recent years . . . a still greater change has come about,
> for many gummata appear, but very few pustules, and those drier,
> while there are hardly any pains, or far less severe. . . .

This seems to me a small hook on which to hang a great theory
of the evolution of a disease. But it is all the substance Fracastor has to give us on this point. Could he have been seeing more
late and less early syphilis simply because it was developing in
his regular patients?

And now as we turn to his chapter on treatment in Book III
of *Contagion*, we are all but lost in the therapeutic jungle of the
time, struggling to find a ray of sunlight here and there in the
often impenetrable thicket of pompous humbug that passed in
those days for therapeutic wisdom.

> . . . be careful to keep up the normal bodily expurgations from the
> nose, skin, palate, bowels. . . . But beware of superfluous evacua-
> tion, of venereal especially. Do not lose your sleep, but on the
> other hand do not sleep too long, or in the daytime, or immediately
> after a meal.

A certain diagnostic acumen emerges here and there. Syphilis
may be hard to recognize "during the initial stage" but

> You may strongly suspect that the patient has this disease, and your
> diagnosis will probably be correct, if he knows that he has had in-
> tercourse with an infected woman.

As for remedies themselves, Fracastor lists a pageful of them
with a degree of approval before coming to guaiac, which "is in
most general use"; among its virtues, it is "sudorific, and can
volatilise, liquefy and absterge the substance of the contagion";
moreover, and somewhat anticlimactically,

> It seems to have a certain medicinal property also, so that it moves
> the bowels.

And so on for several pages, all on guaiac. But if guaiac is not available a variety of other woods can be used:

> juniper, citron, cypress, or pine, turpentine, cedar, ebony, or aromatic calamus with gentian root.

Then we come to details of the sweating method, which had evidently not changed much in the sixteen years since Fracastor's poem:

> The patient should remain in bed two or three hours and sweat; afterwards he can get up, if it seems wise. But it is better not to expose him to the open air until after the seventh day. For the complete treatment about twenty-five days are needed. . . . Meanwhile he must avoid sexual intercourse [presumably for his own sake], and all food that is acid and hard to digest.

Only then does Fracastor come to "drastic methods," including the use of mercury—the only substance in the list which had some real value, and which continued to be used down to recent times. Fracastor gives the following prescription for a mercury ointment:

pork fat	$1/2$ lb.
fresh butter	3 oz.
turpentine and liquid styrax, each	2 oz.
incense myrrh and mastic, each	$1/2$ oz.
aristolochia and gentian, each	3 drachms
hellebore	2 drachms
sulphur	$1/2$ oz.
nitre	1 drachm
juice of elecampane and celery, each	1 oz.
oil of rose laurel	q.s.
vinegar	1 oz.
quicksilver	$1/8$ of the whole

Mix, and make the ointment in an iron mortar.

Two pages further along Fracastor gives another prescription, this time for an ointment to be rubbed on the inner surfaces of the arms for severe headache. This ointment contains goose-grease instead of pork fat, and several new ingredients; but quicksilver is still "one-eighth of the whole."

In footnotes to this account of the use of mercury in Fracastor's book, Mrs. Wright, the translator, tells us that Widmann of Tübingen advocated the use of mercury for syphilis in 1501; but he was not the first to use it. (There are suggestions, as we will see later, that mercury had been used for treatment of disease centuries—perhaps thousands of years—earlier.) As early as 1497 Torella had been one of several who raged against it, calling it "murderous." But Mrs. Wright notes that Vigo, in 1514, had reported seeing a hundred cases healed by the use of mercury ointment alone, although he, like Fracastor, spoke of risks and disadvantages in its use. In the second footnote we learn, among other things, that the proportion of mercury in the "gray unguent" of Fournier's time (1870) was one-tenth, which had been the proportion used by Vigo. (Alfred Fournier was an earlier translator of Fracastor and an eminent French venereologist.) But Vigo used some highly imaginative ingredients, one of which was "live frogs," which, Mrs. Wright says,

> were then considered to have remarkable solvent, aperitive, and detersive properties for sores of all kinds. His [Vigo's] plaster was, in fact, long called "the frog-plaster"; another ingredient is "viper's fat." It is to the credit of Fracastorius that he omits both of these.

But it is too easy to sneer at ancient prescriptions. Let the facts speak only to the state of the art in those days. Contagion was beginning to be understood, but still dimly, still wrapped in the old superstitions. Something that eventually came to be called syphilis was emerging as a distinct disease, and its venereal character was strongly if incompletely suspected. It was generally believed to be new; but notions of its origin were, to say the least, fantastic and confused. The one item of treatment that had merit—mercury—was put forward diffidently in recognition of its dangers. There is a connection between the words "quicksilver," "quacksalver," and "quack."

❧ 6 ❧

Exit Columbus

W E ARE NOT likely ever to know beyond a doubt how syphilis began, or when. But the question continues to be
asked, and answered. A lot of patient research and some furious
argument have been devoted to the subject. We have already
seen that the Columbus story has little besides coincidence to
support it; and even the separate idea that the disease began,
from whatever cause, in the late fifteenth century is hardly more
than a matter of contemporary opinion that might be demol-
ished by convincing evidence to the contrary. But the uncertainty about contagion, and especially about sexual intercourse
as a way of transmitting disease, which prevailed at the time
will always prevent such evidence from being quite final. The
most we can hope for is perhaps a more reasonable theory to replace the one of origin in Columbus's time. Yet if the evidence
we are looking for is unlikely to be of the kind a scientist pre-
fers, it can be of the kind that has sent many a man to the gal-
lows. Readers of mysteries ought to be interested in the details
for their own sake; and as we pursue them we will learn more
not only about VD but also about the distinctive atmosphere of
passion and prejudice that surrounds the subject, a matter just
as important to us as understanding the diseases themselves.

We no longer believe in the extraterrestrial origin of disease, but look for beginnings here on earth. However syphilis started, it must have grown out of something that preceded it. And so we turn to certain diseases *other than* syphilis that may offer the clue we need. There are two groups of these other diseases: first, diseases now known to be quite different from syphilis, but with which syphilis might once have been confused (mainly leprosy); and second, closely related but *nonvenereal* diseases (the "treponematoses"). A close look at leprosy will, I think, dispose of the fifteenth-century-origin idea (which carries Columbus with it) sufficiently to clear the air for a look at the second group; this in turn will lead us to the other theory of origin. Those, in order, are the subjects of this and the next two chapters.

What is important to us about leprosy is, first, that it is recognized on all sides as one of the most ancient of diseases, going back to remote antiquity; and second, that what was called leprosy in early times was in fact not one disease but many.

One of the greatest modern experts on leprosy is Dr. Victor G. Heiser, who was the first president of the International Leprosy Association, in 1931–1938, and was honored on his ninety-sixth birthday, on April 19, 1969. In his book, *An American Doctor's Odyssey*, he says:

> Leprosy is the most ancient and exclusively human of diseases. It has followed man in all his migrations. The ancient records are not precise, and it is impossible to say with certainty that Egyptian papyrus, or Sanskrit *Rig-Veda*, or Chinese parchment, or Jewish *Old Testament* referred definitely to what we know as leprosy. Syphilis and yaws and various skin ailments have clinical symptoms often readily confused with it. One of the oldest works in Chinese medicine, called *Su-yen*, 400 B.C., described a disease which certainly had the characteristics of leprosy. . . .
>
> Leprosy among the Jews is undoubtedly very old, although from descriptions in *Leviticus* [14:4–8], many different forms of disease appear to have been included. . . .
>
> . . . the routes of travel, for trade or for conquest, have been the paths of disease as well. The Phoenicians may have bartered leprosy for sandalwood and spices; the Achaians crossed the wine-dark

sea for Helen, but their slaves may have brought leprosy back to
the shores of Greece; leprosy is supposed to have followed the armies, and was brought by Pompey's legions from the conquest of
the East; and the Soldiers of the Cross who set forth to rescue the
Holy Sepulchre, staggered back bearing the cross of leprosy to the
Christian world.

By the middle of the Twelfth Century leprosy was in Scotland,
Norway, the Shetland Islands, Holland, Denmark, Sweden, and
parts of Russia. . . .

Leprosy is still a serious problem. We are told that there are
more than twenty million lepers in the world today, mainly in
Africa, India, southwest Asia, and northern Latin America—that
is, generally in underdeveloped or impoverished areas. It need
not be surprising that the good treatment now at hand and the
means of prevention that are known are enjoyed by fewer than
20 per cent of all lepers. In addition to the leper colony at Molokai made famous by Father Damien there is another at Car-
ville, Louisiana. In the United States and Puerto Rico 147 new
cases were reported in 1968, the highest number in recent years.
Leprosy is showing up among United States military personnel
after foreign service. In England between 1951 and 1967 a total
of 732 leprosy patients were reported, of whom 196 had been
cured; an equal number were known to be static or quiescent
but were continuing treatment, all as outpatients. Lepers are
known to exist as well in New York City, where fear of ostra-
cism still holds back their recognition, sometimes for several
years. Yet the evidence strongly suggests that except for the
family of one American soldier, none of the known cases were
contracted in England or in the continental United States. Leprosy, says Dr. Howard A. Rusk, *"is much less infectious than
tuberculosis or the common cold."* In this and other respects, it
is very different from syphilis.

Through the ages, long before any clear notion of venereal
disease existed, it was leprosy—or whatever passed by that
name—that was regarded as the most loathsome of afflictions.
To Moses the leper was *unclean;* to the Christians of the Middle

Ages there were retreats or leprosaria ("lazarettos") for the rich,
but those who were afflicted with both poverty and leprosy—or,
to be more precise, the poor who were "accused and convicted"
of having leprosy by an ecclesiastical judge, to quote again from
Heiser:

> were cast out of the world. In nearly all countries the ceremony,
> called the *separatio leprosarum,* was similar and differed little from
> the offices of the dead. According to the ritual of Paris, the leper
> knelt before the altar, his face covered with a black veil, and lis-
> tened devoutly to mass. The officiating priest three times took a
> spadeful of earth from the cemetery and let it fall on the head of
> the leper while saying, "My friend, this is a sign that thou art dead
> to the world, *Sis mortuus mundo.*" And in consolation he added,
> "*Vivus interum deo.*" Thou shalt live again with God.

The leper was forbidden to enter the church, the marketplace,
or any assemblage of people; he must not wash in the brook or
anywhere else, and could only take water to drink with a jug or
cup he carried; he could go only barefoot and in a habit that
marked him as a leper, was forbidden to touch anything he
wished to buy, but could only point to it with his staff; he was
forbidden,

> while going through the fields, to reply to anyone who may ques-
> tion you, except first, for fear you might infect someone, you step
> off the road to leeward.

He must not go by the highway; and on the path he must not
touch hedges or bushes on either side unless he had first put on
gloves. He must not touch little children or any young people,
and was forbidden to eat or drink with anybody but other lepers. He wore a leper's robe of black with a veil over his mouth,
and carried cliquettes or clappers to warn of his approach.

All these horrors were, of course, based on notions of contagion, notions still unformed and intermingled with ideas of
magic. But leprosy was obviously thought to be conveyed by
contact, directly or indirectly through food or water, or through
the air in talking, or even by contaminated hedges or bushes.

Nevertheless at that time ideas of uncleanliness or defilement were all mixed up with the opposite idea of holiness. A. D. White, writing at the turn of the nineteenth century, reminds us that during the Middle Ages there was a belief current in theological circles, said to have come out of the Orient,

> that the abasement of man adds to the glory of God; that indignity to the body may secure salvation to the soul; hence, that cleanliness betokens pride and filthiness humility. Living in filth was regarded by great numbers of holy men . . . as an evidence of sanctity. . . . St. Hilarian lived his whole life in utter physical uncleanliness; . . . St. Anthony . . . never washed his feet; St. Abraham's most striking evidence of holiness was that for fifty years he washed neither his hands nor his feet; St. Sylvia never washed any part of her body save her fingers; St. Euphraxis belonged to a convent in which the nuns religiously abstained from bathing; St. Mary of Egypt was eminent for filthiness; St. Simon[sic] Stylites was in this respect unspeakable—the least that can be said is, that he lived in ordure and stench intolerable to his visitors. The *Lives of the Saints* dwells with complacency on the statement that, when sundry Eastern monks showed a disposition to wash themselves, the Almighty manifested his displeasure by drying up a neighboring stream until the bath which it had supplied was destroyed.

This was many centuries before the aphorism attributed to John Wesley, "cleanliness is near akin to godliness."

There is no reason to assume that the term "leprosy"—however many diseases it may have covered—was the only disease thought of as loathsome at the time; but it was certainly the model for loathsomeness and revulsion through the Middle Ages and beyond. These ideas and associations still cling to the word "leper" today. Somewhere along the way, however, the idea seemed to pass like a contagion in itself from leprosy to syphilis, or *what was being looked upon as loathsome was sometimes actually syphilis and not leprosy.* Scholars have come to this viewpoint reluctantly. Holcomb says:

> The non-technical scholar, too often subservient to terms, either because he knew little of syphilis and less of leprosy, or because he

was a victim of the silence that kept the wicked unmentionable syphilis out of standard works on medicine, unwittingly obstructed any change in the traditional [conception] of leprosy.

There is a good deal of evidence suggesting that some of the ancient leprosy was in fact syphilis. The high contagiousness attributed to leprosy is much more appropriate for syphilis. Even more suggestive are records of the existence in pre-Columbian Europe, and indeed even earlier, of something described as *venereal* leprosy or even as *congenital* leprosy. Leprosy, we now know, has neither of these properties. Syphilis, of course, has both.

Leprosy is certainly a communicable disease, but it is extraordinary how little we know today about the way it passes from one person to another. We know more, it seems, about how it does *not* pass than about how it does. It seems to require *prolonged* as well as intimate contact, favored somehow by poor hygiene and crowding; leprosy, like tuberculosis, to which it is bacteriologically related, is a disease of poverty. That leprosy can be communicated by inoculation *into* or *under* the skin is shown by a record of two American sailors who had been tattooed by the same operator in Melbourne, and who both developed signs of the disease two and a half years later. This very long incubation period is characteristic. Father Damien subjected himself to all the privations of the lepers of Molokai; according to J. Farrow, his biographer:

> he deliberately made it a point to eat from the same dishes when sharing their humble meals and often his pipe was lent to a leper.

He exposed himself to the grossest sort of contamination, as for example when he performed crude surgery on lepers,

> nor did he even have, as he delved into putrid flesh, the comforting protection of rubber gloves. . . .

He did not turn away from the spray coughed by a leper over him while he was hearing confession. Nevertheless he first no-

ticed signs of the disease on himself as long as twelve years after
he arrived at Molokai; he was dead of it after four years more.
The incubation period is said to extend occasionally to as long
as twenty years.

Leprosy is believed to be transmitted mainly by contact of
open sores on exposed skin, or discharges from the nose and
throat, into cuts and scratches in the skin of the receiver. Buret
mentions several instances of healthy persons living among lepers without contracting it, and a particular one of a woman married to a leper for eight years who remained uninfected. Father
Damien is quoted by Farrow as agreeing with the general modern opinion that leprosy is neither venereal nor congenital:

> Marital relations do not always mean infection. There is a woman
> in the village who remains healthy, yet she has buried three hus-
> bands who have died of the disease, and she is now wed to her
> fourth. . . . As for the children of such a union, they are born
> clean.

Damien's biographer adds that "such infants are taken from the
parents at an early age as a precaution against any possible contagion." But this older practice, cruel to both parents and children, has now been given up, since modern treatment can
quickly make the parents noninfectious and lead on to arrest
and cure.

Leprosy is not a venereal disease, but the question of congenital infection is worth a few additional words. A current review
of this general question lists all the common infectious diseases
that cross the placenta to infect the fetus. The most important of
these today are virus diseases, of which rubella, or German measles, has claimed most attention in recent years. Others include
measles itself, smallpox, chickenpox and the related zoster or
shingles, genital herpes, polio, and mumps. There are others,
more obscure. A single protozoan disease is listed, toxoplasmo-
sis. Syphilis is, of course, a prominent member of the group. It is
said that "transplacental bacterial infection is [otherwise] rare."
The article speaks of infectious accidents occurring during birth,

among them gonorrheal infection of the baby's eyes. Leprosy is
not mentioned.

There has been a small and rather neglected group of scholars
who have ransacked the record for evidence that syphilis existed
before Columbus's time. The result is no lack of quantity, but
some of it tends to have an odd quality, faintly suggesting an effort to get through to the totally deaf by shouting. The record
gives hints that their intended audience has nearly always either
been completely indifferent or has given them the curious blend
of gentle but firm detachment usually reserved for foolish children or the mildly insane. It is hard to tell whether these scholars are given to screaming in the first place or are reacting to
the opposition around them. Consider as a relatively mild example a footnote in a paper of 1941 by Holcomb, of which I give
you the full text, with ellipses replacing only references:

> According to Columbus' journal, upon his return from the first voy-
> age he disembarked at Palos. Becker and Obermayer say he landed
> at Cadiz. . . . Montejo says he disembarked at Barcelona. . . .
> Monardes says he disembarked at Naples with a load of Indian
> prostitutes. . . . The official Spanish records of the Probanzas and
> all contemporary Spanish historians say the deserter Martin Alonzo
> Pinzon landed at the Spanish port of Bayona in Galicia. . . .
> D'Arcy Power says Pinzon landed at Bayonia in France. . . . Wins-
> low says one of Columbus' ships touched in France without saying
> which of them, or where it made the landfall. . . . Montejo . . . ,
> Block . . . , Pusey . . . , Jeanselme . . . , and others following
> Ruiz Diaz de Isla . . . say that he or some other Pinzon landed at
> Barcelona, and that he with his crew were suffering from some
> form of epidemic syphilis. The confusion is the result of plain error
> or the imagination of prejudice or ignorance, the truth being
> clearly recorded at the time and amply verified [references are
> given here to Martin Fernandez Navarette, 1765–1844, and to
> two Spanish papers by D. Luis Comenga, both dated 1903].

This will suggest the breadth of scholarship entailed in dealing
with a single historical point; and you are free to decide which
came first—the mildly heated tone of the footnote, or the busy
doctor of 1941, reading (if at all) with a wan smile and turning

back to his patients, his prejudices (if such they were) all unshaken.

And Holcomb may have been guilty of adding darkness to ob-
scurity by being a trifle categorical. He bases his main argument
on the assertion that syphilis

> in a now accepted triad of causation . . . is (a) contagious, (b) ve-
> nereal and (c) congenital, in which triad it stands unique

using as authority a then current U.S. Public Health Service
report. But the assertion is defective. The two first points are re-
dundant, since a disease could hardly be venereal without being
contagious. The second defect is more serious. *Unique* is a
strong word: a single exception is enough to fracture it. The single exception certainly exists in the form of genital herpes,
which, as we saw a moment ago, can be congenital. It can also
be transmitted venereally; we exclude it from the inner circle of
VD, as we will see later, only because it can be transmitted in
other ways as well.

But although I think we can understand and sympathize with
the attempts of Holcomb and others to break through the evident indifference or obstinacy of their audience, it is really too
bad that they let themselves be carried away. There is much in
Holcomb that is worth studying; in fact, his errors are matters of
form rather than of content.

The fact is that herpes would probably not have been confused with either leprosy or syphilis, so that the objection to
the word "unique," although valid, does not really affect Holcomb's main argument.

He begins by telling us what other scholars have also accepted, that the name "leprosy" was applied with great inexact-
ness in the early days. He says the leprosy of Leviticus 13 was
the vitiligo of Celsus (alopecia areata or piebald patchy baldness, now thought to be neurological); the leprosy of the Byzan-
tine Greeks was probably psoriasis, a scaly skin disease; the leprosy of the medieval Christians was a mixture of all sorts of

diseases "too incomprehensible in their scanty details to admit of a natural explanation"; while the

> leprosy of the physicians and surgeons of the Middle Ages was syphilis of the center of the face as now seen to develop in congenital, or, as a late or "tertiary" symptom of acquired syphilis. . . . It had been previously known to the Greeks as elephantiasis . . . and to the Romans as Mentagra.

Holcomb proceeds to point out that this disease had the characters of his triad. He speaks of support in Latin texts describing leprosy dating between 1050 and 1492, but concentrates on the work of Bernard of Gordon, of which he examined several texts, the earliest dating from 1348. Bernard described leprosy as arising in the child within the womb, or from coitus with a leprous woman. Bernard is thus quoted by Holcomb:

> And it will also break forth in him who lies with a woman who has lain with a leper, the seed of whom remains in her womb . . .

with additional details to much the same effect. Bernard's venereal leprosy was transmitted before birth to the child of a leper; a woman could be infected with venereal leprosy and give birth to a leprous child. He averred that leprosy was spread by promiscuous women, who acquired it from the semen of leprous men; he also suggested that such venereal leprosy could remain latent (occult, hidden), and be transmitted, for instance, by a woman showing no sign of illness. All of this is true of syphilis; none of it fits leprosy.

And although the Columbus story keeps recurring like the refrain of a song, the opposite theme is heard now and then in an authoritative quarter. Here, for instance, is what Charles Singer, a noted historian of science and medicine, says in the fourteenth edition of the *Encyclopedia Britannica* (1937). I give the whole paragraph, which is all Singer says of the subject in the article "Medicine, History of." It seems to me remarkable how simply he makes the point, yet how little conviction his words might carry to one already committed to the reverse:

To one infectious disease, syphilis, we must refer more particularly. During the middle ages there had smouldered in various districts an obscure disease known frequently as *lepra*. Toward the end of the 15th century this disease broke out in epidemic form all over Europe, causing great destruction of life. It received various titles, such as "the pox," "the French disease," "the Spanish disorder." Only tardily was it recognized that it was of venereal origin. In 1530, on the suggestion of Fracastoro, it received the cognomen syphilis. From the time of its recognition, syphilis had been pursued by a portentous mass of confused literature. Alarm, misunderstanding, religious feeling, false modesty, wilful misrepresentation, and the change in type of the disease itself, have all contributed their quota of obscurantism and fable to a naturally difficult subject. Fracastoro did something to bring order out of the confusion.

Among students of the history of syphilis the one who seems most painstaking in his scholarship is Dr. Frederic Buret of Paris, who had the misfortune to write a few years too soon, in 1889. Bacteriology was then in its early adolescence. The great victories of maturity in public health were a decade or more in the future, and none of the important discoveries in syphilis—on cause, diagnosis, and cure—had yet been made. The clinical art was by then highly developed, and Buret was obviously an excellent clinician as well as an accomplished linguist and scholar. But if he could have waited he might have avoided diagnostic errors that weaken what is otherwise a definitive case. He is unmistakably partisan. He charges his fellow Frenchman Astruc with responsibility for fastening the Columbus "legend" on the world more than 250 years after the event. Buret would have us believe that few took the Columbus story seriously before Astruc's time. Yet again allowing for errors, admitting that Buret often identifies as syphilis what we can now distinguish easily as something else, he nevertheless amasses instance after instance which can hardly leave the unprejudiced reader in doubt that syphilis was indeed known to ancient China and Japan, to the Hebrews, the Hindus, the Greeks and Romans, and continuously in Europe through the Middle Ages and down to the years preceding the voyages of Columbus. Both its venereal and its congenital aspects were recognized from the beginning. It was often confused with leprosy and called by a profusion of misleading names. But the indurated (hard) chancre was known, as were the spots and figlike sores of secondary syphilis and the destructive lesions of late syphilis.

Buret tells us that the first written allusion to the Columbus story was by a German, Leonard Schmaus, dated 1518, and was little more than the reflection of a contemporary superstition based on the report of another German, Nicolas Poll, a year earlier. Poll had argued that since guaiac, which came from Hispaniola, was the reported cure, "Providence always places the remedy next to the disease." The so-called "facts" arrived afterward, conveniently, from Dias de Isla and Oviedo, embroidering the fantasy of Fracastor. I have let Buret's irony color my words.

Among the hasty statements that must have helped discredit in Buret what is sound as well as what is not is his certainty that syphilis existed in America at the time as well as in Europe, in fact everywhere in the world, from remotest antiquity. He also weakens the fabric of his argument by asserting that there were repeated "epidemics" of syphilis before the one at the end of the fifteenth century, including some, such as the plague of Athens, which we are sure were not syphilis.

But to throw away all of Buret because of his mistakes is itself the same sort of mistake, if not quite so bad, as to throw Shakespeare away for his seacoast in Bohemia, or Beethoven for his *Battle* symphony, or, as the English like to say, to throw out the baby with the bathwater. If we compare Buret with Astruc, it becomes clear that science had made strides in the interval between them. Buret does confess to doubt occasionally; Astruc never does, to the best of my recollection. And if one compares Buret with a more recent historian of syphilis, the widely quoted William Allen Pusey (1933), who achieves the assurance of Astruc in a few authoritative paragraphs, I am inclined to keep Buret with the baby and toss Pusey out with the bathwater. I have the strong and disturbing impression that despite the great advances of scientific skepticism there are still a few scholars who like to lean on authority as those of the Middle Ages leaned on Aristotle and Galen.

Evidence which modern authors, including Pusey, who support the Columbian theory, put forward as presumably the last word on this subject, is that of alleged syphilitic bones, which they tell us are numerous in pre-Columbian America but absent in Europe during the same period. The record, however, is one of the most confused areas of the whole subject, with the experts taking exactly opposite views. C. J. Hackett tells us that where one expert is convinced that pre-Columbian American bones showed venereal syphilis, another (Aleš Hrdlička) says:

> from evidence of thousands of Indian skulls and skeletons predating the arrival of Columbus, there is, as yet, not a single instance of thoroughly authenticated pre-Columbian syphilis.

The record for Europe on this matter of bones is muddled by confusion of syphilis with leprosy, as well as by the known occurrence of bone changes like those of syphilis in the nonvenereal syphilis-like diseases we are going to talk about in the next chapter. Hackett (of whom I will say more), who prepared a report on the origin of syphilis for the World Health Organization, mentions that "some of the leprosy [in bone lesions] of pre-Columbian Europe might have been syphilis." He suggests that the issue may have been confused by other errors of diagnosis and concludes that "all this needs reconsideration." He dismisses the Columbus story as having been "debated with more heat than light."

A detailed examination a few years ago (1966) of pre-Columbian sculpture in America found nothing that clearly depicted syphilis.

But if we accept the probability that syphilis was not brought to Europe from America by Columbus's crew or anyone else but had evidently existed in Europe in much earlier times, we ought still to attempt some kind of explanation for the epidemic

that broke out in Europe at the time, as well as for the failure of
most physicians to recognize it earlier, and the belief of Fracastor and others that it was a new disease. We build as facts on
the occurrence of an epidemic, its widespread recognition by
physicians, and the belief that it was something new. But we assume that it had existed before, "smoldering," as Singer put it,
and that it burst into flame in Columbus's time. If we are to tie
up the loose ends of our story as mystery writers have taught us
to do, we need to look at some of the surrounding circumstances
and events. Obviously this is going to be guesswork.

I think the clue may lie in the nature of the Renaissance, in
historical circumstances which John Addington Symonds, the
English scholar of the late nineteenth century, says "every
schoolboy knows." But I suspect that in the electronic age
schoolboys (and schoolgirls, who didn't count for much then)
have less patience with such things. The significant events are
suggested by such schoolboy dates as the invention of printing
in 1440 and the fall of Constantinople in 1453. There were tremendous upheavals in the very closing years of the fifteenth century that concern us. In January of 1492 the Catholic monarchs
occupied Granada, overthrowing the last Moorish kingdom in
Europe. A few months later they decreed the expulsion of all
Jews from Spain, and in so doing, perhaps, fired off the first gun
in the great war between feudalism and the old Church on the
one hand and a rising capitalism and the new sects on the other
that went on to the Reformation. Buret suggests that the Dias-
pora itself may have helped spread syphilis throughout Europe.
But other groups were in turbulent movement. Symonds says
that in the years 1492–1500,

> the expedition of Charles VIII to Naples opened Italy to the
> French, Spanish and German interference. The leading nations of
> Europe began to compete for the prize of the peninsula, and
> learned meanwhile that culture which the Italians had perfected.
> . . . The same period was marked by the discovery of America, the
> exploration of the Indian seas, and the consolidation of the Spanish

nationality. It also witnessed the application of printing to the diffusion of knowledge. Thus, speaking roughly, the half-century between 1450 and 1500 may be termed the culminating point of the
Renaissance.

And after dealing with the advances and virtues of the period,
Symonds continues:

> Beneath the surface of brilliant social culture lurked gross appetites
> and savage passions, unrestrained by medieval piety, untutored by
> modern experience . . . a succession of worldly pontiffs brought
> the Church into flagrant discord with the principles of Christianity
> . . . the educated classes lost their grasp upon morality. Political
> honesty ceased almost to have a name in Italy. The Christian vir-
> tues were scorned by the foremost actors and ablest thinkers of the
> time. . . . This is apparent to all students of Machiavelli and Guic-
> ciardini [an apparently revolting character who wrote a great his-
> tory of the very period of the epidemic, 1492–1530], the profound-
> est analysts of their age, the bitterest satirists of its vices, but
> themselves infected with its incapacity for moral goodness. . . .
> When Italy between the years 1494 and 1530 became the battle-
> field of French, German and Spanish forces, it was seen to what a
> point of helplessness the political, moral and social conditions of the
> Renaissance had brought the nation. . . .

Making due allowance for the viewpoint of an Englishman of
the Victorian period, we can nevertheless imagine a combination of circumstances—the new diffusion of knowledge and the
liberation of thought; the movement of large groups of people
across national boundaries, and the sexual relaxation that evidently followed the terrible mortality from the Black Death a
century and a half earlier (as well as the promiscuous sexual activity that is always a companion of war)—to give us a vastly
better basis for the rapid spread of VD, from many smoldering
centers, than the notion that it could all have started from one
point, in Naples in 1494. It has been suggested that a mutant
spirochete producing more severe disease may have appeared at
the same time. Such a hypothesis seems to me uneconomical.
The explanation seems to be shaping up without an idea which
is beyond reach of any effort to verify it.

But now consider what Astruc says near the beginning of his treatise, written just 250 years after the siege of Naples. The disease

> . . . was unknown to the Ancients. . . . Its first origin could be traced to . . . Hispaniola . . . whence it was unluckily imported into Europe. That the Spaniards, who arrived there in the Years 1492 and 1493, under Christopher Columbus, first contracted that Disease by lying with the Women of the Country, and thence conveyed it to Naples, which they went to relieve, *An.* 1494. That the French, who at that Time were at War with the Spaniards and Neapolitans, were soon infected by both; and that from these three principal Nations the Contagion was soon communicated to the rest of Europe, and quickly run over most Part of Asia and Africa.

Astruc is convinced to begin with; but he is a scholar, and he bravely marshals evidence both pro and con, always finding grounds to discard the second so as to leave his faith unshaken. It is clear, he says,

> from the silence of the old Physicians, that the Venereal Disease was a Distemper not known in their days. . . .

And similarly with the ancient poets, who were not "altogether so modest"—

> Every one knows what coarse Raillery is to be met with in this Subject. . . . Shall we imagine, that such obscene and abusive writers as *Horace, Juvenal* and *Persius* . . . [or] *Catullus* and *Martial*, who never spare for a loose Reflection,

would have failed to mention the subject if they knew of it? Buret adduces page after page of evidence to the contrary; we will look at some of it later. As for physicians overlooking syphilis, although there may have been more than one reason, we know that they examined women in semidarkness and without removing their bedclothing, and that they refused to treat prostitutes, leaving them to others. Be it remembered as well that the early physicians were usually "gentlemen with clean hands," as Oliver Wendell Holmes, senior, described his contemporaries many centuries later. They left the dirty work to barbers and barber-surgeons and similar inferior folk.

Astruc raises the matter of confusion of syphilis with leprosy and dismisses it, comparing the symptoms of leprosy as Avicenna (980–1037 A.D.) gave them with those Astruc knew for syphilis. Leprosy, he had decided, was contracted by an error of diet, not by infection; and leprosy was incurable. Lumping all venereal disease together, he even argues against the occurrence in ancient times of VD that was evidently not syphilis:

> *Palladius* Bishop of Helenopolis . . . writes "that a certain . . . *Ero,* who was both a Glutton and a Drunkard, and lusted violently after the Fair-Sex, had to do with an Actress, whence by the Just Judgment of Heaven, he was seized with a Carbuncle in the Glans [head of the penis], which made so rapid a Progress, that in a Fortnight's Time his private Parts mortified and dropt off of their own accord. . . .

But this and similar incidents were not VD to Astruc. Ero's carbuncle was anthrax; others were cancer. Even "simple gonorrhea"—confused in the context, as the word was by its inventor, Galen (ca. 130–200 A.D.), with involuntary emission of semen—was not "contracted in a sinful way." None of these diseases could have been VD because

> it is as plain as anything can be, that the Venereal Disease was first brought into Europe only toward the end of the fifteenth Century. . . .

But Astruc's climactic argument is deferred to the ninth and last book of his treatise, in which he appends an account of a careful correspondence he had with two Jesuit priests living in Peking, on the history of VD in China. He approached these gentlemen with a detailed questionnaire to which he received meticulous answers together with a treatise on VD by a Chinese physician, part of which Astruc reproduces in the original Chinese characters. The details are patiently spelled out and then summed up as follows:

The Chinese Physicians are of the Opinion, that the Venereal Disease has been known in the Empire of China in all Ages; and indeed the Books of Physic wrote in the Chinese Language, which are acknowledged to be very old, are quite silent as to the first Appearance of that Disease, nay it is mentioned in them, as being very ancient at the Time when those Books were wrote. Wherefore it is neither known to have been imported from some other Country, nor is it very probable. Certainly it can by no means be inferred from the Names which it goes by in China. . . .

But to Astruc, celebrated physician to King Louis XV, his preconception unshaken, one of the Chinese names, *Chi Tchouang,* meaning *the ulcer of Time,* must mean the *ulcer of the present time,* implying that the disease must be new; and the separate treatment of VD in Chinese books somehow must suggest newness. Despite denials from all his sources, Astruc is persuaded that VD was imported into China by the Portuguese, who brought it to Canton, he says, when they first arrived there in 1517. It is strange, he admits, that the Chinese never spoke of it as the *Portuguese Disease;* but they are, after all, inscrutable.

Buret later went back over the same ground with independent scholarship, and assures us that the Jesuit priests were right. There are records, he says, going back to the third millennium B.C., of the separation of the syphilitic chancre from the one we now call chancroid, of both from gonorrhea, and of the use of mercury for treatment! Exit Columbus.

7

Syphilis and the "Treponematoses"

I N ORDER TO understand the theory of the origin of syphilis which has been put forward in opposition to the one involving a fifteenth-century origin, we must now get down to some details about syphilis, and compare it with the second group of diseases I mentioned at the start of Chapter 6—the related but *nonvenereal* diseases. While we do this we will also be getting at something that is obviously important to us, namely, the nature and characteristics of syphilis itself.

The group of diseases I am going to tell you about now, including syphilis, are all related biologically: they are all caused by spirochetes which even today can hardly be distinguished one from another. The only acceptable name for the group is the technical one, *treponematoses,* based on the name of the genus of spirochetes that causes them, *Treponema.*

It may be helpful to begin with a table which I have taken, with considerable modification of form, principally from a paper by C. J. Hackett, whom I have mentioned before. In the table the treponematoses are divided, as is customary, into four groups, starting with the most familiar one, syphilis, or venereal syphilis proper. The second I have called nonvenereal syphilis; it is also called endemic (as opposed to epidemic) syphilis, and has many

THE TREPONEMATOSES: SYPHILIS AND THE SYPHILIS-LIKE DISEASES

	VENEREAL SYPHILIS	NONVENEREAL SYPHILIS	YAWS	PINTA
	pallidum	*pallidum*	*pertenue*	*carateum*
The spirochete is called *Treponema*		(The four are identical even under the electron microscope; they differ mainly in the disease they produce in man and experimental animals.)		
Infection usually starts in	adults	children	children	children
but may be *congenital*	yes	seldom or never	probably never	never
Transmitted by contact with or between	genitals	mouth or skin	skin	skin
Individual sores are infectious for	a few months	a few months	a few months	many years
The sick person may transmit the disease for	3–5 years	3–5 years	3–5 years	many years
Latency (symptoms disappear but may reappear later) is	characteristic	characteristic	characteristic	probably absent
The first sore is usually on	genitals	mouth	skin of legs	exposed skin
Involvement of bone is	present	present	present	absent
Involvement of heart, brain, and other organs is	present	mild or absent	absent	absent
	The Wassermann and other tests on serum, including specific tests, are positive in all, without differences			
	All are equally treatable with penicillin and other antibiotics			
Original environment	urban	rural	rural	rural
Favoring climate: temperature	cool (any)	warm (any?)	tropical	tropical
humidity	any	dry	humid	humid

other synonyms, a common and short one being *bejel* (bedg'el). Hereafter I will use the word "syphilis" unmodified to mean the venereal form; endemic or nonvenereal syphilis will be identified as such or as bejel. The third disease, yaws, is also known by a name taken from the French word for raspberry (*framboise*) as frambesia—because of the appearance of the characteristic sores on the skin (which are called, in the plural, "yaws"); it, too, has many synonyms. The fourth form of treponematosis, pinta (meaning "painted"—referring to the characteristic change in or loss of pigment in the affected skin) is also called mal de pinto, carate, and again by other names.

The names of the diseases themselves, the species names given to the spirochetes, and other things in the table will suggest that the two forms of syphilis are closely related. It will also be plain that pinta is rather different from the others. It is so different, in fact, that although more than one observer had hinted at a relationship to syphilis beginning as early as 1889, it was not until 1926 in Mexico and 1930 in Cuba that a spirochete was found in pinta, with the result that it was moved out of the class of fungus diseases, where it had formerly been put by error, and reclassified with the treponematoses. Incidentally, it was only with the discovery of the spirochetes of syphilis and yaws, both in 1905, that the relationships and differences among these diseases could begin to be worked out. In fact a leading British textbook emphasized as recently as 1964 that the various treponematoses and their causative agents had not yet been clearly distinguished.

Some of these difficulties are not to be denied. One appears in the parenthetical statement under the first line of the table: we cannot distinguish the four spirochetes. We recognize four diseases, and since they differ, we say we have four spirochetes (although, inconsistently enough, we call two of them by the same name). Three species, then. We assume that the three spirochetes are different; but no specialist in this field, shown any one of them under any microscope, could tell it apart from the others. Nor could he perform any test or series of tests—unless he knew beforehand which one he was dealing with—that would positively identify the species. The fact is that we are not really sure they are different. Apart from the differences in the diseases themselves, there are subtle differences in the symptoms the spirochetes produce in experimental animals—rabbits and hamsters. The pinta spirochete stands out in that it produces nothing in these animals; only recently has it been found infectious experimentally for chimpanzees. Other small differences in the chemistry of the spirochetal cells are disclosed by so-called immune ("antigen-antibody") reactions. They are of the sort we usually associate with differences among strains of the same species (taken, that is, from different people with the same disease) rather than with different species.

We cannot grow these spirochetes in cultures by any of the methods used for other microbes or for viruses. There are cultures of so-called *Treponema pallidum* to which we usually give other names because, even if some of them were once the spirochete of syphilis (which is uncertain), they have changed: they no longer infect animals; they grow rather easily; they even look different. Virulent spirochetes, taken from syphilis in man or experimental animals, do not grow in cultures, with possible rare exceptions. If this happens at all, the culture loses its virulence at once, and there is always a suspicion that it was a different spirochete to begin with. (The nonpathogenic spirochetes *do* grow in cultures.)

Our inability to grow *Treponema pallidum* in cultures is one of the main stumbling blocks to progress, especially in one part of the VD problem I will talk about later—the preparation of a vaccine. Being unable to grow them in this way, we keep them going in the laboratory for experimental purposes by injecting them into animals—rabbits are used universally—and transferring them from one animal to another.

Since progress in the understanding of most microbes did not start until they could be grown in "pure culture," it may seem remarkable that we have nevertheless learned a great deal about the spirochete of syphilis. But we also learned a lot about viruses before they could be grown in fertile chick embryos or in tissue cultures—when they, too, could be studied only by passage through animals.

If we could grow *Treponema pallidum* in culture we could, for one thing, more easily decide whether the different treponematoses are actually caused by different spirochetes. In the meantime we cannot effectively dispose of an argument put forward especially by Ellis H. Hudson in 1946, that there is really only a single disease, *treponematosis*, of which the variants are determined by differences in climate and in man's way of living. This idea conforms to the ancient scholastic rule of Occam, still respected as a principle, that a hypothesis should be as simple as possible. Hudson's idea is nevertheless not taken seriously by many people; but that fact is not evidence against it. It is not with prejudice but only for convenience that we proceed on the assumption of four diseases and at least three spirochetes—more for the sake of its consequences than because we know it to be true. There is, in fact, a little scattered evidence, not enough to be actually convincing, that the clinical differences suggested in the table may change under the very conditions spoken of by Hudson; but this does not happen regularly or predictably: a person with one of the diseases does not give somebody else one of the others. Nevertheless, doubts in this quarter remain unresolved.

The principal differences between the four treponematoses are hinted at in the next three lines of the table, which say in effect that *syphilis is a venereal disease of adults, while the other three are nonvenereal diseases of children*. All are transmitted by intimate contact, but the contact is nearly always venereal only for syphilis. This is an important point, and we must take time to understand it.

These spirochetes are all extraordinarily fragile when they are separated from the living flesh they can grow in, meaning man's except under laboratory conditions. There is a natural treponematosis of rabbits ("cuniculosis") I will do no more than mention. A natural disease of African monkeys that evidently belongs in this group has been discovered only recently. This discovery has caused something of a stir, and has led even more recently to the finding of still another definite simian treponematosis, in the dog-faced baboon of West Africa. It seems possible that if there are two such diseases there may be more; and doubtless they will be looked for. But the four main treponematoses we are talking about are peculiarly diseases of man. The first three can be passed artificially into rabbits, but they are not venereal in rabbits, being propagated from rabbit to rabbit only by taking material from an infected animal and injecting it into another one.

The only means available to the spirochetes to pass from one human being to another is direct and intimate contact. We may include directly transfused blood; but note that even brief periods of storage of blood under ordinary refrigeration will inactivate the spirochetes in it. Other exceptions are sometimes assumed, but usually out of ignorance or wishful thinking, like the perennial toilet seat.

Children with nonvenereal treponematoses live in areas where contact is uninhibited, for climatic or other reasons. The contact is skin-to-skin in humid tropical countries where children go naked, or mouth-to-skin (or mouth-to-finger-to-skin or elsewhere) in drier or cooler places where clothing is used but where what we think of as hygienic conditions are primitive. In all such places the contact is likely to be made before the age of sexual maturity, and by puberty the disease will have become noninfectious or immunity will have developed, so that sex will have nothing to do with maintaining it. The nonvenereal treponematoses are, accordingly, rural and primitive, and for other reasons to be mentioned are believed to be very ancient. The venereal form is thought to have begun as a disease of cities—although it need not remain so—where clothing, improving hy-

giene and various other cultural circumstances limit the possibility of transfer mainly to the only suitable intimate contact
that remains—sexual intercourse—and to the ages at which that
happens. Since the spirochetes grow well in the genital area and
produce sores there, genital transfer is—if I may put it that way
—ready-made for them.

But when it is present in adult tissues without immunity—
which, again, means principally or only venereal syphilis—the
spirochete can go through the placenta and infect a fetus in the
uterus. As we saw before, with rare exceptions it seems to be the
only *bacterium* (as distinct from virus) capable of doing this. Its
capacity to do it may be related to the unusual thinness of the
spirochete, as well as to its shape and movement, which may let
the spirochete go through the placenta as a corkscrew goes
through a cork. The consequence is congenital syphilis.

Syphilis is the best-studied of the treponematoses. It includes
all the features of the next two, if not of all three, so that to
some extent we can speak of them together. But syphilis also has
distinctive features; and pinta is different enough to call for separate description.

All the treponematoses are *slow* diseases, as bacterial diseases
go. The spirochetes have been found to divide in two every
thirty *hours,* as compared with twenty to thirty *minutes* for most
disease bacteria. They probably penetrate only through a break
in skin or a moist body surface, but the tiniest scratch is enough.
We can estimate that several hundred spirochetes are usually
present during the transmitting event, whether it is venereal or
not. Some of them fail to get through and die in the attempt;
and, depending on the stage of the disease in the source—in
terms of relative developing immunity—some may not survive
after they get through. But when the infection comes from early,
active disease, in which there is no immunity or only a trace of
it, all the spirochetes that get in may multiply and keep on
doing so. This is the highest degree of infectiousness we know.

In experiments with rabbits, with the necessary conditions

kept under control, it has been estimated that no more than one or two spirochetes are needed to produce disease. The larger the number introduced, the shorter will be the interval between inoculation and the first symptoms. This interval is, of course, the "incubation period." It seems to depend simply on the number of active spirochetes introduced, their rate of multiplication (which is considered constant at thirty hours), and the number, estimated at about 100 million, which when present all together in a given spot cause enough irritation to set up a detectable sore. You can easily calculate yourself on this basis that a single spirochete might generate the hundred million or so in something more than a month. In fact the incubation period varies over wide limits, influenced by the presence of inactive spirochetes from a partly immune source as well as by the number of spirochetes transferred. It has also been suggested that different "strains" of spirochetes—depending on their source—may grow at different rates. Much longer incubation periods are possible and do in fact occur. But the usual average incubation period of about three weeks would depend, assuming fully active spirochetes of the standard strain, on a "dose"—the word is technical —of the order of 250 spirochetes. These are extraordinarily efficient—*exquisitely adapted*—microbes. If the words sound inappropriate, even heartless, think of something Hudson said: "What do spirochetes know of venery?"

In venereal syphilis there is likely to develop at the point of inoculation, nearly always on the penis or somewhere in the region of the vulva or vagina, a single sore called a chancre or *hard* chancre. "Hard" refers to the ring of rubbery or cartilaginous tissue around the base of the sore, and is contrasted with the similar but *soft* chancre of the minor venereal disease called by that name or by the term "chancroid." This primary sore of syphilis is nearly always single and painless. It grows over a period of days or a week or more from a small pimple to the size of a marble, and tends to break down on top and form an ulcer. The lymph nodes in the area, usually the groin, become large and hard. Spirochetes are present in fluid that can be pressed out of the chancre; they are also in the lymph nodes. Found under these conditions, they establish the diagnosis of syphilis.

No chancre has been recorded, to my knowledge, in any of the treponematoses other than venereal syphilis. It doesn't always appear even in syphilis. The first sign may be what is sometimes called the secondary stage. Terminology can be a little confusing here because it has been changing. The "primary" stage is that of the chancre and its swollen lymph nodes. In the "secondary" stage there is a skin rash and some other things I will explain. These two stages combined make up what is now usually called "early" syphilis, which may also include one or more periods of "latency" in which there are no symptoms. This may happen after the chancre heals and before the rash appears, or between successive crops of what are called in the jargon "secondaries." These symptom-free intervals would be "early latency." After the secondary symptoms heal and disappear, as they tend to do, things happen which are sometimes spoken of as "tertiary" syphilis. But this word has tended to be replaced by the more inclusive term "late" syphilis, in which there may again be periods of latency (now "late latency"). One important reason for this newer terminology is that it is only in the "early" stages that the disease is contagious. Although syphilis may go on developing and, in fact, become most severe and destructive, in its "late" period, the person with such late disease does not transmit it to others.

All of this, except for the general absence of a chancre, applies to bejel and yaws as well as to venereal syphilis.

The chancre heals of itself, and as it does so or some time later a rash appears on the body, all over it or anywhere on it, including the skin of the palms and soles, and in the mouth as well as around the genitalia and the anus. This is the secondary stage. The rash takes a wide variety of forms, and some of the sores of syphilis look very much like those of yaws. These secondary lesions, especially the ones in moist areas, teem with spirochetes and are the most contagious of all the sores in the commoner treponematoses. While some clinicians insist that they can tell the three diseases apart (I am not speaking of pinta), most opinion has it that venereal syphilis may include all the varieties of lesions, and that differences depend on location on the body, and on such factors as skin temperature and moisture, as determined in part by climatic conditions and perhaps by hygiene and clothing.

In syphilis these early lesions are usually painless and not destructive; that is, they heal, with or without treatment, with little or no scarring. A person who does not suspect what they really are may pass them off as of little importance. In yaws the early sores may be more severe and destructive, leaving deforming scars as they heal and even producing damage to bone. But pain and discomfort are not always absent in secondary syphilis; there is often, especially, a sore throat with hoarseness. There may be pain in bones and joints, sometimes only at night. In more severe cases there may be fever and a patchy loss of hair from the head or anywhere else, including the eyebrows and eyelashes. A rare malignant form of syphilis is known to occur; it was described in 1969 and again in 1970, with the suggestion, offered tentatively, that it may have been the same as the "great pox" of the fifteenth century. In such "lues maligna," constitutional symptoms are pronounced, with large ugly ulcers of skin and moist surfaces which tend to form crusts or scabs. Death may follow if the disease strikes a vital organ.

What has happened in the three diseases—syphilis, bejel, and yaws—up to this point is that the spirochetes have multiplied in the lymph nodes that drain the place where the first sore appeared, and spilled over into the blood. Since no first sore is known in yaws and bejel, it may have appeared in such a place, or been so insignificant—or both—that it was not noticed. Having reached the bloodstream—a very early event in all instances —the microbes are carried all over the body. They settle out at the ends of capillaries and grow again, leading to irritation and

damage as their numbers reach a high enough level. These generalized lesions may show themselves in syphilis while the chancre is still present, or as it heals; or there may intervene one or
several periods without symptoms ("early latency"); as much as
six months may pass before new lesions appear.

These early lesions and symptoms tend to heal and disappear,
and may then reappear, heal, and disappear again, over a period, as the table indicates, as long as three to five years. After
that the patient is no longer a danger to the community. Even
without treatment, the U.S. Public Health Service told doctors
in 1968,

> Studies in syphilis epidemiology have recently indicated that
> only early latent syphilis of under 1 year's duration produces suffi-
> cient infectious syphilis to warrant patient interviewing and contact
> investigation. Because of this finding several state health depart-
> ments have already changed the definition of early latent syphilis to
> include only cases of less than 1 year's duration.

It is possible that the patient could marry after this time without infecting his spouse, although no physician would be likely
to advise his doing so. But for the patient himself the worst may
still lie ahead.

A famous study was begun in 1891 at the Rikshospitalet in
Oslo on 1978 patients with early syphilis who were and remained untreated on the tenable ground that the treatment
available at the time was worthless. Reports were made in 1929
and again in 1959, with complete case records of 1404 of the
original cases. Deaths from all causes were found to be more
common in this group than in nonsyphilitics, and this tendency
to a higher mortality from all causes in syphilitics than in others
has been confirmed in independent studies. But between 60 and
70 per cent of the Oslo patients lived on with a minimum of inconvenience even though they had no treatment for early syphilis. *As many as 28 per cent of the total actually seemed to
have recovered completely.* But the remaining 30–40 per cent
had the serious difficulties of late syphilis.

These late symptoms appear after another variable interval of "silent infection" or latency which may last as long as twenty years. They tend to occur with more severity and in greater variety as we go from yaws through bejel to syphilis. The late lesions of yaws are much the same as the early ones, with destructive processes of bone in both. But in yaws they are largely limited to the skin and to bone, whereas in syphilis they may appear anywhere. The most serious ones involve the blood vessels and the heart, the eyes, and parts of the central nervous system. The resulting destruction of tissue and associated symptoms in the cardiovascular or nervous systems or the eye cannot be corrected by treatment, although the disease process itself may be arrested at any time. Neurosyphilis includes the two patterns called respectively tabes (tabes dorsalis, locomotor ataxia—syphilis of the spinal cord, characterized especially by a peculiar halting gait) and general paresis (dementia paralytica, general paralysis of the insane—syphilis of the brain itself).

The table also mentions the Wassermann and other tests on serum (usually called "blood tests"). These depend on antibodies that appear in the blood at about the time the disease becomes generalized—that is, in the early secondary stage. We will speak of them in more detail later. Here the point to notice is the one made in the table: these tests are the same for all the treponematoses.

Congenital syphilis, meaning infection passing through the placenta from syphilitic mother to the fetus in the womb, so that the baby is born with the disease, is most likely to happen if the mother has infectious syphilis after the fourth month of pregnancy. Depending on the severity of the disease, it may lead to spontaneous abortion (miscarriage) at any time after the fourth month, to a baby stillborn at the regular term, or to one born alive with syphilis, prematurely or not. Syphilis in such a baby is already generalized. The symptoms may be secondary or tertiary, or both together. Characteristically there may be a destructive ulcer of the bridge of the nose so that it falls in ("saddle nose"), blindness from opacity of the cornea, and peculiarly shaped permanent teeth as they erupt, especially the upper incisors, the sides of which curve inward toward the biting edge, the edge itself being notched. An associated symptom is deafness due to disease of the auditory nerve. These three symptoms —deformed upper permanent incisors, corneal opacities, and nerve deafness—are known as "Hutchinson's triad" after Sir Jonathan Hutchinson, who first described them in 1859.

Let me emphasize that in congenital syphilis, as everywhere else in this protean disease, wide variation is the rule. The newborn infant may appear healthy, or may have no more than the sore mouth or throat of early secondary syphilis. The congenital syphilitic who survives, like other late syphilitics, may die from a cardiovascular accident or a lesion in some other vital spot, or may live on with more or less deformity. A report from Boston, dated 1970, described 217 persons, average age thirty, with *late* congenital syphilis. Bony deformities were most common, especially of the face, including protruding brows, sometimes creased like a hot cross bun, and abnormalities of the upper jaw, as well as saddle nose and less common bony abnormalities of other areas. One of these latter, uncommon in this group but often described in the past, is "saber shin," a forward bowing of the tibias. Similar bone deformities can be caused by rickets, by injury, or by infections other than syphilis, so that of themselves they are not convincingly diagnostic. But Hutchinson's teeth, found in 171 of these 271 patients, are a much more certain sign of late congenital syphilis.

Whether yaws or bejel can be congenital is uncertain, as the table suggests. As a matter of principle one would expect the congenital form to be rare in both. A new infection in the mother at the time of pregnancy is implied, usually of less than a year's duration. This presupposes adult disease. It requires the presence of spirochetes in the blood of the mother and the absence of immunity. Such conditions are improbable in yaws and bejel, although allowing for youthful pregnancy they are not impossible. Somewhat similar reasoning would apply to venereal transmission of yaws or bejel. This could happen only if infectious lesions were present in the genital area at the time of sexual contact, which is not impossible but is certainly rare.

As the table suggests, pinta is different from the other treponematoses. It is much milder, with symptoms limited to the skin except for involvement of lymph nodes, and entails no physical disability. Its main signs are dry, scaly areas of skin in which there is first a bluish discoloration followed by loss of pigment. These patchy white areas are disfiguring, the more so in the dark-skinned people among whom pinta is most prevalent, and their psychological consequences are often severe. Pinta is usually a disease of long duration. Its lesions appear in successive crops and remain infectious for many years. This continuing infectiousness depends on delayed immunity, reflecting the mildness of the whole process. Loss of pigment is also found in the skin lesions of the other treponematoses, and the signs of pinta have been described as syphilis-like. Experts disagree as to whether latency occurs in pinta.

Looking back over the table and considering what I have said about it, I think you will see a definite trend or gradient from syphilis to pinta. The gradient is in the direction of increasing mildness, increasing difficulty in transmitting the disease to animals, and decreasing destructiveness of late lesions. The implication is that the gradient is also one of increasing adaptation to man, which in turn suggests increasing age, going back through man's history. Pinta would be the oldest of the treponematoses, syphilis the most recent.

There is a set of doggerel verses formerly used as an aid—or a bit of vaudeville—in teaching the symptoms of syphilis to medical students which is worth giving here. I had remembered fragments of it but failed to find it written down anywhere, and finally got a version through the good offices of Dr. James B. Lucas, Assistant Chief of the VD Branch of the U.S. Public Health Service in Atlanta. He did some hunting to find it, and one reason for giving it here is that it seems to be almost forgotten. It is anonymous and may in fact be assumed to be the product of more than one author, so that oldtimers who remember it at all are likely to remember it differently.

> There was a young man from Back Bay
> Who thought syphilis just went away.
>   He believed that a chancre
>   Was only a canker
> That healed in a week and a day.
>
> But now he has "acne vulgaris"—
> (Or whatever they call it in Paris);
>   On his skin it has spread
>   From his feet to his head,
> And his friends want to know where his hair is.
>
> There's more to his terrible plight:
> His pupils won't close in the light
>   His heart is cavorting,
>   His wife is aborting,
> And he squints through his gun-barrel sight.
>
> Arthralgia cuts into his slumber;
> His aorta's in need of a plumber;
>   But now he has tabes,
>   And saber-shinned babies,
> While of gummas he has quite a number.
>
> He's been treated in every known way,
> But his spirochetes grow day by day;
>   He's developed paresis,
>   Has long talks with Jesus,
> And thinks he's the Queen of the May.

"Canker" usually means a small painful ulcer in the mouth; "acne vulgaris" is of course the common eruption of pimples in adolescence; neither has any connection with syphilis. "Arthralgia" means pain in the joints. Dr. Lucas explains "gun-barrel sight" as accompanying tabes dorsalis and resulting from atrophy of the optic nerve, which leads to loss of peripheral vision, so that the image on the sufferer's retina gets more and more restricted until he seems to be looking down a gun barrel; eventually there is complete optic atrophy and total blindness. This symptom of neurosyphilis is becoming increasingly rare.

The rhyming of "Paris" with "hair is" suggests a midwestern U.S. origin of these verses, and the wording of the last verse would seem to date them between 1905, when the spirochete was discovered, and 1910, when treatment with "606" appeared. By the 1930s, as I remember, they had already passed into medical folklore.

⚜ 8 ⚜

The Other Theory

THE ALTERNATIVE to the Columbus idea of the origin of syphilis will be clearer if I say something first about a quite different disease, namely polio. Polio has been brought under control in the United States but is still well remembered by adults. Its conquest was the great post–World War II triumph of American public health.

Earlier in the twentieth century polio was called "infantile paralysis," being mainly a rather uncommon but terribly frightening disease of infants and young children associated with lasting paralysis and deformity in those that recovered. It came to be recognized that *infection* with polio viruses (there turned out later to be three of them) was much more widespread than the occurrence of *disease* would have suggested. Most infections, that is, were "silent," showing no symptoms, or nothing but trivial ones that passed away without damage. Such silent infections nevertheless left strong and lasting immunity, something that tends to be more characteristic of virus diseases than of most others. But the disease was changing even as it was being studied. More and more older children and adults were getting it, and the name "infantile paralysis" was becoming misleading. President Franklin D. Roosevelt was one of its prominent victims; and he exemplified not only this tendency toward paralytic infection well past infancy but another: polio was becoming a disease of the rich as well as, or maybe instead of, the poor, who in the past had always tended to monopolize disease as part of their special burden or inheritance. Not that the poor didn't keep on having polio; but they tended to cling to the older pattern of infection in earlier life, which also tended, with many individual variations, to be less severe.

Although polio continued to be much less common than many another disease, and hence less of a public health problem in the general view, you will understand that this new rich-severe versus poor-mild development raised a certain alarm in particular quarters. Above all, the great catalyst and lubricant of concentrated effort, money, began to flow into centers of research devoted to polio, augmented, of course, by the marching dimes of the poor.

It was after World War II that the effort really got going, making reputations and Nobel prizes, and leading on to spectacular success. These things you know or can easily learn elsewhere. What concerns us here are some of the lessons learned in the process. Polio turned out to be, strange as it may seem, primarily an *intestinal* infection, the virus being excreted in feces and transmitted via fecal material to the mouth. The viruses are comparatively hardy, and the transfer could be much more indirect than is possible with the treponematoses which we have temporarily forsaken. Polio was much more often an *infection,* with only minor symptoms, than a severe *disease;* but the virus tended to get into the blood and elicit a good strong immunity even though little happened that the child who had it knew about. Only exceptionally did the virus break through to the central nervous system and produce what came to be called the major illness—paralytic polio. The immensely important fact was worked out by persistent experiment and much independent confirmation that the virus was always in the blood before such major illness developed. This meant that if the virus could be

destroyed in the blood with an effective vaccine the serious consequences could be forestalled; and this is exactly what came to
be done. Let me mention in passing that something similar happens in syphilis—the spirochetes are in the blood early in the
disease—and the parallel gives us some of the hope we put in
eventual control with a vaccine. But syphilis is not a virus
disease—the difference is profound! and you are not to get your
hopes up too high.

As polio turned out to be an intestinal infection, there was implied, inescapably, a relation to the most basic habits of hygiene, which in turn began to light up what had been happening as the disease moved upward in the class structure as well
as in age. In the same sense it cast a light much farther back,
suggesting what it may have been like in primitive peoples and
ancient times. We think that man once had little of his present-
day aversion to his own excrement; and therefore that transfer
to the mouth of the minute amounts of feces needed to carry
virus from one person to another must have happened universally and very early in life. Perhaps excepting newborn babies,
we would expect paralytic or fatal disease to follow infection
less often the earlier the infection happened. So primitive people
could have been universally infected with polio which either
went unseen in terms of disease or death, or possibly contributed in an undistinctive way in very early infancy to a high
mortality from all causes.

The practices of civilization tend to impede infection from
feces, but they are more likely to delay the event than to prevent it outright. The minute contamination called for is pretty
sure to happen sooner or later. The later it happens with polio
—in older children or in adults rather than in infants—the
greater the chance of serious disease.

It was in the present century, which actually marks the emergence of the flush toilet as well as all sorts of ideas and practices
based on bacteriology, that we were able to push this avoidance
of excrement back to a later age. And since the rich were more

likely to do such pushing than the poor, they were able to defer polio infection and associated immunity into increasingly older age brackets, with the result that when it hit it was more likely to hit hard.

The theory of the origin of syphilis now entertained by the more serious students of this subject, among whom I depend especially upon C. J. Hackett, has points of resemblance to, as well as points of difference from, the polio story. It may be just as well to emphasize that even two related virus diseases would not be identical, so that two diseases as far removed in the biological scale as polio and syphilis could not be expected to have many parallels. The ones we find, in fact, depend on man rather than on virus or microbe: on man's own history, the history of his cultural habits, his migrations, the development of cities, the need for and the uses of clothing, and many related things. I have mentioned before that disease is likely to flare up as a result of an upset in the balance of man and his environment which disturbs a developing or established pattern of adaptation between host and virus or microbe.

Hackett describes something of this sort as the process whereby the treponematoses developed, including syphilis. He reminds us of the close relationship of the four diseases, their clinical similarities, the way they all depend on intimate contact, the near identity of the spirochetes, their dependence on man as the only acceptable host in nature. He goes far enough back to suggest that as man himself evolved from other animal forms, so the spirochete may have come originally—very long ago indeed—from a natural animal disease.

The diagram reproduced in Figure 5 is from Hackett's paper. It points up in briefest outline two alternative ideas, of which Hackett favors the one at the left. You will see that they differ in that the left one shows pinta as having arisen from the stem of a "lost ancestral animal treponeme" somewhere around 15,000 B.C., with the other treponematoses arising from it in succession; while the one on the right gives pinta separate status, as it does

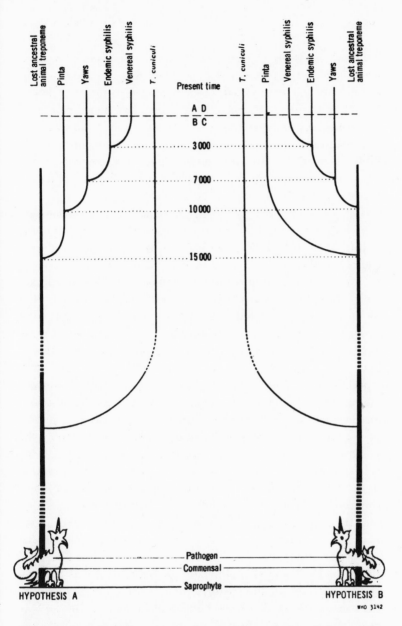

Figure 5. Two hypotheses as to the possible evolution of the syphilis-yaws treponemes. (Hackett, WHO 3142)

to the rabbit disease ("*T. cuniculi*"), each being assumed to have taken off from the primordial stem. The succession, reading up, of "saprophyte," "commensal," and "pathogen" is meant to imply that the primordial spirochete lived a life of its own, apart from any living host, but depending for its nourishment on dead organic matter ("saprophyte"). Sometime later it got into a fairly stable association with some larger living host ("commensal"); and still later, after the balance was upset, it began producing disease ("pathogen").

That the whole idea is only a guess, although a responsible one with a lot of facts behind it, is emphasized by the mythical unicorn at each base. We are warned not to swallow the idea whole; but this is not the sort of fancy that Fracastor indulged in. For instance, saprophytic and commensal spirochetes do actually exist; and it is not wild to suggest that they may have a relationship to pathogenic treponemes something like that of modern orangutans and chimpanzees to man, each set of three being variants which branched out of a primordial form that is now extinct. But the discovery in 1963, the year of Hackett's paper, of a treponematosis of African *Cynocephalus* monkeys adds a dramatic element of support to the idea that the diseases of man grew out of some such source. It is particularly interesting that the natural monkey infection seems to involve only the lymph nodes behind the knees, suggesting infection through the feet, and, as R. R. Willcox says, evoking ideas "of the evolution of pathogenic treponemes from free-living treponemes in mud." The absence in this monkey infection of any evidence of symptoms the monkey himself might have appreciated is, again, testimony to a relatively comfortable and therefore ancient association of parasite and host.

Late in 1970 a brief preliminary announcement was made of the discovery of another natural treponematosis of primates, in this instance in the dog-faced baboon of Casamance, in the Senegal-Gambia area of Africa. This animal shows definite disease, with lesions and typical *pallidum*-like treponemes as well as characteristic blood tests. Possibly this is another branch off the "lost ancestral" root, closer to the four human diseases than anything yet discovered. But the authors of the report do not make any such speculation, and we must wait for more information.

Hackett thinks the primordial human treponematosis may have been pinta. He points to the characteristics of a primitive infection, among them absence of invasion by the spirochete of the deeper tissues that are affected in yaws and syphilis and the long duration of the infectious state. He thinks, arguing from archeology and anthropology, that the original human disease may have grown out of an animal infection somewhere in the Euro-Afro-Asian land mass perhaps before 20,000 B.C., and become distributed throughout the world by 15,000 B.C. He suggests that it passed into the Americas around that time, when the Bering Strait land bridge was intact and ice-free, and that later it became isolated as the polar ice caps melted and flooded the Bering Strait. Pinta is now limited to the humid tropical belt of the Caribbean islands, southern Mexico, Central America, and the north central area of South America.

Somewhere in Afro-Asia, Hackett goes on, by about 10,000 B.C., a warm, humid environment favored mutation of the pinta treponeme into that of yaws, which then spread throughout the world except for the Americas, which were by then isolated. During this period it is assumed that pinta was distributed all over tropical America, including what is now southwestern United States and the whole northern half of South America. Yaws is placed throughout Africa, the southern half of the Near and Far East, Australia, and the intervening islands.

The next change is dated about 7000 B.C., before the dawn of what we call history. It follows the retreat of the last glacial mass and the penetration of man into more temperate and drier regions. At this point endemic syphilis (bejel) emerges in arid warm areas while yaws continues in humid warm ones. Willcox makes the interesting point that bejel tends to occur on the fringes of the yaws areas. Hackett cites experimental evidence,

known to all who study these spirochetes in rabbits, that lower
air temperatures favor development of the disease in these animals, their normal body temperature being a degree or two
higher than man's. It has been reported that yaws spirochetes
may behave more like syphilis spirochetes in rabbits when the
temperature of the animal room is kept rather cool; and the
infection may not take at all if the room gets too warm.

Migration of man into cooler climates would bring clothing
into use, and there would be a growing dependence for transfer
of the spirochetes on the mouth rather than the body skin
among children, leading to the emergence of a bejel-like pattern. Hackett suggests that at this time, before the earliest civili-
zations appeared, yaws was still present across the tropical belt
of Africa and in Madagascar, as well as in most of India, southwest Asia, the coastal fringe of Australia, and the islands; but
bejel now occupied the more northern portion of Africa, Arabia,
south-central Asia, and central Australia. Hackett says:

> The change to venereal transmission might have occurred with
> the growth of big cities, together with increased clothing, in the
> now arid countries of the eastern Mediterranean and south-western
> Asia. . . . This might have been about 3000 B.C. during the post-
> glacial climatic optimum which culminated between 5000 B.C. and
> 2500 B.C., when the climatic zones were displaced towards the
> higher latitudes and temporarily the equatorial/monsoon belts were
> widened and the desert zones less severe. . . . Venereal syphilis
> was probably carried to the Mediterranean littoral by shipping and
> later throughout Europe, which was a treponemally uncommitted
> area, especially after the first century B.C. with the Roman con-
> quests.

E. H. Hudson put forward a similar idea. He speaks of the evolution of villages between 9000 and 4000 B.C. Hygiene was undeveloped and dwellings were closely huddled together. Life in
villages encouraged a proportionate increase of children; and
with their increased contacts in play and the clothing they wore
for protection against the cooler climate, bejel spread from child
to child not so much by skin contact as from lesions on moist

surfaces, probably with the help of the fingers. As cities became established, in Mesopotamia and Egypt, about 4500–4000 B.C., in China about 2000 B.C., in Greece about 800 B.C., and further north, in Scandinavia, not before 1000 A.D.,

> Even the bodily functions of sleeping, eating, drinking, and defecating, parts of the automatic life of the world's villages, were raised to a higher esthetic level. . . . The pleasures of alcoholic beverages were explored. . . . Mating, which in the villages was the uncomplicated concern of man and wife, was gradually embellished, in the relaxed city environment, with a profusion of accessories, such as personal adornment, flowers, perfumes, jewels, and cosmetics. . . . The city produced professional soldiers, priests, lawyers, and teachers, and, simultaneously, professional singers, dancers, and prostitutes. . . .

Hudson continues:

> . . . in a clean and clothed "urbane" society coitus has become the only contact of sufficient intimacy to ensure the transfer of treponemes.

Hackett suggests that at the time of European expansion in the sixteenth century nothing but pinta existed in America, occupying its central tropical and semitropical belt. Yaws had spread across tropical Africa and Madagascar, much of India, all of southwest Asia, and northern Australia and the islands. Endemic syphilis was found then in the more arid northern desert of Africa, and extended across Arabia and northeastward into eastern Europe and Asia. It appeared as well in central Australia and in Bechuanaland in more southern Africa, and as far to the northwest as Scotland. Venereal syphilis is thought to have been present throughout the then civilized world, including Britain, all of Scandinavia, western Russia and the whole Mediterranean littoral. According to this view, syphilis

> was probably carried during and after the sixteenth century to the Americas, southern Africa, . . . India, south Asian countries, China and Australia. . . .

Meanwhile yaws was being transported around the world, but especially to America, in slaves taken from Africa. Hudson, arguing for his idea of a single treponematosis varying only with culture and climate, would have slaves bringing yaws to warm humid areas in the New World, bejel to areas where it was cooler and drier, and syphilis—doubtless carried also, and probably more often, by their masters—to urban or more civilized points. Others, among them Hackett, do not go so far, but agree that black slavery must have been the means for dissemination of yaws. Accordingly, bringing the suggested distribution down to 1900 A.D., he suggests that pinta had receded to its present distribution in the Caribbean area and north-central South America. Yaws had come to line both coasts of tropical South America and had extended up into the Caribbean islands; it was present as well in southwest Asia, northern Australia, the Malay Archipelago, and the islands of the Pacific, with additional isolated foci in India, Ceylon, Formosa, and an adjacent portion of the east China coast—all in addition to its homeland, tropical Africa. Bejel had remained in the Sahara and in East Africa and Bechuanaland, and extended through Arabia northeasterly into southern Russia and Siberia and northwestern China. Venereal syphilis had been carried from Europe into the occupied parts of the United States, Mexico, and Canada, the temperate areas of southern South America, South Africa, Ethiopia, most of India, eastern China, Japan, and Korea, southern Australia and New Zealand. A similar world distribution of the nonvenereal treponematoses, with some minor differences, was described by Willcox in 1955.

There is no reason to assume that Hackett intends his global view as anything more than a suggestion carefully elaborated from much painstaking research. Hudson is not in agreement with all the details. In particular, there have been further changes since 1900, especially as syphilis has followed on the heels of effective treatment of bejel and yaws.

If we can accept this alternative theory provisionally, reserving judgment on details and expecting modifications with more information, we can put the status of the question of the origin of syphilis in some such terms as these: The idea of an origin in the late fifteenth century, including the Columbus story, fell when it appeared that venereal syphilis was present in Europe before that time. It now appears that the other condition required by the idea of a sudden origin in Europe has also been found wanting—that is, the presence of venereal syphilis in America when Columbus's sailors landed. It looks rather as though syphilis was distributed by the white man himself, and as though, where Indians or other dark-skinned peoples were involved, they acted only as agents of the white man's exploitation and cruelty.

PART II

LITERATURE, ART, AND MORALS

❧ 9 ❧

From the Bible to Rabelais

S OMEBODY HAS SAID there is nothing so practical as a good
theory; and in the same sense there is nothing so crippling
as a bad one put forward as true—a dogma. A good theory—an
explanation of natural events which fits the available facts—
always raises questions and leads to answers, to more facts.
Dogma closes the door. As between the two Frenchmen who
lived nearly 150 years apart, Astruc and Buret, we saw in Chapter 6 that both may have been guilty of too much enthusiasm.
But Astruc's view of VD tended to prevail, maybe because it
was simple, possibly because it was attractive to increasingly
predatory white Europeans who were in process of putting
down the darker-skinned peoples of the earth: could it have
been comforting to be able to blame syphilis on one such people?

Anyway, if one turns to Buret prepared to find him more
nearly correct, he proves rewarding. The vast mass of material
he dug up, mainly if not entirely from original sources, from the
ancient Chinese to his own period, is not to be swallowed
whole. In his eagerness to demolish Astruc he certainly went too
far. But if we know that, and add what we have learned from
the alliterative trio, Holcomb, Hudson, and Hackett, we gain

powerful support from Buret for the idea that syphilis has been known, under all sorts of other names, from very ancient times.

Starting with the Old Testament, we find additional supporting material in a paper by the British expert R. R. Willcox, written early in his career (1949), and the more valuable in that he evidently studied the Bible quite independently of Buret, whom he does not mention. The result is that each scholar found things the other missed, and that the two assemble their material in different ways. I have tried to collate the two accounts so as to present them here as one. But be it noted: Buret's story is tendentious: he is out to demolish Astruc. Willcox leans the other way. He amasses eloquent evidence that the writers of the Old Testament were familiar with venereal disease, some of which looks very much like syphilis, including its congenital form. But he nevertheless tries to find a basis on which the Columbian theory might still stand, if only, as he says at the end of his paper, because

> it would be a great pity if someone did produce irrefutable evidence for either side and thus prevent any further such interesting speculation.

Let it be admitted that in the absence of modern blood tests on David, Job, and others, the possibility of coming up with "irrefutable evidence" is slim. It is not proof we look for, but plausibility.

Buret finds a beginning of the story, appropriately, in Genesis:

> 12:17   And the Lord plagued Pharaoh and his house with great plagues because of Sarai Abram's wife.

> 20:17   So Abraham prayed unto God: and God healed Abimelech, and his wife, and his maidservants; and they bare children.
> 18   For the Lord had fast closed up all the wombs of the house of Abimelech, because of Sarah Abraham's wife.

After which, in the old age of both Abraham and Sarah, a son was born to the couple whom they called Isaac (Gen. 21:1–3). But it is suggested that Sarah gave VD (perhaps gonorrhea) to

Pharaoh and all his wives, and also to Abimelech (king of Gerar) and all *his* wives. Bertrand Russell comments on some of these events, in a letter to Colette dated August 10, 1918, which is included in the second volume of his autobiography:

> What a queer work the Bible is. Abraham (who is a pattern of all the virtues) twice over, when he is going abroad, says to his wife: "Sarah, my dear, you are a very good-looking person, and the King is very likely to fall in love with you. If he thinks I am your husband, he will put me to death, so as to be able to marry you; so you should travel as my sister, which you are, by the way." On each occasion the King does fall in love with her, takes her into his harem, and gets diseased in consequence, so he returns her to Abraham. Meanwhile Abraham has a child by the maidservant, whom Sarah dismisses into the wilderness with the new-born infant, without Abraham objecting. Rum tale.

The story of Hagar the maid is given in Genesis 16 and 21. To my knowledge the Pharaoh of Genesis has not been identified by modern Egyptologists.

Willcox suggests that VD may be recognized in the plague which followed the killing of three thousand Israelites after they had made and worshiped the golden calf while Moses was absent on Mount Sinai. Moses had forbidden them to make graven images or "to rear up a standing [that is, phallic] image," or to go awhoring after other gods; but they disobeyed him; so "the Lord plagued the people, because they made the calf. . . ."

Leviticus is particularly rich in references to disease, much of which is called leprosy, but the details often suggest either gonorrhea or syphilis. The "running issue" out of the flesh is evidently gonorrhea. There is much detail regarding sanitation and cleanliness, and clear allusion to the connection between disease and copulation. Willcox points out that present-day fears of catching VD from toilet seats or bicycle saddles can be traced as far back as this book of the Bible:

> 15:4 . . . every thing, whereon he sitteth, shall be unclean.

> 6 And he that sitteth on any thing whereon he sat that hath the issue . . .

9   And what saddle soever he rideth upon that hath the issue shall be unclean.

Willcox also suggests that the association of "leprosy" in the same context with "one that hath the issue" implies that "leprosy" may actually mean "syphilis"; but the case for recognition of venereal disease in the Bible is in fact more direct and convincing in other places. The word "leprosy" may sometimes have meant common bacterial diseases of skin or hair follicles (impetigo, sycosis), as well as true leprosy itself. But mention in Leviticus (13:30) of "a yellow thin hair" suggests syphilitic baldness; and exclusion from the temple of any man "that hath a blemish in his eye, or be scurvy, or scabbed, or hath his stones [testicles] broken," coming soon after mention of "a flat nose" (of which more in a moment), begins to point more strongly to syphilis.

Biblical syphilis becomes more dramatically apparent in the two plagues—of Egypt, and of Moab or Baal-Peor. The words of Moses in Deuteronomy 28 on the results of disobedience to the laws are especially eloquent:

27   The Lord will smite thee with the botch of Egypt, and with the emerods, and with the scab, and with the itch, whereof thou canst not be healed.

28   The Lord shall smite thee with madness, and blindness, and astonishment of heart.

35   The Lord shall smite thee in the knees, and in the legs, with a sore botch that cannot be healed, from the sole of thy foot unto the top of thy head.

59   Then the Lord will make thy plagues wonderful, and the plagues of thy seed, even great plagues, and of long continuance, and sore sicknesses, and of long continuance.

Hudson (1961) provides a scholarly commentary on several of the words in the foregoing passages, noting that "botch" is given in the Revised Version of the Bible as "boil" and that John Milton spoke of "botches and blaines," while Robert Burns used the words "scabs and botches." (We will see in Chapter 11 that John Donne associated "botch" with "pox.") "Emerod" is usually "bubo" or swelling, and might here mean "gumma." The references in 28, if they can be accepted as relating to syphilis, are extraordinarily prescient in recognizing as syphilitic symptoms which were not again related to the disease until the nineteenth century! As Willcox points out, the suggestions of irritation ("itch") or pain ("sore botch") are inconsistent with the idea of syphilis; yet it is hard to identify the whole picture as anything else.

When the people of Israel came to the plains of Moab, east of the Jordan, their numbers and military might appear to have frightened the rulers of the place, who, in an effort to defeat them, tried to induce them to worship Baal-Peor instead of their own god. Accordingly, "the people began to commit whoredom with the daughters of Moab." A plague ensued, the venereal nature of which is implied by the action of Phinehas, Aaron's grandson, who impaled with his javelin a man of Israel and a Midianite woman, apparently while they were copulating. This stopped the plague, although 24,000 had already died. In Deuteronomy 4:3, Moses affirmed that God had destroyed the people of Israel that followed Baal-Peor. All male children were then killed, and "every woman that hath known man by lying with him." That these and other steps, including elaborate measures of hygiene and disinfection, although they seem to have brought the plague under control, did not entirely end it, is suggested in Joshua 22:17: "we are not cleansed until this day" from "the iniquity of Peor." Another reference to the same plague is in Hosea 9:10, where the curious statement appears:

. . . but they went to Baal-Peor, and separated themselves unto that shame; and their abominations were according as they loved.

Another reference to the same plague appears much later, in the New Testament (I Corinthians 10:8), where Paul, having men-

tioned the idolatry of the people of Israel, warned that fornication had been responsible for the great loss of life.

Buret suggests that Solomon's warning against a strange
woman, in Proverbs 5:3–5, has overtones of VD, culminating in:

> 5:11 And thou mourn at the last, when thy flesh and thy body
> are consumed.

Buret also points to the words of Isaiah, which appear in relation to Sodom:

> 3:17 Therefore the Lord will smite with a scab the crown of
> the head of the daughters of Zion, and the Lord will discover their
> secret parts.

A few lines later (24) the words "instead of well set hair baldness" suggest the alopecia of secondary syphilis.

Most striking of all are the suggestions that both David and
Job suffered from syphilis, as well as allusions which strongly
imply the existence at the time of congenital disease which
could hardly have been anything but syphilis. The story of the
seduction of Bath-sheba by David notes that "she was purified
from her uncleanness"; the significant fact emerges that the
child of this illicit union died on the seventh day, whereafter
David made Bath-sheba his wife and she bore him Solomon. But
in the Thirty-eighth Psalm David says:

> 3 There is no soundness in my flesh because of thine anger;
> neither is there any rest in my bones because of my sin.

> 5 My wounds stink and are corrupt because of my foolishness.

> 7 For my loins are filled with a loathsome disease: and there is
> no soundness in my flesh.

Willcox interprets "thine arrows stick fast in me" in this context
as the shooting pains of severe secondary syphilis, and points
also to "the light of mine eyes, it is also gone from me" and to

> 11 My lovers and my friends stand aloof from my sore; and my
> kinsmen stand afar off,

the whole pattern suggesting active secondary syphilis resulting from "mine iniquity . . . my sin," presumably referring to the seduction of Bath-sheba. It is interesting that David evidently recovered, since I Chronicles 29:28 reports that

he died in a good old age, full of days, riches, and honor . . .

As for Job, Willcox suggests the possibility of a treponematosis other than syphilis, since there is no direct mention of a sexual source of the illness. Here are Willcox's words, with a few alterations (in brackets) to convert technical terms into ordinary ones:

"He cleaveth my reins asunder, and doth not spare; he poureth out my gall upon the ground" might be taken as indicating a genital lesion with perhaps an accompanying broken-down bubo. The possibly secondary manifestations which followed included boils from head to toe, a loathsome skin which was extremely obstinate in healing until it was broken "break upon breach" and the face was "foul with weeping". Alopecia at the hairline was another feature, and also severe nocturnal bone pains. Possible [disease of the iris of the eye] is suggested by failing sight, and a foul mouth from mucous patches from his corrupt breath. There were also lack of appetite, intense wasting, nocturnal delirium, insomnia, [shortness of breath], fever, diarrhea and abdominal distension: "Behold my belly is as wine which hath no vent; it is ready to burst like new bottles" which do not entirely fit [the pattern of syphilis], although a certain tightness of the collar might be caused by [swollen glands in the neck].

Whether this disease was syphilis or not, it is not surprising that his wife abhorred him and his friends deserted him. In any event, which would not have occurred in some of the diseases [other than syphilis] which might be considered, he recovered, lived to prosper, to have seven sons and three daughters, and to possess four thousand sheep, six thousand camels, a thousand yoke of oxen, and a thousand she asses. He died old and "full of days."

To complete this account of VD in the Bible with congenital syphilis, I quote again from Willcox:

The Third Commandment, stating that the iniquity of the fathers would be visited upon the children unto the third and fourth gen-

erations is significant, especially as it immediately follows lines for-
bidding the bowing down to images. Even if third generation
syphilis is such a rarity, it may be argued that there is no other
inherited disease sufficiently common to be preferred, especially as
it concerns punishment for possible phallic worship.

In Leviticus 21:18, "he that hath a flat nose" is barred from the
temple, as we saw before. The saddle nose is most likely to indicate congenital syphilis, although it is found as well in late acquired syphilis and other treponematoses (except pinta) and
may occasionally be due to other causes entirely. The reference
in Numbers 12:12 to "one dead, of whom the flesh is half consumed when he cometh out of his mother's womb" is strongly
evocative of a macerated stillborn congenital syphilitic fetus.
The words, incidentally, were spoken by Aaron of Miriam's "leprosy" which, having apparently healed in seven days, could
hardly have been very serious. Finally we again have Willcox
commenting on Jeremiah 31:29:

> The fathers have eaten a sour grape, and the children's teeth are
> set on edge,

which he thinks might have meant the notched Hutchinson's
teeth of congenital syphilis.

Buret has uncovered evidence that knowledge of syphilis and
other venereal diseases goes back to the earliest recorded times,
some of which may well have been before those of the Old Testament. We have already seen that Astruc, trying hard to show
that there was no syphilis outside America before the time of
Columbus, nevertheless demonstrated rather convincingly that
the disease was known in ancient China. Buret speaks of an alleged reference to the use of mercury for syphilis in a medical
treatise of emperor Hoang Ty, who he says reigned in 2637 B.C.,
although, as we saw before, the true date may have been much
more recent. The Chinese of that time knew of the symptoms of
secondary syphilis (Buret tells us)—the coppery rash, the bone
pains, headache, night pains, the mucous patches of throat and

anus, and the sore throat. They even knew of transmission of
syphilis to the newborn. Moreover, we are assured, they distinguished the two different sorts of chancre and separated gonorrhea from syphilis, millennia before all these things were
confused again in eighteenth-century Europe. The French venereologist Philippe Ricord seems to have held Buret's opinion
before him. Buret says he would rewrite the first sentence of the
Bible: "In the beginning God created the heaven and the earth,
man, and VD."

Chinese knowledge, according to Buret, was passed on to the
Japanese; and a Japanese manuscript dated not later than 808
A.D., lost for a thousand years, described details of the course
of syphilis.

The Roman poets, Buret goes on, made repeated references to
VD, often associated with male homosexuality, about which
they were as cruel as men are today. Martial says the debauched Nevolus may have had a contagious disease in the region of the anus, the result of pederasty. Lucillius (b. 148 B.C.),
whose work is known largely through Horace, speaks of an old
man worn out by debauchery with "pimples and red eruptions
going up to the eyes." The word "scabies" is given to this but
means, not the itch, but "scabs." Catullus (*ca.* 50 B.C.) tells us
that Julius Caesar and his pederast, Mamuria, both contracted a
disease whose masked spots have left upon their bodies stains
which will not disappear; both were infected together in the
same bed. A little later Horace speaks of the "shameful disease"
of Cleopatra's soldiers. And the word "scabies" is again used by
the same poet to mean a terrible contagious disease. In Catullus
is also the name *Morbus Campanus,* which may have been the
source for sixteenth-century writers of the term Neapolitan disease. Buret finds additional material in Persius and in Juvenal
as well as in Martial. Some of this may refer to chancroid or
gonorrhea; some—catching Buret with his guard down—looks
to me like trachoma, some like nonvenereal ulceration of the
mouth. Buret may be misled by phrases such as "rotten by de-

bauchery," which, after all, could have been coincidence. But Martial's "De Familia Ficosa" sounds more like syphilis: the wife has figs (ficus), the husband has figs, the daughter has figs, and all the others are attacked by this shameful ulcer. The "fig" —Buret has no doubt—is the flat, moist, wartlike growth of secondary syphilis, called a condyloma, seen especially on the skin around the vulva or the anus. This position is strongly supported by Hudson, in the paper referred to earlier in this chapter. The paper includes a long scholarly review of "ficus, the fig disease," the essence of which may be conveyed by his citation of Forcellini, "a nonmedical man reflecting the beliefs of his day (d. 1768)" who defined the disease, ficus, as

> . . . a sort of ulcer which arises on the head, sometimes in the hair, sometimes in the beard and in other places also, which are covered with hair, hemorrhoids or piles, a kind of ulcer so-called because it pours forth in the likeness to the fruit of the fig tree.

Hudson also refers to Martial at length, including the passage cited by Buret.

Other recurrent phrases in Roman literature certainly sound like syphilis: "shining pustules" (perhaps an allusion to the coppery sheen of the secondary rash); "the malignant ulcer" that comes from kissing; "the mournful disease of the chin" (*mentagra*); "disgusting eruptions." What could the *"morbus indecens"* of the Romans be but VD? But additional references, to the "scabies" of Ansonius (340 A.D.), to a poem by Claudianus (*ca.* 395 A.D.) about spots on the chest as a proof of vice, and a disease contracted by a single contact with "expensive young women" (*meretrices*)—all these and more call for further scholarly reconsideration.

In the ruins of Pompeii and Herculaneum, which were destroyed by an eruption of Mount Vesuvius in 79 A.D. and rediscovered in 1775, among the erotic paintings, sculpture, pottery, and even jewelry are found inscriptions alluding to VD. For instance, Buret tells us, it is written on the wall of a brothel at

Pompeii that "the most beautiful woman of that establishment had the disease capable of producing eating ulcers."

Just before the period of the epidemic of syphilis we find François Villon making several references which Buret labels "vague"; they seem to me more clearly evocative of syphilis than some of Buret's other exhibits. But translators have tended to obscure them. Here are the original French and two modern English versions compared, one in blank verse, the other rhymed and less literal. Both passages are from *The Great Testament*. The first is in "The Lament of the Old Courtesan" (*Les regrets de la belle Hëaulmiere*):

> . . . je n'oubliasse.
> Le glouton, de mal entechié,
> M'embrassoit. . . . J'en suis bien plus grasse!
> Que m'en reste il? Honte et pechié.

. . . to be forgotten.	I had forgotten all for bliss
The glutton, his soul tainted with evil,	(Oh, glutton, evil-soaked within!)
would embrace me. . . . A lot of good it's done me!	Of his embrace. I fed on this!
What have I been left with? Sin and shame!	And now what's left me? Shame and sin!
(*Bonner*)	(*Nicholson*)

Both translators give "mal" as "evil"; but it could as well be "disease." The second is from the famous, or infamous, ballade —the scurrilous one in the form of a curse—which follows verse 141 in the original and Bonner versions (131 in the Nicholson). There are echoes here, in the third verse of the ballade, of a treatment of syphilis that was not supposed to have begun until some fifty years later:

> En sublimé, dangereux a touchier,
> Et ou nombril d'une couleuvre vive,
> En sang qu'on voit es palletes sechier
> Sur ces barbiers, quant plaine lune arrive,

Dont l'ung est noir, l'autre plus vert que cive,
En chancre et fiz, et en ces ors cuveaulx
Ou nourisses essangent leur drappeaulx,
En petiz baings de filles amoureuses
(Qui ne m'entent n'a suivy la bordeaulx)
Soient frittes ces langues envieuses!

In sublimate that's dangerous to the touch	In sublimate whereof men stand in dread;
and in the navel of a living snake,	In sweat from navels of live adders—whew!
and in the blood one sees in barbers' rooms	In blood in basins drying and all dead
drying out in bowls when full moon comes	For leeches' use beneath the full moon—phew!—
that's partly black, partly green as chives,	Some being black, some green as chives; in spew
in sores and tumors, and in those filthy vats	Of chancre-sores and of those filthy crocks
in which wet-nurses wash their diapers,	Where nurses wash the blood from invalids' smocks;
in those little tubs that girls of pleasure use	In little baths the love-girls lie beside
(to understand you have to know a brothel),	(Who knows them not knows naught of stews, by cocks!)
may these envious tongues be fried!	Let envious tongues be fricasseed and fried!
(Bonner)	(Nicholson)

"Sublimate" is presumably a mercury salt; could the word have applied to the method of treating syphilis by "fumigation" using mercuric sulphide (cinnabar, an ore) which "sublimes"—that is, vaporizes directly from the solid state when heated? But surely "chancre" in the context of "bordellos" ought to be enough to encourage scholars to take another look at this, with Columbus put aside.

Rabelais wrote during the epidemic and was familiar with syphilis as it raged at the time; but he makes several references to it, explicitly, as existing earlier. The opening phrase of *Gargan-tua*, which Samuel Putnam, the translator, gives as "Most illus-trious Drinkers, and you, most precious Syphilitics . . ." needs only to be mentioned: these were his contemporaries (Putnam thinks the second part of the toast referred especially to Francis I, who may have been the model for Gargantua). In Chapter 14 of *Gargantua* appears the verse,

> And he died in the year fourteen-twenty,
> Of the syphilis, which he had a-plenty.

This is said to have come from an epitaph composed by Clem-ent Marot, a contemporary of Rabelais who may also have be-lieved that syphilis was not new.

❧ IO ❧

Shakespeare on VD

BY SHAKESPEARE'S TIME syphilis had become common and familiar all over Europe. In other words, the subject was ready for him, and he made the most of it.

But before we get into the details of VD in Shakespeare's works it may be a good idea to prepare the way with a few related matters. It has been suggested, for one thing, that the bard's concentration on VD—syphilis, almost exclusively—implies that he had it himself. I know of no evidence that he did. I am under the impression that Shakespeare actually did not concentrate more on VD than he did on many another subject, such for instance as kingship, jealousy, or murder, or for that matter farm animals or wild flowers. In fact, if such a suggestion is to be taken seriously it would apply equally to me and to writers on VD whose names keep recurring in these pages. It is, at best, a *non sequitur*.

But while Shakespeare interested himself in everything that happened around him—and VD was certainly one such thing! —his focus on VD may well have been sharpened by another concern of his, or one facet of it. Even as an apostle of the High Renaissance, Shakespeare's attitude toward women and the whole range of matters sexual was extraordinarily advanced and sympathetic; he was unmistakeably and ardently anti-Puritan just when Puritanism was a rising menace. Or say it another way: he was a great humanist (without being a professional philosopher), with a love of Man (who, as the old saw has it, embraces Woman) grounded in the broadest sort of comprehension which overlooked no defects or weaknesses—which is not to suggest that he could rise above all the prejudices of his time.

The point is not limited to the periphery of our main topic of VD and is worth pursuing a little further. As far as literature is concerned I am tempted to suggest that neither before Shakespeare's time nor after him has anybody quite achieved his freedom in dealing with the subject of women and sex and romantic love—and hence also with VD. It is known, but perhaps not widely enough, that the modern notion of love as expressed in literature is by no means timeless, having arisen as recently as the late medieval period. It was not at all encompassed in the Greek Eros or the Roman Cupid myths; nor is its modern form recognizable in Ovid. Its origins can be traced to the Arthurian legend, especially to the story of Tristram and Isolde ("courtly love"), and through Dante, Chaucer, Petrarch, and Boccaccio. But even Shakespeare's immediate predecessors and contemporaries, among whom even Marlowe is hardly an exception, did not show the full flowering of Shakespeare's genius in this as in many better-recognized respects. It is revealing to compare the pallid tale "Romeo and Giulietta" by Luigi da Porto (1525), one of a group of sources of Shakespeare's play, with what it became in his hands only some seventy years later. It remained for Shakespeare to give us the compassionate and clear-eyed portrayals of women as people, from Doll Tearsheet to Hermione, from Rosalind and Beatrice to Lady Macbeth and Cleopatra, from Juliet and her nurse to Mistress Ford. *The Taming of the Shrew* is obviously an exception, and a pretty piece of male supremacism. I would put it down as a lapse of the bard's formative period. Elsewhere, including the early poems and the sonnets, Shakespeare seems to have been free, perhaps uniquely free, from the twin taints of puritanism and the nearly universal dogma of the natural superiority of males. Among all the luminaries who followed him, is there anyone of whom we can say as much?

A little closer to my theme, and worth dwelling on as an immediate preamble to it, is Shakespeare's interest in and knowledge of medicine as medicine was known in his day. He knew venereal disease as he knew a range of other diseases, which is to say, very much as contemporary physicians knew them. Again there was nothing unique about his concentration on this subject; much the same can be said for his knowledge of the law, not to speak of statecraft and the arts of war. There is extant a scholarly paper expounding the mathematics of the odds propounded by Claudius and presented to Hamlet by Osric before the duel. But let me get down to cases before I stumble over the conclusion that Shakespeare was a great man.

Shakespeare's knowledge of medicine has been documented in a book by a Scottish surgeon, R. R. Simpson, *Shakespeare and Medicine* (1959). Simpson in turn acknowledges the aid of an earlier study by John Bucknill, dated 1860. Simpson says, "Shakespeare's knowledge of medicine corresponded closely to that prevailing at his time among its professors," being still heavily influenced by Hippocrates and Galen. Yet just as the poet seemed to know nearly everything else that was known in his time, evidently from his own observation as well as from books, so he must have enlarged his knowledge of medicine by what he saw around him. We know that his son-in-law, who married Susanna in 1607, was a physician, reputedly one highly skilled and trusted; but he does not seem to have been important as a source of Shakespeare's information. John Hall arrived in Stratford about 1600; Shakespeare's medical references in the plays reached a peak in *Romeo and Juliet* (1594–1595). In specific references, for instance to drugs, there is little evidence of any influence of Hall, whose own writings on medicine were not recorded until 1617, a year after Shakespeare died. Hall was "a

very religious man" and a Puritan. Nevertheless he had studied
at Montpellier, where the influence of Rabelais, who had been a
professor there, must have lingered. Simpson thinks that the
story told by Menenius in *Coriolanus* of the revolt of the body's
members against the belly, although originally one of Aesop's fa-
bles, had been used by Rabelais and may have come from him
through Hall to Shakespeare. He suggests that Shakespeare's
doctors in the later plays may have been patterned directly
upon Hall, notably the "upright physician" in the sleepwalking
scene of *Macbeth:*

> Certainly no doctor qua doctor appears in the plays until after Hall
> had arrived in Stratford; and all the doctors in the plays are exem-
> plary characters, entirely worthy members of their noble profession.

Dr. Caius in *The Merry Wives of Windsor* is perhaps an exception; but he was French, and from Joan of Arc to the Dauphin
Shakespeare's view of the French was the prejudiced one of contemporary Englishmen. (This prejudice need not be extended to
his use of the term "French disease"—which was common cur-
rency everywhere at the time except in France; but even so it
may be that a special anti-French feeling led him to lean a little
more heavily on the term than he might have done otherwise, as
we shall see.)

Shakespeare's allusions to venereal disease fall into four
classes with indistinct boundaries. There is, first, the glancing
allusion, usually veiled at least to the modern view, which
comes nearest to humor. Then there are more neutral references,
in which VD is mentioned more or less as a fact of life. A third
class contains mention of treatment, always as something as unpleasant as the disease or even more so. Finally, VD is the basis
for invective, including the most savage in all Shakespeare.

In the first group there is an example in *Midsummer Night's
Dream*—usually thought of as the most "innocent" of the plays
(although Peter Brook has given it a different interpretation),
where Quince (I,ii) speaks of "French crowns" which "have no

hair at all"—a reference to syphilitic baldness. But the best examples are in *Measure for Measure*, and most of them are spoken by Lucio, a sort of embittered Mercutio who provides most of what humor there is in this comedy of sex that skirts so dangerously close to tragedy. When the First Gentleman says to him early in the play (I,ii)

> I had as lief be a list of an English kersey as be piled, as thou art piled, for a French velvet,

and Lucio answers,

> . . . I will, out of thine own confession, learn to begin thy health; but whilst I live, forget to drink after thee,

we have a word play on the disease commonly called piles, on the French disease, and on not drinking out of the same cup to avoid infection. Partridge suggests that "*velvet* is an obscure allusion to the clitoris." Two lines later, as Mistress Overdone, the bawd, enters, we have this exchange:

> *Lucio.*   Behold, behold, where Madam Mitigation comes!
> *1. Gentleman.*   I have purchased as many diseases under her roof as come to—
> *2. Gentleman.*   To what, I pray?
> *Lucio.*   Judge.
> *2. Gentleman.*   To three thousand dolors a year.
> *1. Gentleman.*   Ay, and more.
> *Lucio.*   A French crown more.
> *1. Gentleman.*   Thou art always figuring diseases in me; but thou art full of error. I am sound.
> *Lucio.*   Nay, not—as one would say—healthy, but so sound as things that are hollow. Thy bones are hollow; impiety has made a feast of thee.

Shakespeare, in short, knew well enough where the French disease came from. In *Pericles* (IV,ii), as Marina is captured by the pirates as a prize for the brothel, we have first this exchange:

> *Pandar.*   . . . The poor Transilvanian is dead that lay with the little baggage.

Boult. Ay, she quickly poup'd him, she made him roast-meat for
worms. . . .

Partridge gives the word as "poop" with the suggestion of a
nautical origin, and defines it, "to infect with a venereal disease." A little later in the same scene we find this:

Boult. . . . but Mistress do you know the French knight, that
cowers i' the hams?
Bawd. Who, Monsieur Verollus?
Boult. Ay, he, he offer'd to cut a caper at the proclamation, but
he made a groan at it, and swore he would see her tomorrow.
Bawd. Well, well, as for him, he brought his disease hither, here
he does but repair it; I know he will come in our shadow, to
scatter his crowns in the Sun.

And later on, in Scene vi, as Marina, successfully preserving her
virginity to the despair of the bawd, continues to defend it even
against the wooing of the governor, Lysimachus:

Marina. For me that am a maid, though most ungentle Fortune
have plac'd me in this sty, where since I came, diseases have
been sold dearer than physic . . .

Simpson suggests that the following words spoken by Falstaff
reflect contemporary medical difficulty in distinguishing between gout and syphilis:

. . . A man can no more separate age and covetousness than 'a can
part young limbs and lechery. But the gout galls the one and the
pox pinches the other. . . . A pox of this gout! Or a gout of this
pox! For the one or the other plays the rogue with my great toe.
—*II Henry IV*, I,ii.

In Henry VIII (I,iii) there is a glancing mention reminiscent of
Lucio and his gentlemen. Lovell is speaking disdainfully of English courtiers returned after the French wars:

They may *Cum Privilegio*, wear away
The lag end of their lewdness, and be laugh'd at.
Lord Sands. 'Tis time to give 'em physick, their diseases
Are grown so catching.

> *Lord Chamberlain.*   What a loss our Ladies
>   Will have of these trim vanities?
> *Lovell.*   Ay marry,
>   There will be woe indeed Lords, the sly whorsons
>   Have got a speeding trick to lay down Ladies.
>   A French song, and a fiddle, has no fellow.

Later (II,iv), Henry himself makes a remarkable statement which reflects the actual events that have, at least in part, led medical historians to call him syphilitic:

> First, me thought
> I stood not in the smile of Heaven, who had
> Commanded Nature, that my Lady's womb
> If it conceiv'd a male-child by me, should
> Do no more offices of life to't; than
> The grave does to th' dead: For her Male Issue,
> Or died where they were made, or shortly after
> This world had air'd them.

The emphasis on "male" is partly Henry's basis for the proposed divorce: he wanted an heir; but it allows also for the fact that only one of six children Katharine bore him survived, a daughter, Mary (later Mary I of England, "Bloody Mary"). The others were all stillborn or died in early infancy, an event strongly suggestive of syphilis. Katharine's words in the play, earlier in the scene from which the king's statement is taken,

> That I have been your Wife, in this obedience,
> Upward of twenty years, and have been bless'd
> With many children by you,

may be compared with the charge she makes to the king (IV,ii),

> I have commended to his goodness
> The model of our chaste loves: his young daughter,

and the apparently undisputed fact that only this one child survived.

In *The Comedy of Errors* there is a presumptive reference to gonorrhea (IV,iii):

Syr. Dromio.   Master, is this Mistress Satan?

Syr. Antipholus.   It is the devil.

Syr. Dromio.   Nay, she is worse, she is the devil's dam: And here
she comes in the habit of a light wench, and thereof comes, that
the wenches say God damn me, That's as much to say, God
make me a light wench: It is written, they appear to men like
angels of light, light is an effect of fire, and fire will burn: *ergo*,
light wenches will burn, come not near her.

The treatment of syphilis is alluded to in *Henry V* (II,i) by
Pistol:

> O hound of Crete, think'st thou my spouse to get?
> No; to the spital go,
> And from the powd'ring tub of infamy
> Fetch forth the lazar kite of Cressid's kind,
> Doll Tearsheet, she by name, and her espouse.

"Spital" is the contemporary equivalent of "hospital," or place of
treatment; "powdering tub" refers to treatment with mercury by
fumigation: the patient was exposed to the fumes of cinnabar
(mercuric sulphide, vermilion, a mercury ore), which could be
volatilized from a hot plate or chafing dish, to condense as a
powder on the patient's body. "Lazar," properly a leper, is somebody with a loathsome disease. Presumably the word "kite" is
an allusion to the predatory bird.

Later in the same play (V,i) the same character says:

> News have I, that my Doll is dead i' th' spital
> Of malady of France.

In *Measure for Measure* (III,ii) the word "good" in the mouth of
Lucio has the Shakespearean twist of Lear's "fool" and "honest"
Iago:

Lucio.   How doth my dear morsel, thy mistress? Procures she still,
ha?

Pompey.   Troth, sir, she hath eaten up all her beef, and she is herself in the tub.

Lucio.   Why, 'tis good. It is the right of it; it must be so. Ever
your fresh whore and your powdered bawd; an unshunned consequence, it must be so.

Partridge helps us with "beef," which is here, in effect, "flesh" (that is, the body of a prostitute) being prepared for consumption.

The most eloquent of Shakespeare's references to VD are those in which he used it as the basis for curses. The least of these is the common "A pox on it!" Remember Hamlet's exchange with the gravedigger (V,i):

> *Hamlet.*   How long will a man lie i' th' earth ere he rot?
> *Clown.*   Faith, if 'a be not rotten before 'a die (as we have many pocky corses now-a-days that will scarce hold the laying in), 'a will last you some eight year or nine year.

The explicit use of syphilis by Shakespeare as a curse appears in *Troilus and Cressida* and, at its most virulent, in *Timon of Athens.* In the former play it is the bitter Thersites, echo of the whole action, who speaks; and we come now to more explicit clinical suggestions than we have had before. At the end of his soliloquy (II,iii) he says:

> After this, the vengeance on the whole camp! or, rather, the Neapolitan bone-ache, for that, methinks, is the curse depending on those that war for a placket.

"Bone-ache" was a well-known symptom of severe syphilis. "Placket" (a slit or opening) is a metaphoric allusion to Helen, the cause of the war with which the play deals. Later (V,i), Thersites spews out this catalog of symptoms:

> Now, the rotten diseases of the south, the guts-griping ruptures, catarrhs, loads o' gravel in the back, lethargies, cold palsies, raw eyes, dirt-rotten livers, wheezing lungs, bladders full of imposthume [pus], sciaticas, lime-kilns i' the palm, incurable bone-ache . . .

But it is Timon, repudiated by the Athenians to whom he had been so lavish a friend before he lost his wealth, who plumbs the depths of bitterness, even outdoing Thersites. In fact, one might interpret this whole play in terms of a perverted reward for love, or in fact a punishment, of which venereal disease is the counterpart. Shakespeare has Timon obsessed with syphilis, turning it back upon the Athenians, whom he has come to hate, with unbridled fury, in a series of curses. They begin at the end of Act III, even as his onetime friends are showing belated signs of remorse:

> Of man and beast, the infinite malady
> Crust you quite o'er.

And they continue in the soliloquy opening Act IV:

> Lust, and Liberty
> Creep in the minds and marrows of our youth,
> That 'gainst the stream of Virtue they may strive,
> And drown themselves in riot. Itches, Blains,
> Sow all th' Athenian bosoms, and their crop
> Be general leprosy: Breath infect breath,
> That their society (as their friendship) may
> Be merely poison.

A "blain" is an inflamed sore or pustule. It is interesting that Shakespeare uses "leprosy" as an evident synonym for syphilis. The word "minds" is not to be taken clinically. Neither Shakespeare nor any contemporary physician knew anything of neurosyphilis, which was not clearly identified with syphilis until recent times.

In Scene iii of Act IV, Timon, again in soliloquy, returns to the theme:

> Make the hoar leprosy ador'd, place thieves,
> And give them title, knee, and approbation
> With Senators on the Bench: This is it
> That makes the wappen'd widow wed again;
> She, whom the Spittle-house, and ulcerous sores,
> Would cast the gorge at.

A little later there is this exchange with one of the whores of Alcibiades:

> *Phrynia.* Thy lips rot off.
> *Timon.* I will not kiss thee, then the rot returns
>   To thine own lips again.

And a few lines further he speaks to the other whore, Timandra:

> Be a whore still, they love thee not that use thee, give them dis-
> eases, leaving with thee their lust. Make use of thy salt hours, sea-
> son the slaves for tubs and baths, bring down rose-cheek'd youth to
> the tubfast, and the diet.

And still cursing the two women, or the whole world in their
likeness, Timon makes a speech in which a thin thread of venereal disease runs through the fabric of a terrible curse; and then
we come to the climactic passage:

> Consumptions sow
> In hollow bones of man, strike their sharp shins,
> And mar men's spurring. Crack the Lawyer's voice,
> That he may never more false title plead,
> Nor sound his quillets shrilly: Hoar the Flamen,
> That scold'st against the quality of flesh,
> And not believes himself. Down with the nose,
> Down with it flat, take the bridge quite away
> Of him, that his particular to foresee
> Smells from the general weal. Make curl'd pate ruffians bald
> And let the unscarr'd braggarts of the War
> Derive some pain from you. Plague all,
> That your activity may defeat and quell
> The source of all erection. There's more gold.
> Do you damn others, and let this damn you.
> And ditches grave you all.

This is a vivid picture of severe secondary and late syphilis,
with destructive lesions of bones including "saber shins"; sores
of the soles of the feet and the heels to "mar . . . spurring";
the croaking voice from an ulcerated larynx; the flattened "saddle nose" from a gumma of the bony bridge; and syphilitic baldness. When Simpson quoted this passage in the late 1950s he
could say:

> Shakespeare was recording what was in his day a common enough
> sight; but happily how rare it is today!

But that was when the curve of syphilis was down and seemed to everybody to be on the way out: we thought we had the problem solved! Since then the curve has started up again, and we know now that the most horrible forms of syphilis, the malignant and congenital forms, are still with us.

❧ I I ❧

From John Donne to
Modern Times

So far as I know, which in fact may not be very far, there
seems to be a gap in serious literature dealing with VD
which lasted for more than two centuries after Shakespeare's
death. I have not searched the record closely and have undoubtedly missed things; but neither has much material fallen into my
lap as so much unexpected information has, while I sat working
on or thinking of other parts of the subject. So I suspect that this
interval, which ranges (in England) from the rise of Puritanism
to the reign of Queen Victoria, was not a fruitful one for literature on a subject which apparently became shameful precisely
during that time. And English influence, beneficial, baneful, or
whatever it may have been, ranged over the world. That the diseases themselves pursued their course undisturbed will emerge
in a later chapter; and we will also see that scientific interest in
them kept going as well.

There is an illuminating contrast to Shakespeare in the verses
of his near contemporary, the almost equally great poet, John
Donne (1572–1631). Donne, who began life as a Roman Catholic but later took Anglican orders and became dean of St. Paul's,
ranged in his poetry from some of the most sensual verses in all
of literature to the metaphysical and profoundly religious. Even

in his early work, however, there seems to be an undercurrent of a strong belief in original sin, which emerges in the later poems as a passionate appeal to God for forgiveness. I find it extraordinary that Donne could use his magnificent command of language and imagery to describe the topography of a woman, or the steps in her disrobing, without ever seeming to show any feeling for the woman herself. Consider the long "Anniversary" poems on the death of the young virgin, Elizabeth Drury. In them he pours forth torrents of eloquent grief; yet his grief is so far removed from warm humanity that he can interpolate an image such as the movements of the parts of a man immediately after they have been separated by the executioner's axe.

Donne repeats an idea that was evidently current in his day (and has not been altogether forgotten even in ours), which Shakespeare also hints at in Sonnet 129, the anguished sonnet:

> The expense of spirit in a waste of shame
> Is lust in action . . .

namely, that each male orgasm shortens life by so much. Donne says, in "Farewell to Love,"

> Ah cannot wee,
> As well as Cocks and Lyons jocund be,
> After such pleasures, unless wise
> Nature decreed (since each such Act, they say,
> Diminisheth the length of life a day) . . .

And less plainly but to the same effect, in "Epithalamion made at Lincolnes Inne,"

> Even like a faithfull man content,
> That this life for a better should be spent;

and again, in "The First Anniversary—An Anatomy of the World":

> We doe delightfully our selves allow
> To that consumption; and profusely blinde,
> We kill our selves, to propagate our kinde.

Donne makes several allusions to VD. In "Satyre II" he says,

> . . . time (which rots all, and makes botches poxe, . . .)

and in "Elegie: The Bracelet" we find

> Lust-bred diseases rot thee; and dwell with thee
> Itching desire, and no abilitie [;]

which is reminiscent of Thersites. In the sonnet, "The Apparition," he speaks of treatment somewhat as Shakespeare does:

> Bath'd in a cold quicksilver sweat wilt lye
> A veryer ghost then [than] I [.]

In Donne's "Elegie: The Perfume," there is an allusion to leprosy, which in the context is probably intended as syphilis:

> By thee the seely Amorous sucks his death
> By drawing in a leprous harlots breath [.]

After John Donne, as I have said, there seems to be a hiatus. One finds John Dryden in "The Medall" (1682) saying, "and the poxed Nation feels thee in their Brain." In "John Bull," John Arbuthnot (1712) remarks, "Jack persuaded Peg that all mankind besides himself were poxed by that scarlet-faced whore." Jonathan Swift, in his poem, "Cassinus and Peter" (1731), spoke of "the small and greater pox." Thomas Brown mentions the "Neapolitan disease" about 1790. Both early and late in this period, as we saw in Chapter 9, John Milton and Robert Burns used words suggestive of VD. As late as 1818 Lord Byron set down the passage from "Don Juan" which I have used as an epigraph for this book. Unquestionably there is more of this sort of thing to be found scattered in the literature. But there is little reason to expect any of it to amount to very much.

VD as a subject for literature seems to have become submerged under a lid of polite and informal but none the less effective censorship. It seems possible that pressure was building up under the lid, and that eventually it reached an intolerable level. Perhaps some such process can explain Henrik Ibsen's

Ghosts, which did in fact burst upon the world with the force of an explosion.

It is recognized that all over Europe, except in Russia, the theater during the nineteenth century, before Ibsen's time, had gone through a period of decline. In part this is blamed on a playwright named Eugène Scribe (1791–1861), whose theory of the "well-made play" seems to have encouraged stilted and formal romanticism. In Russia a tradition of realism was unbroken from Aleksander Pushkin (1799–1837) through Nikolai Gogol (1809–1852) and Aleksandr Ostrovsky (1833–1886) to Anton Chekhov (1860–1904) and the dramatic theorist Konstantin Stanislavsky (1863–1938). But the earlier figures had little influence on the rest of Europe until a good deal later; and Chekhov was himself influenced by Ibsen. Even so, Ibsen's contemporary, Björnstjerne Björnson (1832–1910), made a sensation all over Europe with his realistic play *A Failure* (1874) five years before *A Doll's House*. Ibsen is said also to have been influenced by his contemporary, August Strindberg. Nevertheless when Nora slammed the door on her marriage the sound reverberated like a punctuation mark in the history of the theater. But it was not the death knell of Victorianism; the patient is still alive.

Ibsen's *Ghosts* came quickly on the heels of *A Doll's House*. We must speak of it for its general influence on the prudery of the age as well as for its more immediate effect—to us—of reopening the question of syphilis to the literate public view. *Ghosts* is less popular than some of Ibsen's other plays, but it is still viable. It is put on fairly often, especially by college groups, and its text is easily available in many different editions. It hardly needs a stamp of approval from me. It is a play of shattering impact, as a well-told ghost story ought to be; yet Ibsen is said to have disapproved of the name *Ghosts*, which was given to it by its first English translator, William Archer. In the original Norwegian the name means, roughly, "Those who walk again"; it is better translated by the French, "*Les Revenants.*"

The play reintroduced the subject of syphilis to a startled

world which for many years had done its best to sweep the whole disagreeable subject under the rug. Through the syphilis theme Ibsen attacked the prudishness and hypocrisy of his time, as he had done in *A Doll's House* by other means. It is hardly surprising that Scandinavian theaters would not touch *Ghosts* even though Ibsen's reputation was already established. His publisher issued 10,000 copies of the text, but most of them remained unsold. The play was published in 1881 but was not translated into German until 1884. The first performance was in May, 1882, by a Danish touring company, at the Aurora Turner Hall—in Chicago!

When *Ghosts* was staged in London later, it was condemned by the critics with such labels as "putrid" and "an open sewer." What must have shocked its early audiences as much as the syphilis theme was the portrayal of disease and death not clearly as the wages of sin—doing so might have softened the blow to Victorian morals—but rather as a punishment for virtue, at least of virtue as it was then understood. The sinful father does not appear on stage. The mother, Mrs. Alving, conforms to all the dictates of the good Victorian woman. By more modern standards she is, of course, a prude, with more than a suggestion of frigidity. Pastor Manders is a credulous fool whose unrelieved puritanism heightens a sense of morbidity that beclouds the whole play. Engstrand is close to being a burlesque villain. Regina, the only healthy character in the play, still lacks a chance for humor in her lines; and Osvald, the play's thematic center, is no more than barely believable. But Ibsen obviously intended the mood of portending sickness and death, emphasizing it with his insistence on Norwegian sunlessness. The people of the time probably needed a powerful cathartic. For today, as part of the treatment we need for VD as a disease of society, this seems to me to be the wrong medicine.

It may be incidental, even unimportant, that the medical verisimilitude of *Ghosts* is pretty thin. Alving, the father who does not appear, is presumed to have had syphilis without outward sign, and to have infected his son without the wife and mother even knowing about it. He has also sired the healthy child, Regina, by another mother. Osvald himself is a congenital syphilitic whose symptoms appear only in maturity and only in the central nervous system. All this is perhaps possible; but even in 1880 it ought not to have been hard to come a little closer to probability.

Twenty years later the French playwright Eugène Brieux tried the theme of syphilis again, but in a very different way. Shaw, who introduced Brieux to the English-speaking world and wrote a preface to the translation of the play, *Les Avariés* (*Damaged Goods*), says:

> After the death of Ibsen, Brieux confronted Europe as the most important dramatist west of Russia. In that kind of comedy which is so true to life that we have to call it tragi-comedy, and which is not only an entertainment but a history and a criticism of contemporary morals, he is incomparably the greatest writer France has produced since Molière.

Damaged Goods was written just a few years before three key discoveries opened up new means toward control of syphilis. It was first performed in Paris in 1901, but was immediately censored and moved to Liège and Brussels, where it was shown on successive days in 1902. The censorship having been lifted, the play came back to Paris on February 22, 1905. Later in that same year came the announcement of the discovery of *Treponema pallidum* by Schaudinn and Hoffmann. The following year Wassermann and his helpers described the blood test still known by his name; and in 1910 Ehrlich reported the first real cure, popularly called "salvarsan" or by the number of the trial chemical, "606." But even though, like his countryman Buret, Brieux would seem to have been a little premature, the fact is that he had the information he needed. Four prominent French syphilologists were godfathers to the play. The French version is dedicated to Professor Alfred Fournier, after whom an institute in Paris devoted to the study of syphilis has been named. The key paragraph of the dedication, which is omitted in the English translation, says something like this:

> I think, with you, that syphilis will become much less serious when we are able to speak openly of it without shame or fear of punishment, and when those affected by it, aware of the suffering they may cause in others, will better appreciate their duty to those others as well as to themselves.

The English version, translated by John Pollock, was first issued in 1907. In his preface Shaw attacks the censorship in England, but gives no facts or dates. One is left with the vague impression that all the Brieux plays were censored there and that none had been staged at least up to 1909, the date of the preface in my edition. News of the great discoveries in syphilis of 1905 and 1906 had evidently not yet reached Shaw, although he speaks of Neisser's discovery of the gonococcus in 1897.

The early history of the play in the United States is furnished in part by Upton Sinclair, whose novel based on *Damaged Goods* appeared in 1913. The play was presented for the first time in the same year, at a Friday matinee on March 14, in the Fulton Theater in New York, evidently a private showing before members of a group called the Sociological Fund. It had been produced by Richard Bennett, the actor, as we are told by M. Moore:

> not as one more play but as the major enterprise of his whole career. . . . He was almost beaten at first by the hostility of censor-managers; and by the fear of actors who "as fast as he gathered them, just as fast did they stray from the fold when their friends began to tell them that every actor who took part in the production would be ostracized from polite society." When he had succeeded in getting a company together, he found it necessary to present the play first under the auspices of the *Medical Review of Reviews,* and persons who wished to see the play bought special memberships in a fund society instead of simply purchasing tickets of admittance.

In spite of these difficulties, the play was a huge success in New York. Sinclair says it was "acclaimed by public, press, and pulpit as the greatest contribution ever made by the stage to the cause of humanity." It had a long run in New York and then toured other cities, according to Moore, "besides bearing fruit in several state laws for the protection of public health." The play was revived in New York at the 48th Street Theater in 1937 and at the Butler Davenport Theater in 1941.

After the earlier performances, we learn again from Moore, "syphilis even began to be mentioned, though rarely, in the public press." But "rarely" is the word to emphasize. Surgeon General Thomas Parran, of whom we will hear more, was not allowed to speak of syphilis on the radio in 1939. It was only in his time that the word "syphilis" finally appeared openly in the newspapers, some twenty-five years after Richard Bennett's crusade. After another thirty years and more, we are still trying.

The central character in *Damaged Goods* is the doctor, who belongs to a species that now seems in danger of becoming mythical. He has the time and the inclination, the patience and clinical skill, and the compassion, to serve as a foundation upon which the other characters and the plot are built. He is off stage only for brief intervals that serve to fill in background or color. In contrast to *Ghosts*, this play is medically authentic and credible; and despite its age and its appearance before scientific diagnosis and effective treatment, it is less dated than one might expect. In fact, I found in it only one really egregious blunder that would be laughable today, although only perhaps in the light of much later experience: the brief passage in the third act in which the doctor recommends prohibition as a preventive of alcoholism. Yet this is itself part of an aspect in which the play is an undisguised period piece. The underlying mores of upper-middle-class Paris in relation to marriage and servants are vintage 1900. But allowing for this the play might be staged today with little or no modification.

The action concerns a young man whom the doctor confronts with the fact that he has syphilis. The doctor advises him not to marry, but he is too far committed—the arrangements are firm, and there is a dowry—and he goes against the doctor's advice. The result, unknown to wife and to husband's mother before the explosive climax at the second-act curtain, is a baby with congenital syphilis showing as mild early secondary symptoms. There is a wet nurse, and the climactic problem is the likelihood that she will be infected by the baby. In the third act, the marriage having broken up, the wife's father, a member of the Chamber of Deputies, is in the doctor's clinic in a mood of vengeance. The play is resolved by the doctor's gentle exposition of the fact that, first, the deputy himself has escaped his son-in-law's plight only by luck; and second, that the damage having been done, the best solution lies in reconciliation rather than vengeance or open scandal. Here are some of the doctor's words in the last act:

> This disease is like other diseases: it is one of our afflictions. There is no shame in being wretched—even if one deserves to be so. (*Hotly*) Come, come, let us have a little plain speaking! I should like to know how many of these rigid moralists, who are so choked with their middle-class prudery that they dare not mention the name syphilis, or when they bring themselves to speak of it do so with expressions of every sort of disgust, and treat its victims as criminals, have never run the risk of contracting it themselves?
>
> There is nothing immoral in the act that reproduces life by means of love. But for the benefit of our children we organize round about it a gigantic conspiracy of silence. A respectable man will take his son and daughter to one of these grand music halls, where they will hear things of the most loathsome description; but he won't let them hear a word spoken seriously on the subject of the great act of love.

These were strong words in 1901, and not less so in 1913. Are they appreciably weaker today? Have we uncovered the problem or only changed its clothes? The Victorian moralism of *Damaged Goods* is old-fashioned but not altogether extinct. The doctor's implied solution of the VD problem is that by education it will be possible to promote abstinence for both sexes except in marriage. But put that way, does the idea sound so old-fashioned?

To my knowledge the drama and serious literature of more recent times have only occasionally made use of VD as a significant part of their theme. An unmentioned gonorrhea is an important detail of the play by Tennessee Williams, *Sweet Bird of Youth* (1959). The male lead had infected his first sweetheart, the ingenue; and, their love having been thwarted by her politician father, the lead has become a gigolo. The ingenue has been operated on; and she says the doctor's "knife had cut the youth out of my body, made me an old, childless woman." More recently a play on Broadway, *Philosophy in the Boudoir,* adapted from the work of the Marquis de Sade, was described by Clive Barnes in a review in the *New York Times* in part as follows:

> The story is nothing but the education by a group of libertines of a young but not too innocent girl into the ways and, more especially, the byways of sex and sexuality. The high point arrives when the mother of the seduced innocent comes to claim her daughter—and is raped by a man with syphilis and then later mutilated.

In refreshing contrast to this horror is the chapter that deals with VD and its treatment in the U.S. Army in World War II, in *The Gallery* by John Horne Burns (1947). To me this is a remarkable document in the literature of syphilis in its own right, and the more valuable for expressing with eloquent artistry the rarely heard viewpoint of the patient. Burns wrote only one other book (*A Cry of Children*) before he died prematurely. The thirty-odd pages of his chapter in *The Gallery* ("Eighth Portrait: *Queen Penicillin*") are recommended reading.

It is good to have a sensitive writer's insight into the experience of being infected with syphilis by a loved one, and how it felt to have it treated as an enlisted man in the U.S. Army in Naples in 1944. We can learn something vicariously here about the depths of human misery, much as we can learn the same sort of lesson from Beethoven's last quartets. There is no bravado, no smirking. There is an evocation of love tragically wounded, yet without hate, even without bitterness; and even the callousness of orderlies and the casual detachment and occasional cruelty of doctors are painted with deft, sure strokes. Penicillin was new then. The first definitive papers on its use in syphilis appeared in that same year, 1944, although it had been under study in the Army for some two years previously. Its value at the time was still not fully established. Nevertheless the treatment was effective, and it was administered efficiently, although more than a little punishment was mixed in with it. The tone of the treatment center is suggested by this exchange with the admitting medical officer:

> "So you got burned?" the major said. "And you'll be losing those three stripes too."
> "Yessir."
> "I don't say: Welcome to our hospital. You're not going to have a good time here. Our whole setup is guaranteed to make you hate everything about us. We don't want men coming back here, do you see? There's no excuse for getting VD. No excuse whatever. We give you treatment here, but we do it in such a way that you won't care to come back as a repeater. . . ."

The artist's eyes, showing us familiar things in a quite new way, as Cézanne did, struck my own special experience with

> desks where microscopes stood in their metal frames like scrub-women resting on their brooms.

Let me leave the story, hoping you will read it all yourself, with these words of the chaplain's, who is afraid to shake hands because "God has made certain diseases highly infectious. . . ." But before that:

> "My boy, if there were no disease in the world, there would be no decency. The fear of God. Our illness is a sign of the disapproval of God for what we did. . . ."

❦ 12 ❦

VD in the Graphic Arts

HAVING NEVER RECOVERED from a childish fondness for books and pictures (beginning, I suppose, with picture-books), I would have enjoyed the chance to take a year or so off and devote it to research for this chapter. But on this as on nearly every aspect of my general subject I have had to put up with something short of a complete survey: otherwise I might have spent twenty years writing this book. In the graphic arts, in view of the special unpopularity of VD, I expected to find very little; yet what I have found suggests that there must be much more. The expectation was at first bolstered by a remark in a recent scholarly paper by Timken-Zinkann that "we rarely find works of art which we can connect directly with syphilis"—in contrast to plague and other diseases. The same paper contained a group of examples that were new to me. Since then I have found more in older sources; and I am back to the impression typical of most of these chapters that one could keep digging and keep finding more.

Not that every shovelful is rewarding: one turns up tin cans and old shoes as well as nuggets. The Columbus theory is rampant, forcing the idea that nothing could have been syphilis in Europe before his time, but that anything in America might have been.

For example, on the second point: there is a disappointing photograph of a black, presumably earthen figure entitled "Syphilitic woman with her child," a piece of Mochica art from the northern coast of Peru dating from the fourth century A.D., reproduced in a book on medicine in art, edited by J. Rousselot. The picture shows what may represent a saddle nose, the flat bridge that Shakespeare knew, a mark of late congenital syphilis. But it is the mother in this figure, not the child, who shows the defect. The text speaks of mutilation of upper lips and noses, evidently done with a knife and attributable at least in part to sacred and punitive incisions. This nose might well have been mutilated rather than diseased. The child's nose looks healthy to me in the photograph of the figure. Its teeth are not clearly shown and are not mentioned in the text. But the mother shows her upper front teeth, and there is nothing syphilitic about their squareness. This single observation would be in accord with the conclusion of the writer, mentioned in Chapter 6, who found nothing clearly identifiable as syphilis in a detailed study of pre-Columbian American sculpture.

On the other hand, there is a drawing in black and white, reproduced in the same book from a Persian treatise on surgery dated about 1300 A.D., called "Cauterization of leprosy lesions," by an anonymous draftsman. Its three figures are stylized, with a doctor squatting at the right with his cautery in his extended hand, and what I take to be two images of the same patient, back and front, nude but for turban, with spots symmetrically in the front view on body, face, legs, arms, feet, and especially on what would be the backs of the hands. The rear view, if that is what it is, shows only a row of spots along the middle of the backbone, and perhaps two more in the midline of the neck. The text suggests that the drawing had been recopied several times, so that it may have undergone changes. The evidence is not enough to diagnose syphilis; but it seems to me more likely to have been syphilis than leprosy.

Another picture in Rousselot is entitled "Josaphat as a child,

meeting a leper and an old cripple at the gates of Jerusalem"
(see Figure 6). It is dated mid-fourteenth century. Here the alleged leper has spots on every exposed skin surface—face, neck,
ankles (not clearly shown), and hands, including what is seen of
the palm of the extended right hand, which is grasping a clap-
per. Today, only somebody committed to the fifteenth-century
origin of syphilis could be comfortable calling this leprosy.

But apart from these examples I leave the question of VD in
pre-Columbian art to others and come down to the period of the
epidemic. Here we strike gold at once in the form especially of
several works by an artist of the first rank, Albrecht Dürer, and
some by lesser hands. Dürer made a well-known woodcut enti-

Figure 6. "Josaphat as a child, meeting a leper and an old cripple at the
gates of Jerusalem." Miniature taken from the *Miroir Historial* of Vincent
de Beauvais. (Bibliothèque de L'Arsenal)

tled "The Syphilitic," to illustrate what is said to be the first printed medical article on the disease, a broadsheet by Diedrich Ulsen, town physician of Nuremberg. It is easy to agree with the opinion of a recent writer that the drawing is uninspired; and in fact its poor quality, with perhaps the additional fact that it lacks the master's usual monogram, has led to doubt of its authenticity. It shows the figure of a man with spots—described as "ulcers" but drawn as irregular rings, much as our contemporary satirist David Levine draws what must be freckles. In the presumed Dürer the spots are shown on all parts of the body not covered by hat, cloak, and boots. The face wears an expression vaguely sad or disdainful, perhaps in line with Fracastor's suggestion of the characteristic melancholy of syphilis. There are spots on the extended right palm. Above the figure is a sphere bearing the zodiac and marked 1484, the date of the great conjunction of Saturn, Jupiter, and Mars. I have not seen the accompanying verses by "the Frisian doctor Ulsenius."

Dürer is said to have revealed in some of his letters that he had a mortal dread of syphilis, and there are suggestions here and elsewhere that he may have had it himself. He abandoned his wife a few weeks after he married her in 1494. He made a drawing a year earlier of a nude female bathhouse attendant in Strasbourg, the earliest known German drawing of a nude woman from life, so that he was evidently familiar, as Timken-Zinkann says, with "houses which later proved to be hotbeds of luetic infection." Some of his finest works in this early period (1494–1503) deal with a theme that might have been related to syphilis, that of "Woman, Death, and the Devil," one of which, "Young Woman attacked by Death," appears to represent a rape. It is described by the same author as bordering on the obscene: "No German artist prior to Dürer dared to show such a subject and to shock the viewer in such a manner."

But a most significant as well as excellent work of Dürer's not only furnishes one of my best exhibits (see Figure 7) but supports the idea that the artist was himself syphilitic, and had by

Figure 7. Self-portrait of Albrecht Dürer, circa 1503.
Schlossmuseum, Weimar. (Bettmann Archive)

this time passed into the late stage. It is a three-quarter-length
nude self-portrait done with pen and brush with white high-
lights, showing an abnormal left testicle (right in the mirror
image), which has been identified as a syphilitic fibrosis, something now rare but well-known and clearly identified with
syphilis before 1900. The drawing was evidently made for purposes of consultation at a distance. A better-known self-portrait

sketch by Dürer shows him pointing to a circled area on the left side of his abdomen (again, in the drawing, the right side). A handwritten inscription above is translated as reading, "There, on the yellow spot, where my finger is pointing, is where my pain is." One assumes that the doctors of the period could do about as well with the sketch of a fine draftsman as with the patient in the flesh.

A number of Renaissance artists besides Dürer are said to have illustrated syphilis, and I have seen reproductions of a few of the pictures. Among them is an anonymous engraving in Rousselot called "The routing of the Spaniards from the city of Naples on the arrival of the Duc de Guise," described as "an allegory showing us the Spaniard sweating out his pox enclosed in a barrel and undergoing a mercury fumigation." Another in the same source is an engraving by Giorgio Ghisi, "Venus wounded by thorns"; and still another is a sketch by Nicolas Manuel Deutsch showing the ravages of the disease. A drawing by Jan van der Straet (or Stradamus), engraved by Jean Galle, shows in the right-hand corner a guaiacum tree being chopped down and stacked while a syphilitic patient lies at the left with a doctor applying salve.

I have seen reproductions of two woodcuts of this period, both apparently anonymous. One appeared on the title page of a book, A mala Franczos, by Bartholomew Steber (see Figure 8). It shows two patients, a woman in bed and a man sitting on a stool at the bedside, the woman covered with bedclothes to the waist, the man vaguely clothed across the hips. Both patients are marked with undistinctive spots, most of them crescent-shaped and so perhaps meant to represent ulcers. There are no spots on the face or hands of either patient, nor on the exposed feet of the man. A doctor stands on one side gravely examining a flask of urine, and another kneels in front of the man, applying something from a jar to the patient's leg with a long spatula in his left hand, and incautiously using his free right hand to steady the patient's knee. There was probably a

Figure 8. Woodcut, frontispiece to Steber's *A mala Franczos*.

good deal of syphilis among doctors in those days, acquired in this nonvenereal way.

The other contemporary woodcut is the frontispiece of another book, *Tractatus de Scorra* by Grünpeck (Grunspeck), which is reproduced in Rousselot. It shows an enthroned queen holding a spotless baby in her left arm while a crown, in her right hand, is extended toward an already crowned and armored prince, also spotless, who kneels at her right. Kneeling at her left are two supplicating women spotted on their exposed faces, necks, and hands. At the feet of the queen, in the foreground, is the supine figure of a man—a corpse?—clad only in a breech-clout. This figure has crescentic or ring-shaped spots all over him except for face and hands.

A detail of one of the panels of the altar at Isenheim painted by Mathias Grünewald (or Neithart), called "The temptation of St. Anthony," completed in 1514, has been suggested as representing syphilis. The detail is reproduced by Timken-Zinkann and described as "a man stricken with St. Anthony's fire." It shows a man in an attitude of agony. His belly is swollen and his hands are mutilated. His body is covered with large sores in different stages, some pointing, some weeping. It is possible that a man with active late syphilis might also have come down with St. Anthony's fire (ergot poisoning), which was widespread at the time, the result of eating bread made from grain contaminated with the ergot fungus.

Two seventeenth-century drawings included in the treatise by W. A. Pusey show the treatment of syphilis. In one, several patients and attendants appear in various positions. A patient is covered except for his head in an enclosure or cabinet, with a towel hanging from his head. The other is described as coming from a collection of engravings by Jaques Laniet illustrating famous Parisian proverbs. It shows in the small window of a large oven the head and shoulders of a figure with a hat and a dress or shirt to the neck. An attendant manipulates the fire below. On the wall of the oven under the window are lettered the words, "POVR VN PLAISIR MIL DOVLEUR IL SVE LA VEROLE," which means, "For one pleasure a thousand sorrows: he sweats out the pox." The first phrase is multiplied by ten from Villon, the last line of whose ballade, "La belle Hëaulmiere aux filles de joie," (see Chapter 9) reads, " 'Pour une joye cent doulours.' " These were the wages of foolish love to Villon; he put the phrase in quotation marks, so that even in 1460 it must have been an old saying.

There is a painting by the Italian Pietro Falca (Pietro Longhi, 1702–1785) called "The Apothecary", which is reproduced in color in Rousselot. It shows what is said to be a young prostitute, having an apothecary look at her syphilitic sores. Several men are also shown, but no other women; and it may be that the mere presence of an unattended young woman in such circumstances was enough, at the time, for both conviction and diagnosis. In fact, the buxom young blonde reveals no outward sign of disease. She is shown standing, facing the apothecary, who is stretching her mouth a little with an instrument as he peers into it. If indeed she has mucous patches there, the apothecary looks wiser than he is: his bare hand is perilously close. The rest of the description goes this way:

> The scene takes place in the classical pharmacy among flagons, pots, phials, mortars and pestles. An assistant is seated at a table filling out a prescription while two [male] clients await their turn on a bench. In a corner, a young assistant is working at a stove, doubtless heating a cauterizing-iron.

A further detail shown in the painting is a pot of aloes in the right foreground. Aloes were used for treating amenorrhea as well as for skin ulcers.

Hogarth has given us the following words on gonorrhea in a woman, a subject which, as we will see, would be extremely hard to illustrate. It appears in his series, "A Harlot's Progress":

> "Once out of the hospital, Margot continues to ply her trade. Do you know one of these creatures that has not had the clap?
> "Our Margot has had it. Elixirs, pills and emetics had so exhausted her, and she's tired of living.
> "In short, she dies. . . . Her maid, upon seeing her dead, starts to yell and scream.
> "The doctors blamed each other. Slim (one of the doctors) is furious, knocks over a table and treats his friend as a madman. . . .

"It was your pills that killed her," says Squage (the other doctor)
"and not my elixir."
"While they are blaming each other, a scrawny woman is filching
from her chest."

William Blake is said to have evoked plague "and other calami-
ties, such as venereal disease," but if he did so in his drawings I
have not seen them. Blake is, however, quoted by Rousselot as
saying:

> "Let the brothels of Paris be opened
> With many an alluring dance,
> To awake the physicians thro' the city!"
> Said the beautiful Queen of France. . . .

There are suggestions of a Rembrandt, a portrait, perhaps
more than one work, dealing with syphilis; and of another, by
Felicien Rops, called "Mors syphilitica"; but I have seen no
other details. I have no doubt there is more; but what little
searching I have been able to do turned up nothing further until
we come down to recent times. I have pored over what I found
easily available of works by artists known for their interest in
medical subjects, among them Johannes Wechtlin (1490–1530),
Rowlandson, Gillray, Cruickshank, Daumier, and Goya. I have
been disappointed especially to find nothing in the works of
Hieronymus Bosch or Pieter Brueghel the Elder—both of whom
must have known of syphilis; and I would think they were of a
temperament to draw pictures of it. Perhaps they did, and perhaps their pictures have been put discreetly apart from less disagreeable subjects. By the time of Goya, Rowlandson, Gillray,
Cruickshank, and Daumier, VD may have got itself buried
under too deep a cover of puritanism even for them. And while
Beardsley and Toulouse-Lautrec might not have been stopped
by the same obstacle, they may have found other reasons for
avoiding the subject. But I suspect that a diligent search would
be fruitful.
Several people have mentioned to me that there is a mural in

Mexico by Diego Rivera showing Cortez with marks on him recognizable as syphilis, but I have not seen this and have no more information on it. But another mural by Rivera is of the greatest interest. This is the one the great artist started in 1933 in the lobby of the new RCA Building at Radio City in New York, which soon landed him in trouble. He attempted to present his own view of the world in a panorama on each side of a worker who is operating a giant machine in the center. On the worker's right there is a presumed progression of capitalism from Darwin at the extreme left of the panel to decadence near the center, the latter suggested by groups of people drinking, smoking, dancing, and playing cards. On the worker's left a progression of communism moves from Karl Marx at the extreme right to Lenin in the area near the center corresponding to the wastrels opposite. The mural is crowded with much more, including faces, many identifiable, as well as animals, plants, microbes, and other biological material and a profusion of instruments and machines. There is a microscope of a sort that was advanced in 1933; but Rivera drew it with an incredible tuft of eyepiece tubes sprouting from its body.

The mural kicked up a storm at about the point at which the face of Lenin became recognizable. The work was stopped and the mural was destroyed. Whereupon the painter, after doing a few more jobs in New York, went home and re-created the complete mural on the third floor of the Palace of Fine Arts in Mexico City. At least a piece of it will be found reproduced in many collections of Rivera or of Mexican muralists.

Why do I speak of this mural here? Radiating out from the machine operator at its center are four long petal-shaped panels, of which the one extending obliquely upward from his right, forming the roof of the segment showing capitalist decadence, contains the fantastic microscope I mentioned and many other things, including unmistakable gonococci in a white blood cell (as they typically appear) as well as many other bacteria, among them spirochetes. The gonococci and the phagocytes are stylized much as one would expect them to be in this master's hands. He must have looked through a microscope in some medical laboratory. Whoever showed him spirochetes showed him the wrong ones, probably for lack of better. Living *Treponema pallidum,* seen under the best optical microscope, is as stylized to begin with as any artist could wish it to be. Rivera undoubtedly intended to show the spirochetes of syphilis; and nobody who knows his work could imagine that in drawing what look like the borrelias of relapsing fever the fault could have been the artist's. Anyway, this criticism ought to be thought of as of microscopically small importance.

❧ 13 ❧

The Famous and the Infamous

SCATTERED BETWEEN the lines of history, seldom plainly visible, are names of famous people—almost all men—who are known or thought to have been victims of VD. Almost all men, with a woman of course implied in nearly every instance, sometimes referred to, nearly always anonymously, usually scurrilously: but of women's names we have very few. Even so, the diseases are hardly ever named or even suggested in the usual history books, nor in most biographies or biographical notes in encyclopedias, nor even in medical histories. Generally the subject's VD is delicately expurgated, as it might be in books intended for children. When VD is mentioned it is nearly always syphilis, although we need not doubt that gonorrhea has always been much more prevalent. Syphilis was spoken of freely during a brief interval in the Renaissance. Before that it was not recognized, although we assume now that it existed; and afterward the Puritans buried it, especially in polite parlance, but even to some degree among physicians. Ever since the period of the Great Epidemic, syphilis has exercised a fascination over medical historians and certain physician-scientists; but it is probably not surprising that case histories of syphilis in people of note have not been so common as similar reference to, say, bubonic plague or tuberculosis.

There have been several studies of the influence on human history of plague, tuberculosis, typhus fever, and of acute epidemic disease generally. I do not know of any similar assessment of the effect of venereal disease, although it could hardly have been less. There are isolated exceptions, not always reliable, as witness the presumed effect of the great epidemic itself when it first struck the armies of Charles VIII of France and made him lift the siege of Naples. Later in this chapter we will let Thomas Parran speak of the effects of syphilis on Henry VIII of England and other kings, and through them, in suggestive terms, on history. But as we have already seen, VD is unlikely to have devastated armies as faster-moving and more fatal epidemic diseases have often done. Its effects are exerted more insidiously; and perhaps its most dramatic consequences have resulted from the acute pain of a blocked urethra in gonorrhea or by way of the paranoiac cruelty of syphilitic insanity, both especially among absolute monarchs. One can hardly do more than guess at the effects of such symptoms, especially the second, on philosophy and art. This latter effect may actually have been exaggerated, as when both world wars have been attributed to the influence of Nietzsche—who died with syphilitic insanity—on Kaiser Wilhelm and on Hitler, respectively, which seems to me a ludicrous oversimplification, if not altogether false. And if the profound works of Beethoven's later years—the piano sonatas beginning with the "Hammerclavier" and the late quartets— were a direct consequence of his deafness, which has been attributed to syphilis (but as we shall see, the point has been strongly disputed), I would still be loath to credit *Treponema pallidum* with a wholesome effect.

What cannot be denied is that the spirochete and the gonococcus have, through the ages, induced an enormous toll of human suffering. Some of the suffering has been passed on to others—sometimes to thousands of others, as in the instance of Ivan the Terrible—in a manner that did not entail transmission of the disease itself. Some of the suffering may well have influenced philosophy, art, and literature as any sort of suffering may influence them. Yet the whole thrust of this book will be blunted if, as we come now to speak of individual victims of VD, we lose sight of the fact that they were diseased, and that disease is an unmitigated evil. Let us be consistent. If we slip into the notion that Henry VIII of England or Casanova "deserved" to have VD —if we accept disease in such men as just punishment for sin— we have tacitly accepted a principle, and we cannot make exceptions of John Keats or Franz Schubert.

Obviously the names that follow are a drop in the bucket— names I have happened to run across in my study of the rest of the subject. For many of them I am indebted to Mr. A. Dickson Wright, a doctor of Wimpole Street, London, who did me the extraordinary favor of letting me have a copy of his unpublished manuscript, "Venereal Disease among the Great." I mention other sources in their places. Still others are qualified acquaintances who are best left anonymous, just as Mr. Dickson Wright was reticent about some of his word-of-mouth informants. But it may as well be admitted that the drop in the bucket is not merely a small sample; neither can its chemical purity be guaranteed. Most of my names predate modern diagnostic methods; even today we occasionally make mistakes in diagnosis (as we shall see later), and if we are better tomorrow we are not likely to be perfect. I speak only of the dead. It is worth mentioning that even when the person himself proclaimed his venereal disease, as did Ulrich von Hutten and Benvenuto Cellini, or gave evidence of it that seems clinically convincing today, as did Albrecht Dürer, the possibility of error is not excluded.

The most reasonable order seems chronological, and I have arranged the names by birth date when it was available. Yet it has also seemed convenient to lump together in groups kings and other political figures on the one hand, and artists and other nonpoliticians on the other.

To begin with, let me repeat from Chapter 9 the biblical figures Abraham and Sarah, the Pharaoh of Genesis and King Abimelech of Gerar (and all the wives of the last two), Miriam, David, Bath-sheba, and Job. Perhaps we should not overlook the ill-fated first-born of David and Bath-sheba. The list contains three kings, initiating a pattern. From a nonbiblical source I have the name of the obscure Ramses V, assigned (by Breasted) to the twentieth Egyptian dynasty, some time before 1090 B.C., whose mummy showed signs of what may have been congenital syphilis.

Among Romans and notables of the Roman world a succession of rulers continues: Julius Caesar (named by Catullus, according to Buret) and his bedfellow, Mamuria; Cleopatra herself (Dickson Wright) as well as her soldiers (Horace, via Buret). There is also Herod, king of Judea, who, according to Astruc, had private parts that were "putrefied and eaten up with worms," and who is the first king reported to have been subject in his later years to insanity which made him bloodthirsty (Matthew 2:16). The emperor Tiberius is said to have become so suspicious that he killed his chief aid and confidant, Sejanus, presumably as a result of syphilis, since earlier he had suffered from the facial sores and falling hair typical of the early generalized disease. Buret also lists the Roman emperor Commodus, son and successor of Marcus Aurelius.

It is perhaps not surprising to have a blank covering the fall of Rome and some centuries thereafter. I have an unverified suggestion that Charlemagne, king of the Franks and emperor of the West (742–814) may have been a sufferer; if in fact he had VD, his is the only name for many centuries. Buret refers to Weston, Dean of Windsor, as the most debauched canon of his time (1356), who had the "burning," or, according to a phrase of the period, had been "bitten by a Winchester goose"—which Beckett identified with the pox because of the stews (brothels) which were under the charge of the Bishop of Winchester.

Thereafter we find Charles V of France (1337–1380), who Dickson Wright thinks was syphilitic, and John of Gaunt, duke of Lancaster (1340–1399), who is said by Buret to have displayed his "rottenness" to King Richard II; Astruc also tells us that the same John died of a "putrefaction of the genitals" which this author attributes to "carnal copulation." Other pre-Columbian syphilitics named by Buret are King Ladislaus of Poland, evidently Ladislaus II (1350?–1434), and Wenceslaus, presumably the fourth of that name (1361–1419), king of Bohemia, who is said to have been given to drunkenness and violent fits of temper and to have died in a rage. He was evidently *not* the "good" king of the Christmas carol, who was more likely to have been the one who died in 936 and is known as the patron saint of Bohemia.

The next name on my list is François Villon, the great poet of the underground, who was born in 1431 and disappeared from Paris in 1463 to die nobody knows where or how. We have seen that he used the word "chancre" and seemed to know of the mercury treatment of syphilis. Dickson Wright thinks he may have had the disease himself, noting that others had suggested as much before. The argument rests in part on Villon's ballade "a s'amye," (to his girl friend), a lacerating poem addressed to "you filthy slut" (Bonner) or "you dirty whore" (Nicholson), a lady "au nez tortu"—words given by the two translators respectively as "twisted nose" and "nose turned in"—possibly suggesting saddle nose. But Dickson Wright also tells us that Villon suffered from condylomas ("figs"), which were likely to have been syphilitic, and also from complete baldness, which in the general context would point in the same direction. If Villon was in fact syphilitic, he was the first in my record of a series of great poets and artists to be so afflicted.

Still in the pre-Columbian period, although written from the perspective of the epidemic, we have two references in Rabelais, both in *Pantagruel*, Book II, and dealing with Sixtus IV, who was pope from 1471 to 1484. The first, in Chapter 17, mentions that the pope was cured of "a chancrous bump"; and a footnote tells us that this pope was noted for his liberality and debauched life. The second, in Chapter 30, has the same pope "greasing up syphilitic patients," a phrase plausibly interpreted by Buret as meaning that he anointed them with mercury ointment.

The period of the epidemic may as well begin with Columbus himself. Thomas Parran, the great American expert of whom we will hear much more later, argues that he had syphilis. The "severe attack of gout" during his third voyage, as well as the mental disorder which appeared at the time, are his clues. He continues:

> He began to hear voices and to regard himself as "ambassador of God." Perhaps it was for this reason that he was sent back to Spain in chains by Bobadilla, the newly appointed governor of the islands.
>
> In spite of his disabilities, Columbus made a last voyage and returned in 1504 so ill that he had to be carried ashore. With his whole body dropsical from the chest downward, like that which is caused by injury to the valves of the heart, his limbs paralyzed, and his brain affected—all symptoms of late, fatal syphilis—he died on May 20, 1506.

Let me separate sufferers in this important period and speak, first, of kings, popes, and politicians.

Dickson Wright lists three popes in a row: Alexander VI (1431–1503), who reigned during the siege of Naples, when the epidemic is supposed to have begun; Julius II (1443–1513), and Leo X (1475–1521)—all as having had syphilis, but without details. Parran tells us that Charles VIII of France, the besieger of Naples, was himself syphilitic, "as is strongly indicated by the deaths in infancy of his four children who were the last of the Valois dynasty"; and that Francis I probably came to the throne as a result. That Francis was syphilitic is presumably the basis for some of the allusions in Rabelais (Chapter 9). There was a contemporary jingle about it:

> L'an mil cinq quarante sept,
> François mourut a Rambouillet
> De la vérole quil avait fait. [sic]

> In the year fifteen forty-seven
> Francis died at Rambouillet
> Of the pox he had.

Parran says that the reign of Francis I

> presents a vivid picture of what happens to a nation when its abso-
> lute ruler is governed by the impulses of irritable inconsistency
> and the delusions of grandeur which accompany one type of late
> syphilis.

And the same author speaks of the contemporary of Francis:

> Henry VIII of England often has been cited to illustrate the im-
> pact of this disease upon the fate of a nation. Catherine of Aragon,
> his first wife, bore him four children, all stillborn or dying immedi-
> ately after birth, before the birth of her single living child, a daughter,
> later to reign as "Bloody Mary." Mary herself showed many
> evidences of congenital infection—the face prematurely old and
> scarred; the thin, motheaten hair; the square head with grotesquely
> protruding forehead; and the extremely bad sight, which probably
> was due to interstitial keratitis [scarring within the cornea of the
> eye]. Her sudden death at the age of forty-two is supposed to have
> been due to a syphilitic aneurism [a "bubble" formed on a large blood
> vessel by thinning of its wall].

Dickson Wright tells us that Henry VIII suffered from ulceration of the legs above the knees which did not respond to
hundreds of remedies, the prescriptions for which are still extant. The same commentator adds that Henry's cruelty in later
life—he is charged with having executed 3 per cent of the population of London, as well as most of his wives—may have resulted from general paresis or syphilitic insanity. Cardinal
Thomas Wolsey (1475–1530), Henry's confidant and virtual ruler
of England during much of his reign, was one of those executed.
Wolsey, Dickson Wright says, admitted having the pox. Buret
cites Hume's *History of England,* Volume 4, as recording that
the king had ordered Wolsey beheaded because the Cardinal
had infected the king by whispering in his ear—possibly additional evidence of the king's irrationality.

Ivan the Terrible, the first czar of Russia (1530–1584), is known to have suffered a grave illness after the death of his first wife, Anastasia, in 1560. He became gloomy and paranoid, changing from a good king to one afflicted with wanton cruelty. Dickson Wright says he became a sexual maniac, and attributes the symptoms to late syphilis.

Astruc lists a group of contemporary monarchs:

> Charles IX of France [1550–1574] had a Caruncle [sic] from a violent Gonorrhea, which was cured with Cathareticks [sic]. . . . Henry III [of France, 1551–1589], returning into *France* from *Poland* upon the death of *Charles* IX, was infected with a Clap by a Courtezan, whom he had to do with at *Venice*. . . . And, not to mention Instances in the Princes of other European Nations, *Charles* of *Lorrain,* Duke of Mayenne [1554–1611], the famous Head of the League, or rather Chief of the Rebels against Henry III and Henry IV was in like manner infected with this Distemper. . . .

Dickson Wright adds that Henry IV (1553–1610), son of Henry III, himself is reputed to have had gonorrhea several times; an account survives of his catheterization to overcome painful closure (stricture) of the urethra and consequent retention of urine.

The contemporary list of nonpolitical figures begins with Konrad Celtes (1459–1508), the first poet laureate of Germany, followed by the great Dutch humanist Desiderius Erasmus (1469?–1536). It has been reported that Erasmus thought syphilis to be inevitable; according to Moore, he "said that in his day a man who did not have the pox was accounted a rustic and not a polished gentleman."

And now a group of notable people whose lives extended over a century who, in one way or another, directly or indirectly, told us of their syphilis themselves, sometimes even making their own diagnosis. The French disease was presumably familiar to knowledgeable people of the day, and the diagnosis has usually been accepted by later commentators, including medical men. It is therefore worthwhile to mention that some of these victims did not seem to suffer very much from their syphilis, a circum-

stance that would contrast with the commonly held view that
the syphilis of the day was much more serious than it became
later.

First in this group is Albrecht Dürer, whose evidence was described and illustrated in the preceding chapter. The second,
whose illness seems to have been more serious than that of others, was Ulrich von Hutten (1488–1523), the German humanist,
friend of Erasmus and supporter of Martin Luther, who wrote a
book on syphilis especially to advance the virtues of guaiac as a
cure. Von Hutten acquired syphilis at the age of twenty-three
and died eleven years later, having in the meantime had the stiff
joints and lightning pains characteristic of severe syphilis, and
painful gummatous ulcers on his arms and legs. He thought
guaiac had cured him. Another contemporary, the satirist poet
Pietro Aretino (1492–1556?), did not to my knowledge give evidence on the point himself, but he is described casually by his
modern biographer Thomas C. Chubb (1940) as having had the
French disease with no suggestion that he suffered any marked
inconvenience from it.

More eloquent and convincing testimony to similar effect is
provided by Benvenuto Cellini (1500–1571), the great sculptor
and goldsmith, equally noted for his autobiography and his dar-
ingly ingenious innovations in bronze casting. His words, as
translated by John Addington Symonds, seem to me worth paus-
ing for:

> It is true indeed that I had got the sickness; but I believe I
> caught it from that fine young servant-girl whom I was keeping
> when my house was robbed. The French disease, for it was that,
> remained in me more than four months dormant before it showed
> itself, and then it broke out over my whole body in one instant. It
> was not like what one commonly observes, but covered my flesh
> with certain blisters, of the size of sixpences, and rose-coloured.
> The doctors would not call it the French disease, albeit I told them
> why I thought it was that. I went on treating myself according to
> their methods, but derived no benefit. At last, then, I resolved on
> taking the wood [guaiac] against the advice of the first physicians

in Rome; and I took it with the most scrupulous discipline and rules of abstinence that could be thought of; and after a few days, I perceived in me a great amendment. The result was that at the end of fifty days I was cured and as sound as a fish in water.

[But some time later, after staying out in marshland in winter,] I fell a hundred times more ill than I had been before. I put myself once more under doctor's orders, and attended to their directions, but grew always worse. When the fever fell upon me, I resolved on having recourse again to the wood; but the doctors forbade it, saying that if I took it with the fever on me, I should not have a week to live. However, I made my mind up to disobey their orders, observed the same diet as I had formerly adopted, and after drinking the decoction four days, was wholly rid of fever. My health improved enormously; and while I was following this cure, I went on always working. . . . After fifty days my health was reestablished. . . . When at last I ventured to relax my rigid diet, I found myself as wholly free from those infirmities as though I had been born again.

The first of these episodes is a good description of secondary syphilis, not remarkable for severity. The second, with clinical details lacking, might have been a recurrence or a different kind of illness; but the two periods of latency, including the one that may have followed an unnoticed chancre, support the sculptor's diagnosis. The response to guaiac is irrelevant. The events, not precisely dated, seem to have occurred around 1531 or somewhat later. In Cellini's account of his next forty years he never mentions the disease again, nor any symptoms that might be thought of as late manifestations of syphilis. His strength of will, which led him in the quoted passage to oppose his own ideas of diagnosis and therapy against those of "the first physicians of Rome," continued to characterize his behavior throughout life; the turbulence and strife of his later days are, of course, among the qualities that make his autobiography such good reading. During the climactic casting of the great Perseus, which is dated about 1550, he has occasion to speak of his "powerful constitution"; and, in fact, the details of the heroic operation make clear enough that he was not exaggerating. We can conclude at least,

Fracastor and others to the contrary notwithstanding, that there
was mild as well as severe syphilis in the epidemic period.

The English poet, Thomas Carew (1595?–1645), Dickson
Wright says, was characterized in the following lines by Sir
John Suckling as having had the "chaud pisse" of gonorrhea:

> If it be so his valour must I praise
> That being the weaker yet can force his ways
> And wish that to his valour he had strength
> That he might drive the fire quite out at length;
> For truth as yet the fire gets the day,
> For ever more the water runs away.

For the seventeenth century the names of two political figures
are contributed by the same commentator, Dickson Wright. The
first is Cardinal de Richelieu (1585–1642), who is listed with
some diffidence as having had a large abscess in the area between the genitals and the anus that was "possibly" of venereal
origin. It led to retention of urine while the cardinal was traveling to Bordeaux, and he was catheterized several times in the
standing position, with results—the release of half a gallon of
urine—that gave His Eminence "une joie inconcevable."

Louis XIV of France (1638–1715) had fourteen acknowledged
children, and hence we are assured that he could not have had
syphilis, although so long a lifetime, it seems to me, could have
been compatible with both. But this monarch may have had
gonorrhea. The presumption is based on an alleged willingness
to copulate with almost any woman if one of his four official
mistresses were not within easy reach. Yet such wildness seems
to have characterized Louis's early years only—and perhaps it
is part of the argument against syphilis; after he met and secretly married Madame de Maintenon he is said to have become
a model of puritanical rectitude. The pattern is not unfamiliar.

Our story continues during the seventeenth and eighteenth
centuries with a group of nonpolitical figures. The English poet
and playwright Sir William Davenant (1606–1668) suffered from
both gonorrhea and syphilis and lost the bridge of his nose

from the latter, according to Dickson Wright. John Aubrey (1626–1697), biographer of both Davenant and William Harvey, among many others, said of himself, Robinson tells us, that he had suffered a number of "accidents," including ague, violent fever, "measills, but that was nothing . . . small-pox at Oxon" but also, "1656: December: *Veneris morbus.*"

Dickson Wright reports that Molière (Jean-Baptiste Poquelin, 1622–1673) died from what was more likely to have been syphilis than tuberculosis, as is often reported. After eight years of chronic invalidism, during which he consulted many doctors and many quacks so that he came to ridicule them all, he died of hemorrhage from the throat after a convulsion at the fourth performance of his *Le Malade Imaginaire.* This may have resulted from rupture of an aneurism of the aorta, the great artery of the heart, which could well have been due to cardiovascular syphilis.

The same commentator speaks of the Venetian adventurer and author Giovanni Casanova (1725–1798) as having suffered four attacks of gonorrhea, five of chancroid, and one of syphilis, all between the ages of nineteen and forty-one.

Details of the gonorrhea of James Boswell (1740–1795) have been gleaned from Boswell's private papers, which began to be published only as recently as 1928. William B. Ober says:

> Neither reticence nor prudery inhibited Boswell from recording his vices along with his virtues. As a result we know more about him than any other character of the eighteenth century, down to the most intimate details of his daily life. His journals record 19 episodes of urethritis

of which a dozen appear to have been fresh gonorrheal infections, the others recurrences. He was first infected in 1760 by a minor actress named Sally Forrester, whose name I am glad to repeat in the interest of fairness to women. Boswell began to keep his famous "London Journal" in 1762, and there he records his second bout of clap from his affair with "Louisa," now identified as Anne Lewis, whom he had sought out in quest of "a winter's safe copulation," as he described it. Having discovered the nature of his illness, he returned to upbraid Louisa, who admitted having been infected three years earlier; but she had thought herself healthy for the last fifteen months. "Silent" and persistent gonorrhea in women was not then understood. Many more details of Boswell's sexual life and of his subsequent attacks of gonorrhea are given in Ober's papers, including the extraordinary fact that he was brought up as a strict Calvinist Presbyterian, a teaching which evidently failed to inhibit him noticeably but racked him with guilt from the time of his masturbation in boyhood through his relations with prostitutes long after his marriage in 1769. Ober continues:

> He was a man trapped by forces beyond his control, his motives deeper than his insight, driven to a life of chronic anxiety, ridden by a continuing sense of guilt and need for punishment, intemperate and incontinent, impairing his manhood by courting (and receiving) venereal disease in expiation, and finally dying of its sequelae.

Returning to political personages with VD in the late seventeenth and eighteenth centuries, we come upon Peter the Great of Russia (1672–1725), who became czar at the age of ten and is thought of as the founder of the prerevolutionary Russian state. He is known to have suffered from convulsive fits and is described widely as having died of his excesses, presumably as a result of neurosyphilis.

Frederick the Great of Prussia (1712–1786), Dickson Wright reports, wrote the following in one of his numerous letters to Voltaire:

> J'eus l'honneur
> De recevoir par mon malheur
> D'une certaine imperatrice
> Une bouillante chaud pisse.

> I had the honor
> To receive, worse luck!
> From a certain empress
> A boiling hot piss.

Which is to say, of course, gonorrhea. Frederick had married Elizabeth Brunswick-Bevern in 1733, but it is recorded that the marriage did not last long, and that for the rest of his long life he had no interest in women. At some time after the letter to Voltaire, which Dickson Wright dates 1760, the king developed a severe inflammation of the testicles which required that he be castrated. One assumes that all these events are interrelated.

Certain circumstances regarding Catherine the Great of Russia (1729–1796) are relevant here, and some of them suggest that she had syphilis. Her natural son, Paul I, who succeeded Catherine as monarch, was evidently a congenital syphilitic, having developed a saddle nose at the age of ten as well as subsequent insanity manifested in part by unpredictable fits of rage. A suggestion that his syphilis may have come from a smallpox inoculation may or may not have been an effort to clear his mother's name. It is said of Catherine that she had syphilophobia, which led her to select her numerous lovers by screening them through a committee of six women, "les Epreuveuses" (testers), who were allowed six months to pass on them. Catherine is also described (by Dickson Wright) as having died of apoplexy while seated on her Polish throne, a commode, and as having built the first VD hospital in the world, at St. Petersburg.

Dickson Wright records that Napoleon Bonaparte (1769–1821) contracted gonorrhea while he was a young army lieutenant in Paris, and became syphilitic during the hundred days after Elba.

There is a long list of well-known nonpolitical figures ranging over the eighteenth and nineteenth centuries who are believed or known to have had VD. The first of these is Ludwig van Beethoven (1770–1827), on whom there has been a spate of new commentary in connection with the observance of the two hundredth anniversary of his birth in 1970; but it will be enough to select one of these as most definitive. The only symptom the great composer had which has been attributed to syphilis is his deafness. This symptom was linked to syphilis by so formidable an authority as Grove's Dictionary of Music, and the idea is given in several biographies. It has also been disputed. We are fortunate to have a recent critical review of the whole question by two Denver otolaryngologists, Stevens and Hemenway, who reproduce in translation the original report of the autopsy performed by one Dr. Johann Wagner, who was at the time assistant director of the Pathological Museum in Vienna. Part of this report is paraphrased in Grove's Dictionary. A footnote in Grove, incidentally, which argues that the diagnosis of syphilis "is confirmed by the existence of two prescriptions" is a piece of nonsense which the two otolaryngologists do not dignify by mentioning.

In brief, the opinion of these doctors, which seems to cover all the relevant facts, is that among the three possible explanations for Beethoven's deafness—namely syphilis, typhoid fever, and a localized disease of the inner ear—the last is most logical. They admit that such a diagnosis might have been supported if Beethoven's temporal bones had not been lost, presumably when the grave was opened in 1863 or again in 1888 for examination of the skull. Of syphilis these authors say:

. . . this would ask us to accept a very unusual course for syphilis to have taken. With an onset at age 27 one must assume either a late congenital or an acquired form of the disease. The first is unlikely as Beethoven had none of the other stigmata so commonly associated with congenital syphilis.

It would be unusual to develop acquired tertiary syphilis at age 27, except in the face of a very virulent infection. Also a virulent disease with a documented 25-year span of activity should have produced other lesions within the [central nervous system] or elsewhere. . . .

They argue further that syphilitic deafness would almost certainly have included vertigo, or dizziness, which Beethoven did not have, and that in other respects as well the character of the deafness as Beethoven himself described it in his letters was not typical of syphilis. But they admit that their own retrospective diagnosis of "cochlear otosclerosis" is weakened by absence of the temporal bones. They conclude their account with the words, "Perhaps in a forgotten cellar in Vienna a small formalin-filled jar holds the answer."

To continue with eighteenth- and nineteenth-century sufferers, putative or known: The painter Goya (Francisco José de Goya y Lucientes, 1746–1828) is described by Dickson Wright as a copybook case of cerebral syphilis, although the symptoms seem to have been limited mainly to the lining membranes of the brain (meningovascular syphilis) without involving the cerebral cortex itself. At the age of forty-five he had blinding headaches, a right paralysis (hemiplegia), loss of speech and sight, as well as dizziness, ringing in the ears, and a deafness that became complete. He died of a stroke at the age of eighty-two.

For the next great name on my list there is again doubt. Johann Wolfgang von Goethe (1749–1832), who has been ranked in greatness with Shakespeare, is known to have had a serious illness in early life. It is recorded that his dissipations at Leipzig ended in 1768 with a hemorrhage and a long convalescence. Dickson Wright says that his only surviving son may have died of syphilitic insanity acquired congenitally; his other children were stillborn or died soon after birth. Perhaps qualified scholars can be induced to look further into this question for publication in 1982.

William Hyde Wollaston (1766–1828), who was secretary of the Royal Society and the discoverer of the elements palladium and rhodium, died of cerebral syphilis. The philosopher and noted misogynist, Arthur Schopenhauer (1788–1860), contracted syphilis while a student at Göttingen, underwent protracted mercury treatments, and survived to the age of seventy-two to die of pneumonia.

The great poet John Keats (1795–1821), himself trained as a doctor with a license from the Society of Apothecaries, is said by Roberts to have had a venereal disease; Dickson Wright says he took mercury at least twice, presumably for syphilis. He is known to have died of tuberculosis at the tender age of twenty-six. His contemporary and almost exact parallel in these lugubrious respects was Franz Schubert (1797–1828), who contracted syphilis at the age of twenty-four, received treatment with mercury, and died aged thirty-one of the combined effects of poverty and tuberculosis. Born in the same year but surviving longer was another poet of the first rank, Heinrich Heine (1797–1856), whose syphilis began similarly at the age of twenty-four but continued, with severe secondary and late symptoms including neurosyphilis, leading to paralysis in the last years of his life. Keats, Schubert, Heine! It is a tribute to the basic decency of man that we have elected to remember them for their priceless gifts; but how would we think of them if the fact of their syphilis were more widely known? I wonder if we remember them tenderly for one side of their lives only by the device of blotting out the other? But if we face that other, can we condemn these three men as immoral? Could the poetry and music they left us possibly be reconciled with the idea that the men who wrote them were evil?

This period is crowded with the names of great sufferers, but the chapter is getting long; and I have moved some of them to the back of the book (see Notes).

Friedrich Wilhelm Nietzsche (1844–1900) contracted syphilis in a brothel in 1865, Dickson Wright tells us, and showed signs of syphilitic meningitis at least as early as 1873, when he was no more than twenty-nine. General paralysis of the insane developed eight years later and continued with remissions until his death. Anatole France put forward the idea, which was taken seriously, if at all, only for a brief period, that general paralysis contributed to genius, providing the drive and restless energy needed for human advancement.

King Edward VII of England (1841–1910), who, according to legend, liked to chase naked women through the woods, contracted gonorrhea at Karlsbad and gave it to his queen consort, Alexandra. His nephew Prince Alfred is said to have died of cerebral syphilis in 1899. According to the *New York Times* of November 8, 1970, the Duke of Clarence, elder son of King Edward VII and brother of King George V, is charged by "informed speculation" not only with having died at the age of twenty-eight of syphilis of the brain, but possibly with having been the notorious undiscovered murderer of women known in London in 1888 as Jack the Ripper. And, to bring the list of political notables down as close to date as we dare, we have among others the name of Lord Randolph Churchill (1849–1895), who had syphilis, presumably well before the birth of his son, who became Sir Winston.

Dickson Wright completes our list of politicians by naming both Benito Mussolini (1883–1945) and Adolf Hitler (1889–1945), with the comments that the former undoubtedly had both gonorrhea and syphilis, having received prolonged treatment for the second while he was a refugee in Switzerland; yet he adds that the autopsy showed no sign of either disease. Hitler, he says, probably contracted gonorrhea while he was studying art in his youth.

Of the more modern nonpolitical figures I select only the best-known. Paul Gauguin (1848–1903) had syphilis when he went to Tahiti, hoping for a cure in the sun. It must therefore be admitted that his syphilis had some connection with the best of his paintings. August Strindberg (1849–1912), the Swedish playwright and novelist, had been a doctor's assistant in early life, was married and divorced three times, and is known to have passed through several episodes of insanity; I have heard this diagnosed as schizophrenia, but Dickson Wright says syphilis (he could have had both). Guy de Maupassant (1850–1893), died at the age of forty-three from general paralysis of the insane. Vincent van Gogh (1853–1890) is known to have become insane, and his derangement, associated with some of his most cherished paintings, is again attributed to syphilis by Dickson Wright. Oscar Wilde (1854–1900) undoubtedly suffered from syphilis, according to the same reporter; he acquired it from a certain Oxford harlot known as "Old Jess" when he was an undergraduate there. Mercury treatment damaged his teeth, but he married and had two healthy sons; later on he had a recurrence of symptoms of syphilis. His homosexuality is not implicated in this sequence of events, nor is there special reason to assume that his illness had a particular effect on the special quality of his genius—an effect, for instance, in eliciting his quips about humbug and death, which might have been provoked by any sort of pain or suffering.

It seems appropriate to close this mournful chapter with a group of doctors and scientists. The name of William Wollaston has already been mentioned. An earlier instance, John Hunter —being rather special—is saved for Chapter 15. We may add the great German bacteriologist Emil von Behring (1854–1917), known especially as the co-discoverer with Shibasaburo Kitasato of antitoxins; von Behring died of general paralysis of the insane. Dickson Wright is sure he had not acquired it as a laboratory infection. Von Behring was not noted for studies of syphilis, which has in fact been communicated to a succession of laboratory workers since 1912 as a result of accident while handling infected rabbits.

Niels Ryberg Finsen (1860–1904), Danish Nobel laureate (1903) for applications of light to medicine, had tabes, or syphilis of the spinal cord, in later life. Dickson Wright gives us the names of Karl Westphal, German neurologist, who died in 1923 of general paralysis, and of three Parisian physicians, Professor Giles de la Tourette, Dr. de Savarene, and Dr. Delpech (given thus without further identifying detail), all of whom, he says, caught syphilis from the same prostitute while they were interns at the Salpêtrière, and all of whom died with syphilitic paresis. The story is credited to a Dr. Louis Chauvois.

The list, as I said before, is no more than representative or symbolic, small as a sample, wide in its spread over varieties of men. Something more needs to be said about these people, but a special talent which I lack—something of the quality of Edgar Lee Masters—would be required to say it. The author of *Spoon River Anthology* mentions a few diseases, including syphilis, but in passing, without a suggestion of the insight into such matters he might have needed: he was concerned with other things, but suffering and death were close to the heart of them. If somebody with the necessary talents could have the people named in this chapter speak from their graves as Masters had his characters do, he would make up for my inadequacy. Kings, popes, poets, painters, doctors, scientists; men pious and profane, and women doubtless equally so; men who bloodied the pages of history, others who enriched our heritage beyond price—and some of those whose names are forgotten: ordinary people who suffered just as much but were permitted to go out quietly with no stone either to mark their graves or to throw at their good names. In short, men and women like all the rest of us.

❧ 14 ❧

Disease, Sin, and Punishment

FROM VERY EARLY TIMES and in many cultures sexual practices have come to be surrounded with an aura of taboo. This happened many thousands of years ago, before man thought of disease in naturalistic cause-and-effect terms. Masturbation and fornication, and any behavior in young people which looked to older ones as though it might lead to such activity, were frowned on or forbidden, partly, perhaps, because serious work was not possible during periods of arousal, but doubtless also because such unbridled pleasure was felt by the older folk to be sinful. Long before Job the gods meted out punishment on terms that must often have seemed baffling. Danger and calamity lurked on every hand; and beyond the elementary means toward sustenance and protection that could be learned by experience were all sorts of hazards whose nature and mechanism were inscrutable. But man cannot be content without explanations. A child counters his father's honest "I don't know" with, "But, Daddy, what do you *think?*" If primitive man didn't know and had no way of finding out, he had to guess, both for his own sake and to satisfy the young. In giving them a mollifying story he also nourished a proper respect for older folk, upon which rested his authority and the cohesion of the group. And after the story had been repeated, even though it was no more than plausible at first, both old and young came to believe it.

It must have been true from the beginning, as it is today, that the prohibition of sexual activity seldom worked. The impulse is too powerful. As the growing child is warned that masturbation is sinful, he nearly always finds ways to release his libido in secret. As he (or she) is told that the act is not only against God but physically harmful as well, he adds crime to desecration in the burden of his guilt and goes on masturbating. The attempt of authority to impose its will succeeds only in generating neurosis; and no doubt in so doing it sets up the means of passing the injunction down to the next generation.

In the late Middle Ages similar prohibitions may have driven the serfs into practices which were condemned as witchcraft. Feudalism was being supplanted by developing mercantilism, weakening their meager livelihood. Recurrent plagues multiplied their woes and their fears, and the emerging powers of the Church, whose Latin service they could not understand, deprived them of almost the last of their comforts. Virtually the only pleasure left in their bitter lives, sex was looked upon as sinful unless it had the legitimate purpose of procreation. The result was to force them into the secret heretical acts we glimpse in the paintings of Hieronymus Bosch and some of the drawings of Pieter Brueghel the Elder. As a culmination of such a conflict of authority with irrepressible human impulse, the doctrine of original sin became the manifestation of ultimate terror. J. Michelet, in *Satanism and Witchcraft*, says:

> One is filled with amazement to see all these widely different epochs, all these men of varying cultivation, unable to make one step in advance. But the explanation is simple; they were one and all arrested, let us rather say, blinded, hopelessly intoxicated and made cruel savages of, by the poison of their first principle, the doctrine of Original Sin. This is the fundamental dogma of universal injustice: "All lost for one alone, not only punished but deserving punishment, undone even before they were born and desperately

wicked, dead to God from the beginning. The babe at its mother's breast is a damned soul already."

Very early in the background of our own culture, and doubtless in others as well, disease came to be entangled in this conception of sin, of punishment for misbehavior. In earliest times, according to Sigerist,

> . . . disease was a great curse and the position of the sick man in society was aggravated particularly by the view that illness was a punishment for sin. This at least was the case as soon as the Semitic influence became strong.
>
> Here we encounter a view which, transmitted through Judaism to the West, was to play an extremely important part to our very days. The sick man was a sinner. He had stolen, killed, committed perjury or adultery, had spat into a river, drunk from an impure vessel, done whatever the society of which he was a member considered sinful, and as a result his god or guardian spirit had abandoned him, whereupon he fell an easy prey to the demons. He was sick and suffered, and deserved it. His suffering made his sin apparent to all. . . .
>
> This concept that disease was a punishment for sin was dominant in the Old Testament. God has revealed his law. He who obeyed it piously lived in happiness but he who transgressed it was punished, and illness and suffering at large were the chief punishments. This was a thought of pitiless logic and simplicity. Christianity endeavored to overcome it by glorifying suffering but never quite succeeded. Throughout the Middle Ages and later, epidemics were frequently considered visitations inflicted by God upon mankind. . . .

But even before the Jews—in Chaldea, Egypt, and Persia— disease was attributed not to gods but rather to devils. This idea was echoed by St. Paul, who, as A. D. White said, looked upon the gods of the heathens as devils:

> everywhere the early Christians saw in disease the malignant work of these dethroned powers of evil. The Gnostic and Manichaean struggles had ripened the theological idea that, although at times diseases are punishments by the Almighty, the main agency in them is Satanic. The great fathers and renowned leaders of the

early Church accepted and strengthened this idea. Origen said: "It is demons which produce famine, unfruitfulness, corruptions of the air, pestilences; they hover concealed in clouds in the lower atmosphere, and are attracted by the blood and incense which the heathen offers to them as gods." St. Augustine said: "All diseases of Christians are to be ascribed to these demons; chiefly do they torment fresh-baptized Christians, yes, even the guiltless, newborn infants."

In line with such ideas it is to be expected that the first explanations of syphilis, during the epidemic, were made in terms of punishment for blasphemy rather than for sin. Yet as the venereal nature of the disease came to be understood, the result was merely to add sin to blasphemy among the crimes being punished. During the rise of humanism a major effort was made to counter this attitude. One result was a certain bravado to be found among writers on VD from Rabelais to Shakespeare. Before the Reformation blasphemy and heresy were much more serious crimes than sexual transgression; blasphemy threatened the very power of the Church, and it was an open secret that the popes themselves could not resist the lure of the flesh. But with the rise of Puritanism the emphasis shifted to sex, and even the witchcraft to which the Puritans, like the Inquisition before them, applied the torch, may by then have had a more clearly discernible basis in sex than in heresy as such.

The Puritan view prevailed, and by no means only in England and its colonies. By the mid-eighteenth century Astruc was setting down the by then crystallized idea of VD as direct punishment for sin. The italics are his:

> . . . in the midst of sensual Pleasure there arises something bitter, nay very bitter, and we frequently meet with the Cause of Death in the very Fountain of Life. . . .

But Astruc is at pains to reconcile this idea and his evident piety with his hobby-horse—his preconception that VD was new. He opens Chapter I of his Book I with these words:

> That the *Venereal Disease* was sent into the World by the Disposition of Providence, either to restrain, as with a Bridle, the unruly Passions of a sensual Appetite, or as a Scourge to correct the Gratification of them, is an Opinion highly probable. . . . But we must not conclude from hence, that this Disease in the Form it now appears, has been therefore known to the Antients, because the Lewdness of Mankind has always stood in need of a present Correction. . . . let us enquire, not what God should have done, but what he has done; not whether he ought at all Times to have inflicted the *Venereal Disease* as a Punishment for the Lewdness of Mankind; but whether he has in reality so punished him or not.

And he goes on to assure us that it was God's wisdom to begin the punishment in this form with Columbus's returning sailors. Divine wrath had earlier taken different forms, as in the instance of Ero, whose "carbuncle" Astruc calls anthrax. Later we have this further interpretive item:

> When the Venereal Disease first made its Appearance in Europe, it was not known that the Infection was propagated by Coition, the diseased either cautiously concealing the manner how they were infected, in Order to hide their Wickedness, or it may be not suspecting that so severe an Illness could possibly be contracted by Copulation solely, as it seemed so unusual a Way of conveying Contagion. . . .

The efflorescence of VD appeared just as the forces of the Renaissance were attempting to liberate the human spirit and to abolish notions of divine vengeance, whether by rationalizing them or by dissolving them in laughter. The conflict raged between such humanistic impulses, which affirmed a pride in the nature of man and a willingness to accept his weakness while glorying in his strength, and those which sought to restrain his natural impulses for the sake of a presumed reward after death. The attempt to free the human spirit fought against original sin. The submergence of VD—or the denial of its existence in literature and art, as part of the denial of man himself—is a token of the drift of events: humanism lost the struggle.

VD as a subject for literature and art was forced under-

ground, as masturbation is, by threat of punishment. We know
that in the eighteenth and nineteenth centuries there was a
great flowering of the sort of literature usually called pornography. Here and there in it we find mention of VD, but usually in
veiled, indirect, or "polite" terms. Here is an example from the
memoirs of Casanova, written in 1793 but not published until
the 1820s:

> *Surgeon.* . . . I have made a good deal of money . . . and it is to
> you, captain, to you—may God bless you!—that I am indebted
> for my present comforts.
> *Captain.*   But how so?
> *Surgeon.*   In this way, captain. You had a connection with Don Je-
> rome's housekeeper, and you left her, when you went away, a
> certain souvenir which she communicated to a certain friend of
> hers, who, in perfect good faith, made a present of it to his wife.
> This lady did not wish, I suppose, to be selfish, and she gave her
> souvenir to a libertine, who in his turn was so generous with it
> that, in less than a month, I had about fifty clients. The follow-
> ing months were not less fruitful, and I gave the benefit of my
> attendance to everybody, of course, for a consideration. . . .

This sequence of events has a modern flavor, as we will come to
see; except that the recipients of what is called the "souvenir"
evidently had no hesitation in coming to receive the "benefits"
of the surgeon's "attendance," which would also have been a
good deal more dubious then than now.

VD continued to be written about by physicians in literature
intended for professional eyes alone; but practicing physicians
persistently avoided it, tending to leave treatment to others. In
England a certain Richard Alison, described by Roberts as a
tailor, was accused in 1516 of practicing physic and surgery
without a license; but because syphilis was regarded as a new
disease he was not prosecuted even though he admitted the
charge:

> For he was learned in confections and medicines for the treat-
> ment of certain diseases called "pokkes or the great pokkes" the

cure of which pertained neither to the faculty of physic nor to the faculty of surgery.

Two years later, in 1518, the Royal College of Physicians was chartered and undertook to discipline "surgeons and other humble practitioners" who treated VD. But the physicians of the time tended to be philosophers or theorists rather than practical chemists; hence the so-called surgeons, who somewhat earlier had been "barber-surgeons," branched out and became surgeon-apothecaries. Many of them, as Roberts says, performed no surgery as such but

> still tended to treat skin complaints, dress ulcers, and the like; indeed it was "the Cure of Venereal Disease, upon which alone the Subsistence of three Parts in four of all Surgeons in Town" depended.

When Boswell acquired gonorrhea, he called a surgeon rather than a physician; and John Keats did the same for his syphilis.

As late as the 1870s in New York, at the first meeting of the American Gynecological Society, Dr. Emil Noeggerath, described by Robinson as "an inordinately lean, tall man of saturnine mien," shocked the attending physicians by saying:

> About ninety per cent of sterile women are married to husbands who have suffered from gonorrhea either previous to, or during, married life.

By asserting that most acute and chronic genital inflammation in women came from what he characterized as "honeymoon gonorrhea"—which could result from a latent infection in the husband as well as from an active one—he brought down on his head the wrath of physicians from all over the world. Noeggerath's ideas were nevertheless sound. By reactivating interest in the subject they led directly to the work of Credé, to whom we owe the method of preventing gonorrheal blindness in babies by dropping a solution of silver nitrate into their eyes at birth (1884). Just before that, in 1879, Neisser, using the recently developed methods of Robert Koch, had described the gonococcus, thus taking the first step in the scientific study of venereal disease.

We can get an idea of attitudes toward sex and VD in the late nineteenth century from several exhibits. The science of bacteriology was then flourishing, and no educated person could any longer doubt the *fact* of contagion; but there was still confusion as to its *means*. The following item from the page of the *Journal of the American Medical Association* (June 2, 1969), which quotes from "JAMA 75 years ago," throws a sidelight on 1894:

> The Sanitary Committee of the Orange, N.J. Board of Health has recommended that a circular be issued to the people "urging every one to desist as much as possible from kissing, as the touching of lips is likely to convey contagion; one of the persons might have disease germs in the throat and communicate them to the other."
>
> It was also proposed by the same Committee that a second circular be sent out warning ladies against long dresses and advising them to have their skirts cut sufficiently short to avoid all danger of contagion. These gentlemen are certainly inviting destruction. The exercise of sanitary authority is none too well liked at best; when it excites ridicule, its days are numbered. The advice against long dresses might be defensible if it were necessary; as a matter of fact women whose health is worth preserving don't sweep the streets with their dresses. As for the other proposition—that may be safely left with the young people of both sexes.

VD seemed to be farthest from the minds of both the Orange Board of Health committee and the commenting editors: such a phrase as "women whose health is worth preserving"—implying that there is another sort—would be unlikely to appear today.

Traces of the sanctimonious had not disappeared from official U.S. medicine as recently as 1964, when a paper by C. L. Hudson, a trustee of the A.M.A., outlined the history of the organization's efforts to deal with VD, going back as far as 1874. The paper reads like a political tract prepared with the chief object of offending nobody, or nobody important. The A.M.A. has always stood bravely in the forefront of efforts at proper education tinged with appropriate piety, against prostitution and alcoholism, and in favor of sexual continence as "compatible with health and . . . the best prevention" of VD. But one finds this sort of thing also in the medical literature that is primarily technical rather than political. Here are words spoken in 1955 to dermatologists by a Boston physician, J. G. Downing, on the subject of syphilis in industry, conveying a sagacious wariness of the victories that seemed to have been won over the disease at the time. It was just about then that the curve of VD hit bottom; but that may be the reason for the speaker's unhappiness:

> with the advent of penicillin and its short-term treatment, whatever fear the amateur [who seemed then to be supplanting the professional prostitute] had of long and arduous treatment lasting for a year and a half, was completely dissipated. Whatever effect the arsenical and bismuth era [that is, the era of "long and arduous treatment" which began in 1910 with Ehrlich's "606"] had in preventing sexual promiscuity no longer exists. Promiscuity in this country is on the increase. Penicillin will not eradicate syphilis, for no disease in the history of man has been treated out of existence.

This extraordinary statement is worth a careful reading. It mixes a prophetic insight—penicillin has indeed failed!—with a rock-ribbed puritanism certain that only the fear of hell-fire can save us from damnation. It is true that no disease has ever been abolished by treatment (no disease, in fact, has ever been abolished at all!); but neither has there ever been a treatment so brilliantly effective as penicillin for an infectious disease. Failure to control syphilis has not been due to penicillin, whether to its effectiveness or to its shortcomings. To assume that the long, disagreeable, and expensive treatment for syphilis which penicillin supplanted had an effect in "preventing sexual promiscuity" —and I grant that the speaker's "whatever" implies doubt in his own mind—is to argue that capital punishment prevents murder. Many people continue to believe both ideas, but nobody has ever come up with credible evidence for either.

Nobody need be surprised that vestiges of this idea of disease as divine punishment still persist, that they are not restricted to

VD, and that they crop up where we might least expect to find them. A New York City Health Department official—is anyone likely to be less unsophisticated?—was quoted in the press in 1970 as saying, apparently seriously, that recurring infections contracted in hospitals (a problem rivaling VD, and like VD, getting worse) are looked upon by many doctors "as a visitation from an avenging god punishing them for their sins." Oh, well, they would say if faced with the point, a figure of speech, not meant literally. Or possibly they wouldn't; but the persistence even of such a figure seems to me eloquent enough.

Thomas Parran, who as surgeon-general of the U.S. Public Health Service just before World War II was a conspicuous pioneer in the effort to break through puritanism within medicine and elsewhere, has given us an insight into efforts along these lines during World War I. VD mounted rapidly in wartime, as always happens; and strenuous attempts to lift taboos were made by Public Health Service officials "under the urge to create a nation fit to fight." But after the war the effort faltered and failed. "Congress apparently thought the spirochetes of syphilis were demobilized with the army." By 1926 all federal aid to the states for VD work had been terminated. Dr. Parran gives us the substance of a "sales talk" presented by lobbyists in Washington seeking military camps in their communities:

> Of course, we are only a small community and do not have at present all the facilities you may be looking for. But if we can have your assurance now that a camp will be located in "X," in six weeks' time we can bring in enough women and set up gambling houses and saloons so that the boys would be assured of recreation.

(As of February 14, 1970, according to the press, President Nguyen Van Thieu of the Saigon government had approved a plan to operate brothels within entertainment and gambling centers there, with an admission charge to limit the customers to the rich, which is presumably a Saigonese euphemism for American.)

Under Parran's leadership in the years before World War II a great campaign was undertaken to open the subject of VD for public discussion. The word "syphilis" came to be mentioned in the newspapers for the first time; and a serious effort was started to work toward control of the disease. Again the advent of war interposed insuperable obstacles. Nevertheless, after 1945 the effort was begun again, with penicillin promising victory. But the promise failed to materialize. It was not for lack of knowledge, or means, or even, this time, for lack of money, although there was never quite enough especially of the last. Nor was it for lack of clear-sighted effort on the part of public health workers here and elsewhere in the world, effort that continues in the U.S. Public Health Service and in comparable national services elsewhere with the massive assistance of the WHO. Nor was it, I suggest, for lack of sufficient punishment, lack of "discipline" exerted by the old upon the young.

We have made some progress since Victorian times, but pretty large vestigial lumps of the old punitive approach to VD control are still in evidence. It is said, for example, that the U.S. Armed Forces do not punish men for contracting VD today. Punishment was not official policy in World War II, when John Horne Burns described a VD treatment center. There are ways of inflicting punishment without using a lash or leaving physical scars. It is significant that as late as 1969, D. L. Nathan said that "many servicemen at home and abroad tend to avoid military physicians when they suspect" they have VD.

In the absence of anything better to tell the young, we keep repeating the old injunction against sex before or outside of marriage. The argument is phrased differently today and accompanied by a little more patient information and fewer blood-curdling threats; but there has been no basic change. It is a legacy tracing back through puritanism to the doctrine of original sin and beyond. The idea has no roots in hygiene or in a knowledge of human behavior. Maybe for that reason—or whatever the reason may be—the prohibition has never worked. Young people today are speaking up more and more plainly, in actions as well as in words, telling us they recognize this bit of hypocrisy as part of the tissue of deception with which we cover them as the moral equivalent of their baby blanket. We are likely to reply that one of the consequences of their disobedience is the current resurgence of VD. This idea is plausible, but like the story of the Columbian origin of syphilis, it is not necessarily true. We have arrived at the heart of our subject, which is necessarily technical.

PART III

FACTS AND
FIGURES

※ 15 ※

VD and Not VD

IT IS TIME to be more explicit about VD, especially what the different forms look like and how we tell them apart. As I mentioned before, we all agree in listing two diseases, chancroid and lymphogranuloma venereum (LGV), in addition to syphilis and gonorrhea as "true" venereal diseases, plus another which we are now finding reason to separate from the group, plus a miscellaneous collection of still others on which there is disagreement. Syphilis and gonorrhea are the major venereal diseases; they are the core problem which has resisted massive world-wide attempts to solve it; they are commoner than the others and better understood. It looks as though the two other undisputed ones, chancroid and LGV, could be controlled without much trouble, and are in fact getting less common.

The clinical aspects of syphilis are described in Chapter 7 and need not be repeated; but all the others are worth looking at— major, minor, doubtful, and disputed.

It may be just as well to be specific here about the meaning of the word "venereal." The specialist is apt to take it literally: a venereal disease is simply one contracted through sexual intercourse. But to ordinary people the word has all sorts of piercing and rasping overtones, especially if it refers to symptoms they happen to show themselves. Not all specialists take this casually, and I am among those who would restrict the definition so as to avoid causing unnecessary pain. Here is a doctor who tends to agree: W. K. Bernfeld of Wales, who wrote a one-page paper entitled "Iatrogenic venereological complaints," which opens with a few words that explain the title:

> "Iatrogenic" means "produced by doctors," although by analogy with "pathogenic" it should denote "producing doctors." "Complaint" has the double-edged meaning of ailment and accusation.

Dr. Bernfeld has a wit appropriate to his mission, which is expressed in four terse case reports. Three are cases of false diagnosis, two of gonorrhea and one of syphilis. In one the patient's wife had left him, although she later returned when the facts were established. The fourth case records an explosion between husband and wife over the husband's conclusion that trichomonads found in the wife's vagina implied unfaithfulness. Dr. Bernfeld, as though proving that Brieux's idea of a doctor is still viable, mentions that

> I saw both patients in the clinic together for a whole hour, to let him air his suspicions and recriminations, and to persuade him that the findings did not necessarily prove her unfaithfulness.

And he ends the paper by quoting from the United Kingdom statute of 1916:

> "Venereal disease" means syphilis, gonorrhea, and soft chancre.

Let me remind you, first, that we have been able to make clear distinctions between these (and other) diseases only within the past century or less. Many of the names we use go back much further; but names of diseases in their early uses often meant something other than what they mean today. Celsus (25 B.C.–50 A.D.) described what was probably soft chancre or chancroid; and we know that gonorrhea goes back a good deal further; syphilis may be even more ancient. But as late as the mid-eighteenth century it was possible for Astruc to lump them all together in a single "venereal disease." Another monument to confusion is the adjective "Hunterian" to describe the "hard" chancre of syphilis. John Hunter, an eighteenth-century English practitioner, did in fact distinguish the chancre of syphilis from the "soft" chancre of Celsus. But in his time the germ theory had not yet been born, and not enough was known to do a decent experiment; just the same it was an age of inoculations. Hunter actually thought he *proved* that syphilis and gonorrhea were the same by deliberately inoculating his own penis with pus from a man known to have gonorrhea but who had an unsuspected syphilis as well. This was in 1767. The intrepid investigator was rewarded by developing both diseases, and could announce triumphantly that "matter from a gonorrhea will produce chancres." The separation of gonorrhea from syphilis is usually credited to Philippe Ricord in 1837. Ricord (whose suggestion to improve the Bible was mentioned in Chapter 9) was a French doctor born in Baltimore. But even earlier Benjamin Bell (1749–1806) in Edinburgh and Edouard Bosquillon (1744–1814) in France seem to have done as much; and in 1812 Jean-François Hernandez was able to inoculate convicts at Toulon with gonorrhea without producing syphilis. Such experiments were not as convincing in their day as they seem to be now, with the hindsight of the germ theory of Pasteur and Koch, a product of the end of the nineteenth century. Neither the cause nor the specificity of gonorrhea could be known with assurance until 1879, when Albert Neisser (1855–1916) discovered the gonococcus. The bacillus of chancroid dates from 1889. The agents of both granuloma inguinale—the odd-member-on-the-way-out of the minor VD group—and syphilis were found in 1905. LGV, although distinguished clinically as early as 1786 (again by John Hunter) was not clearly recognized as a venereal disease until 1912–13 and yielded up its causative agent only in 1932.

That these five diseases are widely different is underlined by the great disparity among their causative microbes. We have a roughly spherical coccus for gonorrhea and a corkscrew-shaped spirochete for syphilis. For chancroid and granuloma, respectively, there are two easily distinguished rod-shaped bacilli. The agent of LGV was at first thought to be a virus but is now classified among the marginal or atypical bacteria, partly because it is sensitive to penicillin and other antibiotics, which have no effect on viruses.

So Astruc, poor fellow, was pretty far off the beam. Nothing so clearly shows the differences among diseases as such easily distinguishable microbes. Given these differences, fortified with specific antigen-antibody reactions, one can go back to clinical differences with confidence. Yet Astruc may just possibly have been right when he suggested that a case of genital ulceration might have been *anthrax*. It is improbable—I have never heard of such a case—but not impossible. Anthrax comes to man from the skin or hair of animals that have died of the disease. Its spores are very hard to kill. Cases turn up in people today mainly as an occupational hazard. It is possible to imagine someone using a contaminated blanket or fur piece, or something of the kind, as an aid to masturbation! We hear of bobby pins sucked into the bladder through the short female urethra, and penises caught in the tube of a vacuum cleaner. Almost anything is possible.

A case described in 1957 by Willcox may suggest the possible range of variation. A twenty-one-year-old woman had a lump in the groin which turned out to be swollen lymph nodes. Examination showed her to have a cluster of small blister-like sores on what is called the mound of Venus (mons veneris)—the pubic area—the hair having been shaved off to show them. These vesicles, which developed typically during the next two days, proved to be vaccinia or cowpox; and their presence was explained as having followed intercourse a week or so earlier with a man who had a fresh and painful vaccination on his arm preparatory to going abroad. The woman had never been vaccinated except in this rather unusual way.

But let us get down to specific diseases. Gonorrhea, the most important member of the VD group apart from syphilis, usually starts a few days—three to five—after contact, typically as a urethritis in men and as a vaginitis in women. It begins suddenly, with the urge to urinate frequently in men, with burning pain and with much thick pus in the urine. Women may not notice any symptoms, or may have a discharge of pus from the vagina with pain as in men. In many cases of gonorrheal vaginitis, the rectum is also infected. A common direct consequence of gonorrhea in women is invasion of the Fallopian tubes which extend from each side of the uterus. When this happens it often leads to sterility by closure of the tubes. Complications following the initial symptoms may affect both sexes. When they appear it is usually after an intervening period of latency or apparent good health like that in early syphilis, during which the disease remains fully transmissible. The commonest complications involve the joints as arthritis or the lining of the heart as endocarditis; but many other tissues and organs may be affected.

Gonococcal vaginitis or vulvovaginitis, in young girls before puberty, was once put down to contact with contaminated towels and such things, but VD is not communicated that way. Direct contact, usually with infected adults, is now known to be the means of infection here as elsewhere. Gonorrheal infection of the eyes of babies at birth—so-called ophthalmia neonatorum —results from contact with an infected vaginal wall during the birth process. The symptoms appear a few days after birth and usually lead to blindness. The use of silver-nitrate solution, or penicillin, or another antibiotic routinely dropped into the eyes of the baby at birth, has largely controlled this problem. With decreasing incidence of this disease, such treatment of babies' eyes was stopped in some places. With a rising prevalence of gonorrhea, ophthalmia neonatorum has been reappearing both in this country and abroad; and routine prophylaxis is accordingly being restored.

Chancroid, or soft chancre, shows itself as an acute painful destructive ulcer of the genitals followed by buboes or swollen lymph nodes in the inguinal (crotch) area. In LGV there is also a primary sore on the genitals, followed by buboes in the groin; but the initial sore may be small and go unnoticed, especially in women, while the buboes in LGV break down and discharge pus, typically through several openings, and heal forming scar tissue. The LGV infection may spread to neighboring lymph nodes in the abdominal area or in the rectum and lead to painful contracting scars.

Granuloma inguinale takes the form of a slowly spreading destructive ulcer of the genitals which grows and heals at the same time. The abdominal wall or the rectum or both are often affected. There are no buboes. This disease is sometimes called Donovanosis after the man who first described tiny structures inside the cells of its sore, by which it can be diagnosed.

Chancroid, LGV, and granuloma can be told apart with certainty only by demonstrating their different causative microbes or the specific antibodies which appear in the blood during the disease. All three of these diseases seem to be limited for obscure reasons to the very poor and wretched—or to artificial wretchedness of the sort found among troops in combat. This circumstance suggests debilitating predisposing factors, but nothing is known about the nature of such factors if they exist. The combination of venereal disease, poverty, and an insufficient prevalence to make the problem economically important is sufficient to explain why not much interest has been taken in the first and third of these diseases. LGV happens to belong to a biological group caused by borderline agents—between viruses and bacteria—which have attracted interest in their own right; and so we know more about it than we do about the others. If the association with war continues, we may look for more research on all three; although the problem under those circumstances is likely to get worse faster than it can possibly get better. Fortunately all three diseases can be treated effectively with antibiotics; and if we could bring major VD under control, the minor diseases would be unlikely to persist separately.

Granuloma inguinale, as I have said, has had its place among the minor venereal diseases disputed. This is a good place for the details, partly as a transition to the larger group of diseases whose venereal status is not unanimously accepted. Granuloma has been traditionally a minor venereal disease, and it now looks as though it may have been included in the group uncritically or only because the sores often appear on the genitals. Possibly the fact that it is a tropical disease most often found in dark-skinned peoples has encouraged a certain amount of carelessness in its classification by mainly white observers. It has been known for a long time that granuloma appears in many body locations other than the genitals. Julius Goldberg, a Chicago researcher who has given many years to the study of this disease, has pointed to its occurrence in a two-year-old child, in newborn infants, and in an adult male whose penis had been amputated sixteen years before he acquired the disease. But the evidence most damaging to the idea that granuloma is venereal, brought out by Dr. Goldberg, is that a bacterium that seems to be identical with the microbe of the disease may also be found in the intestinal tract and is, in fact, related to some of the commonest normal microbes of feces. The granuloma microbe itself is not easy to handle and has not been studied quite enough to establish it as a member of the normal life on man. If this were done, it would exclude granuloma from the venereal category, even though sexual activity were shown to have some part in its development. Goldberg's opinion, in fact, based on his knowledge of the microbe and on a lot of clinical observation, is that the disease often develops in male homosexuals as a result of pederasty. Predisposing factors seem to be required which are not compatible with VD status. His conclusion is that "venereal transmission of the disease is not consistent with the observable facts." The opinion has been gaining ground.

Similar reasoning applies to some of the other diseases that have been loosely, and I think wrongly, included in the VD category. This is a wide and miscellaneous collection, hard to characterize as a group in a few words. Some *can be* transmitted by sexual intercourse but have other ways of getting around as well. In others venereal transmission is lightly assumed but not actually known. Others are infectious processes that merely happen to be found in the genital area. And some of them, as seems likely for granuloma, are due to members of the normal life on man, kicking up mainly because something else is wrong that may have nothing to do with sexual intercourse. Patients, actual, prospective, or even possible, are likely to understand that once we accept these diseases as venereal we can't help attaching to them the whole aura of shame, disgrace, and prejudice that clings to the idea of VD no matter how much we turn our backs to it. But let's have a look at the group so that we can dispose of it.

I have two technical papers before me as I write that may help me focus this general idea. One is by a Philadelphia physician, John F. Wilson, dated 1964 and entitled "The nonvenereal diseases of the genitals." Dr. Wilson lists no less than sixteen groups of diseases embracing more than seventy-five separate items, and gives details and illustrations of many of them with the purpose of helping other doctors exclude them from the VD category by what is called "differential diagnosis." It would be nice if I could just repeat the list, or abridge it to give you the commoner diseases; it would save a lot of bother. But although Dr. Wilson agrees with my main thesis, he spreads his net so wide that all kinds of exotic fish fall into it. In speaking in this context, for instance, of erysipelas and acne, which are about as far from VD as one can get, he seems to me to raise irrelevancies that may actually encourage error. Just the same he makes it clear that many signs of disease which appear on the genitals are *not* VD.

My second exhibit notes a tendency to broaden the definition

of "venereal." This is a paper by the well-known London venereologist C. S. Nicol, who mentions that in recent times the official British regulations have been broadened to include not only
LGV and granuloma, but also "nongonococcal urethritis" (in the
male); and he continues with this suggestion:

> If by venereal disease one means any disease *usually transmitted by
> sex contact* then certain non-gonococcal genital infections in the fe-
> male, including trichomoniasis, and a number of other minor
> infections or infestations seen in both sexes might be considered.
> The inclusion of the last group clearly remains controversial.

Here are some of the more important "controversial" diseases:
Condyloma acuminatum, or venereal warts, or genital warts,
are thought to be ordinary warts that happen to be found on
genital surfaces. Warts are benign tumors of the skin. There are
different kinds. Some are known to be caused by a virus, and
there is evidence of their transmission from man to man. Such
warts on the genitals might therefore be transmitted by sexual
intercourse; but the evidence that this actually happens is very
circumstantial. We can safely put this condition outside the pale
of VD until we know more about it.

Scabies is an infection of the skin with the itch mite, *Sar-
coptes scabiei,* a tiny animal near the lower limit of visibility
without a microscope. It likes to live in the groin but is not particular, and is transmitted by any kind of intimate skin contact,
including sexual contact. It can also be transmitted indirectly on
what Fracastor called "fomites"—such as towels or bedclothing.
It is obviously not particular enough for our club.

There is also a louse with a predilection for the pubic region,
called *Phthirus pubis* or the crab louse, distinct from body and
head lice (genus *Pediculus*). Two Edinburgh doctors recently
reported finding these parasites in 26 of 110 delinquent schoolgirls in Edinburgh, whereas during the same examination only
two were shown by culture to have gonorrhea. Another paper
suggests that infection with crab lice is increasing sharply in

England and Wales, and gives much detail about the causative insect. These lice have a marked preference for the pubic hairs, apparently because the relatively wide spacing of these hairs is just right for *Phthirus pubis* to cling to an adjacent pair; but they will also spread to the hair around the anus and elsewhere, including the armpit; and in children they are sometimes found on the eyelashes.

Candida or Monilia infections. Microscopic yeasts called *Candida* (commonest species *Candida albicans,* also called *Monilia albicans*) are part of the normal microbic life in the vagina and are normally harmless, so that merely finding them there in a microscope slide or culture has no special significance. But they tend to overgrow under provocation, especially in diabetes and during prolonged treatment with certain antibiotics, which don't affect them but kill off their competition and upset the local ecology in other ways. Another predisposing factor recently blamed is the contraceptive pill. Overgrowth of candida may lead to a vaginal discharge or "leucorrhea," with irritation of the vulva; but similar symptoms may have other causes:

> A fastidious woman in an overzealous effort to keep herself clean may cause a chronic vaginal discharge by douching,

said the A.M.A. *Journal* in an editorial in 1954. Candidal vulvovaginitis may spread by sexual contact and produce irritation of the penis. There is an antibiotic effective against candida (nystatin or mycostatin), but treatment must get at the underlying cause.

Trichomoniasis. A protozoan, *Trichomonas vaginalis,* like candida, frequently lives harmlessly in the normal vagina; but it may be found there in abnormally large numbers in the presence of a leucorrhea which in this case may contain pus; so that the condition has to be distinguished from gonorrhea. There are parallels here with candida infection, but important differences, too. One is the pus; a more important one, especially to a bacteriologist, is the fact that this protozoan can produce disease in animals experimentally (not VD!) under conditions which don't work with candida. The provoking factors, furthermore, are not as obvious or as well understood as they are with candida, although there is no doubt that they are necessary. This trichomonad is large as protozoa go, enormous compared with the bacteria that always accompany it (and on which it feeds) and perhaps fierce-looking, especially when alive and in vigorous motion. In short, it *looks* dangerous. Nearly identical trichomonads live in the mouth and the gut but are not likely to be seen in VD clinics, and when seen elsewhere are seldom given a second thought. Oddly enough, *Trichomonas vaginalis* is usually not found in males, and when it shows up is not likely to be associated with any symptoms: an exception, NGU, is described in the next paragraph. Trichomonads are always found with overgrowths of bacteria, some of which may be more harmful than the protozoa. The pus comes from the bacteria. But as with candida, when trichomonads are found in both of a pair of sex partners with symptoms of disease in either, the symptoms are unlikely to clear up until the protozoan is cleared from both. An effective drug is metronidazole, also called flagyl. The disease needs to be treated, but ought not to be called venereal.

Nongonococcal urethritis (NGU) and vulvovaginitis (NGV) are a pair of clinical miscellanies into which some doctors throw genital candidiasis and trichomoniasis as well as a lot of other things. The principal importance of the category—apart from the fact that it entails diseases of men (and usually not of women) and of women (and usually not of men)—is that these are conditions suspected of being gonorrhea in which no evidence of the gonococcus is found. The point is sharpened by a recurrent inability to find the gonococcus in female gonorrhea. Accordingly the conditions are most likely to show up in VD clinics. All of which tends to suggest that the category is listed as VD, when it is, by a kind of default or frustration. The urethritis group and the vulvovaginitis group do not always or necessarily mix; just as candida infections and trichomoniasis are mainly diseases of women, so forms of urethritis are mainly diseases of men; and although sexual intercourse may sometimes be instrumental in passing some of them around, they are not essential or primary factors in doing so. A more common uniform factor, again, is that the microbes found in these conditions are likely to be members of the microbic life on man. They cause trouble only because some provoking reason has let them get out of control. The category is a common one and therefore an important medical problem; but it can only be made worse by calling it VD.

Gangrenous balanitis (inflammation of the penis) or vulvovaginitis seems to be a disappearing condition, if absence of recent reports is an indication; my most recent one came from Costa Rica in 1962. It is a disagreeable disease (not, of course, that there is really any other kind), corresponding in the genital area to a disease of soldiers and students that was called "trench mouth" in World War I. This is, again, disease arising out of an overgrowth of "normal" microbes under severely debilitating conditions. It seems to be the consensus today, maybe only by omission, that it is not VD.

Herpes (simplex) is not so easily disposed of. The word "herpes" means a sore made up of clusters of tiny blisters or vesicles. When used alone, the word usually refers to herpes simplex as distinguished from herpes zoster—a quite different disease popularly known as "shingles." Herpes simplex is commonest on the lips, where it is called "cold sore" or "fever blister"; some people suffer from it repeatedly; others never get it. The cause is a virus, of which several types have been distinguished in recent years. Most adults, whether they suffer from cold sores or not, tend to have antibodies in their blood that neutralize the virus, evidence of an earlier infection which, when severe, is recognized as "primary" herpes. This can be a transient illness with fever and other symptoms lasting some two weeks but is occasionally much more serious and may even be fatal. After the patient with primary herpes recovers, the virus is believed to persist in the affected area in latent form. The antibodies present may give incomplete immunity; recurrent attacks are induced by predisposing conditions suggested by the words "cold" and "fever" in the popular names. Many conditions may be involved, including psychosomatic upsets.

Primary herpes tends to be a childhood illness, but as with polio (Chapter 8), and perhaps for similar reasons, contact with the virus may be put off to a later age so that the first infection appears in adult life. The location of such an infection may be almost anywhere—including the fingers of hospital personnel and broad areas of the skin in wrestlers!—but the commonest locations are mouth, eyes, and genitals, the last especially in women. It is well established and entirely consistent with the pattern that primary herpetic vulvovaginitis or cervicitis (infection of the mouth of the womb) is likely to be contracted by sexual intercourse between a man who has a recurrent "cold sore" on the penis and a woman having no immunity against herpes. And so it comes to be described as a venereal disease; but clearly the definition doesn't need much tightening up to exclude it.

The genital location is only one among many possible ones, and, in addition, direct contact, although effective, is not essential. There is a report which speaks of twins, aged two years, who both had primary herpes around the anus, confirmed in one by isolation of the virus and presumed in the other. Both were traced to application of an ointment which had previously been used by the father on his "cold sores."

Even recurrent herpes of the genitals has been thought of as a venereal disease, but the circumstances are peculiar. D. C. Hutfield says it

> often breaks out with each successive intercourse as a result of the reactivation of virus latent in cells at or near the site of primary infection. This may be related to the trauma of intercourse, or

may possibly have a psychosomatic basis, since there is often an associated syphilophobia.

Which is a good example of the difference between what a patient thinks of as venereal disease and the way the term may be used by a doctor to describe a disease related to sexual intercourse even though transmission of infection is not involved. What is thought to happen here is "reactivation" of a virus already present; and one of the psychosomatic factors in causing it is fear of syphilis! We could as well speak of a complication of pregnancy as VD.

There is an even more dramatic instance of loose usage of "venereal." It is semantically correct (and, in fact, innocently intended), but is nevertheless bound to be misleading and unfortunate. I am again speaking of herpes, but this time of a special type of the virus. Since about 1965 there has been increasing evidence of an association between a variant "type 2" herpes virus and cancer of the uterine cervix. The association appears especially in women who began having intercourse relatively early in life and have had several sex partners. An association is also suggested with uncircumcised men. All of this is of intense interest to people studying cancer and viruses; and there is no denying the seriousness of the question or the potential importance of the research. But the suggested circumstances are fundamentally different from those of VD as a currently significant public health problem. The single transmitting event we think of as leading to VD is hidden in this herpes-cancer pattern—at least up to now—in a long series of multiple contacts. It seems probable that cancer will eventually prove to be caused by viruses; but we cannot predict that its form will be that of classical infection, and it may turn out rather different. Here again, as with candida infections, trichomoniasis, and nongonococcal urethritis and vaginitis—but in a condition that hardly needs anything added to its intrinsic seriousness—the restriction of disease to a single sex plus the suggestion of VD convey all the soul-shattering implications of original sin. Forethought may suggest the use of a few extra words, perhaps "transmitted by sexual intercourse" to avoid the misuse of the word "venereal." But it will not be easy to get editors of technical journals and books to cooperate.

❧ 16 ❧

Fruits of the Germ Theory

"HE WHO KNOWS syphilis, knows medicine," said the great physician Sir William Osler; and the famous remark heads Chapter 1 of a little book called *Syphilis: a Synopsis* written for doctors by the U.S. Public Health Service and dated 1968. Somewhere the book admits that "many physicians have been graduated without an adequate knowledge of the many faces of syphilis"—which was possibly the polite understatement of 1968. It is often true today that he who knows medicine, knows little or nothing about syphilis. The little book is terse, simple, straightforward, and clearly illustrated with color photographs. If the question comes up, the doctor can get a usable answer from it in minutes. But more often than not the question doesn't come up: it doesn't enter the doctor's mind. Hear one of them, Dr. H. Pariser, speaking earnestly to others in a 1964 symposium on syphilis:

> To find syphilitic lesions we must snoop around corners so to speak; that is, spread the vulva and buttocks, pull back the foreskin, stretch the scrotum, evert the lips, check the mucous membranes carefully, examine the skin by cross light, pay particular attention to the palms and soles, the sides of the nose, the corners of the mouth, and palpate for the presence of adenopathy [swollen lymph

nodes]. . . . We should constantly check the impulse to rule out
the possibility of syphilis in the well-dressed and well-educated
purely on socio-economic considerations, to regard every eruption
as syphilitic in the venereal disease clinic, and, by contrast, to ig-
nore the possibility of syphilis in other clinics and in our private offices.

Syphilis turns up in premarital blood tests, or when and if the
private physician does blood tests routinely, usually once with a
new patient. It emerges by accident, or when the patient himself
or herself suspects VD and goes to clinic or doctor with the
question. Much the same is true of gonorrhea. Since all the venereal diseases can now be treated effectively, we could go a
long way toward stamping them out if we could reach the point
of diagnosis, especially if the diagnosis could be made and treatment begun before the patient passed the disease on to others.
But patients do not seek and doctors do not look; and if and
when either one happens to turn up the fact, each for his own
reason often fumbles or runs away. The public health people are
trying to re-educate the doctors and to spread the word among
people who are or may some day be patients. They are not succeeding very well. I am not criticizing them: I know what they
are up against.

The public health people don't need me to tell them they are
not succeeding very well. They are not giving up, but they show
signs of discouragement. Partly for this reason they are trying to
get at the problem in other ways. One is to try to devise new
techniques, or to perfect old ones, so that doctors who are busy
with other (more important?) things will have less excuse for
not bothering. The new techniques or wrinkles are coming up
slowly; but the fact is that the old ones would serve if they were
used.

The techniques we already have, as I say, could do the job if
they were used. Not that we know everything; but ignorance is
no longer the reason for failure. The very growth of technical
detail, which is getting to be forbiddingly complex already, may

even possibly slow us up. The little book is almost pathetically simple to a reasonably well-trained doctor. It speaks arithmetic while the researchers wrestle with differential equations. The gap between the stripped-down rules in the little book and the technology of the experts is wide and getting wider; and there can be a suspicion that the doctor's job may be getting harder rather than easier. The doctor is, of course, not expected to handle the technology: he just sends a sample to the laboratory. But the good doctor understands what he is doing, and why; and to do this in VD is getting harder all the time, even as science is trying to make it easier.

It is fairly obvious that this is only one sector of a wider dilemma of our technological age. People generally cannot hope to be expert in all the different technologies that are needed to run the world. The technologists concentrate on their own specialties, which are likely to be consuming enough to leave them little time for anything else. An intermediate group of people, among whom the politicians are most visible, is supposed to direct the technologists, but in many areas besides VD it looks as though they are not doing very well. We put our faith in education as the solution of the riddle, and then find education training technologists and turning out politicians and thereby doing little, if anything, more than maintaining the dilemma. Perhaps we could break through if enough people could come to understand enough technology. Possibly they could manage without being experts—if they knew just enough to let them exercise the power which democratic theory says is theirs. If they can't, it seems to me that democracy can never hope to work.

It is not easy, or it would have been done long ago. Here in our particular bailiwick I may as well admit that we are starting on the toughest chapter in this book. I will do my best to make it simple, but I ask you to face the fact that it can't be done without more loss than gain. If you want to understand VD you must know some of its technology. I will try to select the essentials and keep them palatable and digestible.

The first step is to be sure we know certain things about infectious disease, a subject on which misconceptions have been increasing since the new drugs encouraged the idea that the whole problem would soon be cleared up. Most people know that virus diseases like colds, influenza, and hepatitis have not been taken care of yet. But did you have any idea that there were 450,008 cases of serious streptococcal disease (streptococcal sore throat and scarlet fever) reported in the United States in 1969? Reported, mind you: many such cases never get to a doctor; the actual number must have been much greater. This is baterial disease; it is potentially very serious, but the streptococcus is killed by penicillin. Such streptococcal disease is the most prevalent reportable infectious disease in the United States next to—you guessed it—gonorrhea, which leads the lists with 534,872 cases, and as we will see later, the reported cases for gonorrhea, too, are only the visible tip of the iceberg. Although streptococcal disease—and many others still prevalent—are not shameful like VD, they, too, are still part of the unfinished business of public health. So the first thing to know about infectious disease is that, quite apart from VD, it is still with us.

I have been working at an idea all along in this book, and I come back to it once more. We could not start to control disease—any disease—until we recognized it as something *natural*. We had to get rid of the idea that diseases are visited upon us by gods or devils, or that they spring out of certain conjunctions of planets and stars. It happens that *infectious* diseases were the first to be understood in this way. Pasteur and Koch and the other early bacteriologists showed us that there are effects that result from causes, that the causes—microbes and viruses—can be isolated, characterized, distinguished one from another, and in separated form used to produce the disease in question. They made the point clear beyond a reasonable doubt.

Diseases which we think of as having a *single* cause—a particular kind of microbe or virus, or a vitamin deficiency—are the simplest diseases we know, and generally the easiest to control. The problem entails no more than to keep the microbe or virus away from its host, or to make sure the vitamin supply in the diet is adequate. But even so the process is not simple, as witness the fact that infectious diseases and vitamin deficiencies still exist in the world. There are always complications, difficulties, especially with *world-wide* disease control.

The venereal diseases are all caused by single microbes and ought therefore to be as near simplicity as we can get. Moreover, they are all bacterial diseases and therefore—unlike virus diseases—treatable with antibiotics. There are nevertheless some technical difficulties. For one thing, we can't grow the spirochete of syphilis in culture. If we could, possibilities would open up, of which the most important might be the development of a vaccine for syphilis. We might also develop a better diagnostic test, but we already have good ones.

We can grow the gonococcus, although it gives more trouble than most bacteria. Improved culture methods are coming along, and work is in progress that may possibly lead to a vaccine. Gonorrhea badly needs a quick, reliable diagnostic test like the blood tests now highly developed for syphilis. Such a test is being worked on, and we may have one before long. It will help, although I doubt that anybody expects it to solve the problem.

Our main business in this chapter is diagnosis. We need to know enough about it to understand what is done to identify VD, even though we will certainly not try to do much of it ourselves. It is important for us to suspect the possibility: the opening paragraph of this chapter will have suggested that it may be unwise to depend on the annual checkup. If we know we have been exposed to VD and we see on ourselves any of the signs I have described—any kind of sore on the genitals, a skin rash not definitely explained in other terms, a painful discharge from urethra or vagina (or rectum)—we should go to a VD clinic or a physician. The clinic is likely to be a little better; we will see why in more detail later. For persons under age, many states require parental consent for treatment, which of course calls for parental knowledge, and thickens the plot. I will do my best to thin it out.

In the chancre stage of syphilis, diagnosis depends on identifying spirochetes in the sore, or sometimes in the regional lymph nodes. The best way to do this is with a darkfield microscope, which means having the patient and the microscope not more than a few feet apart, so that fresh fluid can be put on a slide and examined before it dries. VD clinics are equipped to do this and have people who know how. Even the doctor who has a laboratory attached to his office seldom has a darkfield microscope; nor is there much chance that he or his technicians were ever taught to use one. Given the equipment and the necessary skill, the test can be done in a matter of minutes. The finding of any number, down to one, of spirochetes showing typical form and movement is enough to establish the diagnosis (see Figure 9). Occasionally even skilled technicians make mistakes in this test, identifying as *Treponema pallidum* either something that is not a spirochete at all, or one of the "normal" spirochetes found in the mouth or around the anus. The experienced technician, faced with a sore on such a place, may get around the difficulty by drawing a drop of fluid out of a nearby lymph node. If the fluid comes from such a lymph node, or from a sore on dry skin, the chance of error is small. A positive darkfield with appropriate clinical signs and history justifies starting treatment; and treatment ought to be started at once.

A good deal of research is being put into the development of a test for spirochetes that could be done on dried material, so that the doctor could send a specimen to a laboratory, if necessary by mail. There are such tests, based on antibodies and a fluorescent dye, which, as we will see, are also the basis of certain blood tests. As a direct test for spirochetes this method looks promising.

The darkfield test can also be used on the rash of early infectious ("secondary") syphilis, and is again more reliable with skin

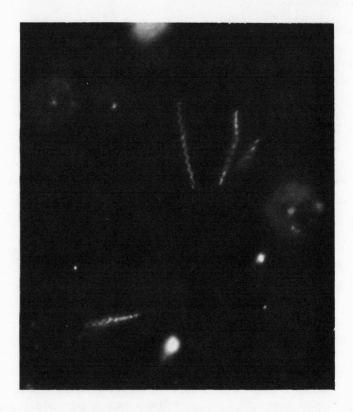

Figure 9. The spirochete of syphilis, *Treponema pallidum* (darkfield, from a living specimen, X2000).

sores than with those from moist surfaces where there may be spirochetes that are not *Treponema pallidum*. But by the time the rash comes up, antibodies have usually been formed, and tests on blood for their presence become the basis of syphilis diagnosis.

There are three different groups of blood tests for syphilis. The first group, still the most widely used, is based on the test discovered by Wassermann and his team in 1906, and his name is still given to the particular form of the test he discovered. These tests, surprisingly enough, all depend on an antibody which has no direct connection with the spirochete of syphilis. This curious fact came to light soon after the test was first announced, and caused a lot of confusion, which subsided when it became clear that the test is reliable just the same. From the time of its discovery, the variations of the Wassermann test— that is, the tests based on this peculiar Wassermann antibody, which is called "reagin"—have come to make up what is probably the most widely used diagnostic test in the world.

The second group of tests became available only as recently as 1949. They are based directly on an antibody to *Treponema pallidum*. The original and key member of the group is the *Treponema pallidum* immobilization (or TPI) test. To obtain spirochetes for the test, they are taken from an infected rabbit and injected into the testicles of healthy rabbits, where they multiply abundantly, so that in a week or so the testicles are much enlarged and full of active, virulent spirochetes. As I have mentioned before, this is the nearest we can come to a culture method for the spirochete of syphilis.

In the third class we find a single test dating from 1957, based on a noninfectious spirochete called the Reiter treponeme, which can be grown in ordinary culture and is therefore obtainable more easily and in larger quantity. Its antibody is again not exactly that of syphilis, but it is nearer to it than reagin.

These three groups of blood tests give us somewhat different information, and although, as you would expect, the TPI test is the most reliable of the three, there are good reasons for continuing to use all of them. Both Wassermann and TPI tests, in their original form, are technically elaborate and difficult, and attempts have been made to simplify them and make them easier to do. This usually entails a loss in the value of the test, although often not enough to offset the technical advantage. Some of the details are important.

We measure the reliability of these tests in terms of two qualities, which we call *sensitivity* and *specificity*. The words are
clear enough if you will think about them. A sensitive test picks
up more cases of syphilis, misses fewer cases, does not turn up
as many *false negatives*. A specific test tends to be positive only
in syphilis; it is less likely to be positive in other diseases or in
the absence of syphilis; in other words, it shows fewer *false positives*. You will gather that no test is perfect in either respect. Errors are, in fact, uncommon in general, but when they do happen they can obviously be serious. The tests that make use of
rabbit-virulent *Treponema pallidum* are best in both respects, as
you would expect; but they are also the most complicated and
expensive. Just the same, that is only one reason why the older
Wassermann-type or reagin tests are still the ones used most
widely. The experience behind them is irreplaceable; and the
particular information they give has its special value. Besides,
some of their variants are the quickest, simplest, and cheapest
blood tests for syphilis of the lot.

Syphilitic reagin, as I said, is an antibody, but not to the spirochete of syphilis. It is an antibody to something produced as a
result of the disease. Certain normal tissue extracts—fatty substances, most of them obtained from healthy beef hearts—are
used to show the presence of reagin in human blood. When reagin is found in this way in human blood, it nearly always
means that syphilis is present. But reagin has nothing to do with
immunity in syphilis. Wassermann happened on it by a clear
case of serendipity, which is as good a way as any of finding
something useful, even though it can't be planned or predicted.
His original test, as I have mentioned, is not simple. It is done
in several steps and requires careful preliminary adjustment of
unstable materials for each day's lot before the test can be set
up at all, and then a battery of controls to make sure everything
is working right. Notwithstanding all these complications, the
practical value of the test is shown by the fact that today most
good-sized hospitals all over the world have laboratories

equipped, and technicians specially trained, to do it—with
minor technical variations. This remains true even though these
elaborate tests are no more sensitive or specific than a simplified
test, again because of the experience behind the Wassermann
test, and perhaps because its built-in controls, in the hands of a
good technician, help to guard against technical error.

A simpler test was worked out at the Venereal Disease Research Laboratories of the U.S. Public Health Service at the
Center for Disease Control in Atlanta, and is known by the initials of the laboratories, the VDRL test. It is the one most
widely used now for premarital screening, preliminary tests, and
tests done routinely for private physicians; and it has been coming into use all over the world. There are many other variations
of the reagin test, and attempts are still being made to devise
new ones. For our purposes only one other needs to be mentioned, the so-called RPR or *rapid plasma reagin* test, perfected
in 1962 and designed for rapid screening under field conditions.
It is done with three drops of blood on a plastic-coated card. It
has the advantage that it can be used for testing field groups
such as migrant workers, and is good for testing babies because
it asks no more of them than a finger-prick. The results compare
favorably with those of the VDRL test. The fact that when the
test is done outside of a clinic it is hard to keep the results confidential has been mentioned as a drawback by public health
workers. The intent with the RPR test is that a positive result
will always be checked with one of the more standard reagin
tests.

Otherwise checking of reagin tests is seldom called for unless
there is good reason to doubt the results, especially when they
are positive. If the clinical indications and history point strongly
to syphilis, a negative test naturally raises the suspicion of a
technical error and calls for a repeat. But it is the positive test
in the absence of history or clinical signs that gives the most
trouble, including a special sort of torment to the patient. Some
of these tests are "technical false positives"—technicians being

human—and are easily rectified when a repeat turns out to be negative. But when repeated tests are unequivocally positive, something more is needed. At this point the doctor may remember to "snoop around corners" and double-check the patient's story. If a suspicious spot is found somewhere a positive dark-field may bring in the verdict.

But the false positive may be real, which is to say "biologic" rather than technical, meaning that reagin is present, but *false* in the sense that syphilis is absent. Positive reagin tests are found, that is, in the absence of syphilis. They remain positive for shorter or longer periods, and one variant of the reagin test, like the Wassermann test, may confirm another, like the VDRL. These are the most troublesome diagnostic errors in syphilis, and more than a few homes have been wrecked by them. Some of these "BFP's" (biologic false positives) are transient ("acute"), reverting to negative without any treatment within six months; others are more persistent ("chronic"). They result, obviously, from formation of reagin antibody in the blood by something other than syphilis. The transient sort sometimes follows various other infectious diseases, or appears after smallpox vaccination or other immunizations. The chronic ones are always present in the nonvenereal treponematoses (as we saw in Chapter 7); they may also appear in leprosy and malaria, and in narcotic addicts. Pregnant women and old people sometimes give BFP's. In pregnancy and certain other cases they are thought to depend on underlying serious illness of the "collagen" or "auto-immune" type, especially lupus erythematosis. A BFP may therefore have the value of uncovering a disease, even though it is not syphilis.

When a BFP is suspected, one of the more specific tests is called for, of which the TPI is the court of last resort. But the Reiter test is often used for screening BFP's, being more specific than reagin tests, although somewhat insensitive, especially in syphilis of many years' duration. In spite of its difficulties and limitations, this test is used fairly widely, because it can be done in hospital laboratories, whereas the third group, those based on rabbit-virulent spirochetes, are performed only in specialized laboratories, most of which in the United States are operated by state or federal government agencies.

The virulent-spirochete tests would probably replace all others if they were easier to do, and they would be easier, for example, if virulent spirochetes could be cultured. But they still have a few drawbacks, and it is possible that reagin-type tests would continue to be needed in any event. The reagin tests usually become positive earlier—in a few weeks after the chancre appears —whereas TPI-type tests may not be positive for several months; so that tests like the VDRL are very valuable for early diagnosis. Furthermore, the TPI test may remain positive longer after clinically successful treatment of late syphilis; and hence a positive reagin-type test may be a better guide to the need for continuing such treatment. Yet this, too, unfortunately, is not quite so simple. A positive reagin test in late latency, in the absence of any symptoms or recent history of progressive syphilis, does not usually warrant treatment. People are not infectious under these conditions, and since their syphilis is quiescent and may be healed, one lets them alone. But there is some reason to believe that a persistently positive TPI test in late syphilis without symptoms may mean residual infection not entirely eliminated by treatment. I will tell you more about that in the next chapter.

The TPI test is the most elaborate and technically demanding of all blood tests for syphilis. Two circumstances are made use of in it. The first is a way of keeping the spirochetes alive and moving for eighteen to twenty-four hours or so—no easy trick, but it can be done. The second is the fact that when such spirochetes are mixed under exacting conditions with certain materials, including blood serum which has the syphilitic antibodies in it, the spirochetes stop moving and are killed. The mixture is kept for the eighteen to twenty-four hours during which spirochetes without added antibodies would still be found moving. The test is read under the darkfield microscope. It is positive in syphilis and in all the nonvenereal treponematoses, but negative in all other BFP's; and it is used especially to resolve such cases.

A good deal of work has been done to try to simplify a test based on the TPI principle—that is, a test using the same spirochetal antigen and its antibody but without the need to keep the spirochetes alive. The best of these, which has come to be widely adopted, is called the FTA–ABS test, meaning "fluorescent treponemal antibody-absorption." It uses the same rabbit-virulent spirochetes but kills them so that they keep for some time, making it possible for the laboratory using them to do without a rabbit colony and without the need to keep inoculating and processing testicles. And it includes a fluorescent dye which, when mixed under the right conditions with the spirochetes and syphilitic blood serum, makes the dye stick to the spirochetes so that, when seen under a modified darkfield microscope, they look greenish and fluorescent against a dark background. At first this test was found to be *too sensitive;* it was positive with normal human serum which contains antibodies to "normal" spirochetes. But if the test serum is first treated with the Reiter treponeme, these "normal" antibodies are removed. This is the "absorption" part of the test. The specific antibodies still remain to fluoresce with rabbit-virulent spirochetes.

The FTA–ABS test is almost as specific as the TPI test and may be even more sensitive, especially in early syphilis. Nevertheless it appears that some blood specimens which are reagin-positive and FTA–ABS negative still prove to be positive by the TPI test, so that they cannot be called BFP's; and oddly enough, the Reiter test is also still found useful in some of these cases.

But granting that a margin of error can never be entirely eliminated from such biological tests and allowing for the complexity, the time it takes to do a battery of them, the expense, and the agony that is sure to be felt by the person being tested, it still remains true that we have adequate means for the diagnosis of syphilis.

With the recent increase of *congenital* syphilis several new problems have arisen. Clinical signs in the infant may be absent or inconclusive. The mother's history may call for blood-testing the baby, but the results of such tests, whether positive or negative, may be ambiguous, first because the baby may not yet have begun to produce typical antibodies in sufficient amount for a positive test, and second because antibody that is found may have come from the mother through the placenta rather than from the infant himself. But antibodies can now be distinguished by special methods, and those capable of passing through the placenta can be separated from those that are not. FTA–ABS tests based on such separation and pointing therefore to antibodies produced by the baby himself have been developed. There has also been a suggestion that X-rays of the infant can help identify congenital syphilis by showing typical bone deformities.

Further improvements are in the works, including automated methods which for an RPR card test can process a hundred samples per hour; automation is also being applied to treponemal antibody tests and may be one way of simplifying them. But the fact is that errors are few; I have dwelt on them to explain them, but they are not as important as might appear from the space it took to describe them. The current reports on automation and other refinements seem to me to go a little further than the circumstances may warrant. There is a suggestion in the reports, between the lines, that the problem of syphilis, like war and the poor, will always be with us. It looks as though we are becoming resigned to failure to control the disease. If we can control it, the refinements are unnecessary; if we can't, they are unimportant.

The problem of diagnosing gonorrhea is different and in some ways tougher. The part played by medical ignorance or lack of interest, and by technical carelessness or incompetence, is much the same for both diseases. But syphilis can be diagnosed if it is suspected and if the patient can be induced to stay around for the necessary brief interval. Given this much, the worst problem is the occasional biologic false positive; and with time and money—which is not to suggest that lack of the second is trivial —this, too, can be worked out. In gonorrhea, if there is pus and pain the diagnosis can be made tentatively in a few minutes and confirmed in twenty-four to forty-eight hours. The main trouble is that, especially in women, there may be neither. The infected woman may have no warning, and if she has had only one sexual partner, and is unaware that he has had others, she may have no basis at all for suspicion. Even when compulsory examinations are made—of prostitutes or prisoners—the routine tests may fail if the infected area is missed by the examiner's swab. The following remark by two U.S. Public Health workers, Garson and Barton, may sound like a joke but was made in deadly earnest:

> the most sensitive, practical indicator of gonorrhea in the female is the anterior urethra of a susceptible male.

The paper is dated 1960. There has been progress since then, but the difficulty has not been altogether cleared up.

The oldest and still most widely used way of making a tentative or presumptive diagnosis of gonorrhea is to examine a drop of pus under a microscope using a quite ordinary stained slide. The procedure is painless to the patient and can be done, all told, in five minutes. Diagnosis is based on the appearance of typical paired gonococci inside so-called pus cells (phagocytes), usually crowding the cells (see Figure 10). But the picture is not always typical, and it may be mimicked by somewhat similar bacteria that are not gonococci, making up part of the problem

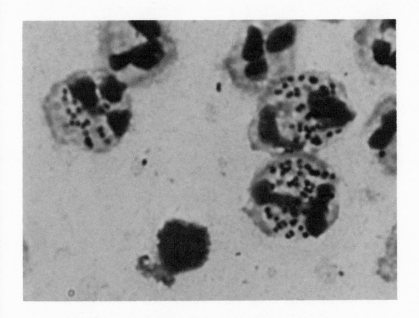

Figure 10. The gonococcus, *Neisseria gonorrhoeae*, as
it appears within phagocytic cells, dried and stained
(X1800).

of nongonococcal urethritis (Chapter 15). Part of this problem
has resulted from the widespread use of antibiotics for other diseases in recent years. So that again we have false negatives and
false positives; but both are much more common in gonorrhea
than in syphilis.

The usual way of resolving such ambiguity is to make a culture of the gonococcus, in which it can be identified without
question. The culture grows out in twenty-four hours; another
day may be needed for final identifying tests. But these things
are easier said than done. To make a culture, the specimen must
be sent to a laboratory, and if the doctor is at any distance from
an appropriate one, special means must be used to keep the
fragile gonococcus alive in transit. The gonococcus requires spe-

cial culture media and growth conditions. These are, however, within the capacity of any good hospital laboratory. But all the little pitfalls have made the whole procedure a good deal short of perfect.

Nevertheless, in recent years both culture methods for the gonococcus and ways of keeping it alive in transit have been greatly improved, so that errors and missed cases are getting less common. There is little doubt that this diagnostic problem will be solved. The details belong in Chapter 20.

In addition to improved culture methods, attempts are being made to improve the specificity of the slide technique with the now widely used fluorescent antibody trick. Antibodies specific for the gonococcus can be produced by injecting them into rabbits, even though the rabbits develop no disease. Such antibodies can be coupled to fluorescent dye. The resulting fluorescent antibody attaches itself specifically to the gonococcus when the two are brought together and identifies it under the special microscope by its greenish fluorescence. The fluorescent antibody technique applied to the gonococcus has so far been most effective when combined with cultures by the newer methods.

Gonorrhea diagnosis has no blood test and would certainly be improved by one, if only because it is easier to take a small blood sample from the arm than to squeeze pus out of the penis or explore the whole vaginal surface with a swab. Blood tests have been devised, and a few have been fairly extensively tested; but up to now none has been accepted. Intensive work is going forward, however, although only in a few laboratories; and success may be around the proverbial corner.

As for the minor venereal diseases, the recognition of lymphogranuloma venereum is based first on clinical signs and confirmed by a group of laboratory tests. Ordinary cultures show nothing useful: the LGV agent grows like a virus, best in the yolk sac of fertile hens' eggs. The agent can be identified microscopically. The common confirmatory method is an allergic skin test ("Frei test"), which is done by injecting killed LGV agent obtained commercially. A tiny amount injected into the skin so as to raise a small bleb, with a control injection in the other arm of yolk-sac material without LGV (to eliminate allergy to egg), shows, in positive cases, a pea-sized swelling only in the test arm after two or three days. The test becomes positive a week or so after infection starts, and remains positive permanently with or without treatment.

There is also a blood test for LGV based on antibodies to the agent. Both Frei and blood tests have a tendency to be positive in related nonvenereal diseases, including psittacosis, or parrot fever (a form of pneumonia), and trachoma, a serious disease of the eyes. These diseases are clinically so different from LGV that there is seldom any problem in distinguishing between them. Yet another member of the group known as TRIC agent is found fairly often in nongonoccocal urethritis.

The diagnosis of chancroid is confirmed by demonstration of its bacillus in the soft chancre either microscopically on a stained slide, or, better, by means of a culture, which can be done without special difficulty.

Granuloma inguinale is usually diagnosed by identifying the distinctive so-called "Donovan bodies" inside the cells in material taken from the sores. The microbe can be cultured, but the technique is difficult and is not used much. A blood test for antibodies to the microbe also exists but, again, is seldom done.

❧ 17 ❧

Cure and Curability

AN OUNCE of prevention, says grandma, is worth a pound of
cure. Few people take her seriously. Unless we are singed
by the fire before being snatched to safety, we are not likely to
know that anything has been prevented; and mass prevention
seems anonymous or impertinent and elicits no gratitude. We
still like to have the doctor give us something in response to a
complaint; and few doctors can restrain the compulsion to leave
the patient with a prescription, although the best ones admit
doubts, even dangers. Here in the age of science the patient's
gratitude still overflows when relief or recovery follows the
doctor's ministrations; yet most of us know the fallacy of *post
hoc* . . . In medicine the age of bacteriology, when we began to
understand disease and treat it rationally, gave way to the age
of pharmacology—although it isn't called by that name—and we
see something like a reversion to the prescientific custom in
which there was a remedy for every symptom. Medical reports
attempt to bypass clinical errors with tests of new drugs called
"double-blind" and even "reversed double-blind"—in which
code-marked drug and placebo are given without being identified by either giver or taker; and where possible the groups are

then reversed to eliminate all prejudice. But we still tend to re-cover from disease without drugs and to die with them, possibly as often as the opposite. There are times, we have pretty good reason to believe, when it is the smile and the kind word, the simple act of concern of one human being for another—the ex-pression of love—that is more therapeutic than anything the chemist can fabricate.

Nevertheless there are drugs that cure, and none do so more dramatically than the modern remedies for venereal disease. Possibly something associated with the very fragility of the mi-crobes that dictates their venereal way of life, that makes them easy prey to harmful influences generally, also makes them the more susceptible to therapeutic drugs. But if that is true, you would hardly have believed it before Paul Ehrlich gave us "606" in 1910, or perhaps even before the modern age of sulfonamides and penicillin, which started only in 1935. Even today, after the first flush of therapeutic victory has begun to fade, we are begin-ning to think, again, that grandma was right.

Of all drugs used for VD before Ehrlich's time, only mercury for syphilis and silver nitrate to prevent gonococcal blindness in newborn babies can now be thought to have had any value. Of these, the second, introduced in the early 1880s by the Leipzig obstetrician Karl Siegmund Franz Credé following the work of Noeggerath (Chapter 14), is still in use today. Mercury has gone the way of guaiac, of which nothing more need be said. Mercury probably never did more than relieve symptoms, although an ointment of calomel (mercurous chloride) rubbed into the geni-tals, proposed in the early 1900s following experiments with chimpanzees, seems to have had value as a prophylactic for syphilis. In 1949, as the crest of optimism in the penicillin era ap-proached, Evan Thomas, an eminent New York syphilologist, said:

> Antisyphilitic therapy with mercury, a protoplasmic poison, is prac-tically obsolete. If mercury is used at all, the best method of admin-istration is by inunction.

Thomas Dover (1660–1742), an Englishman, still remembered for a powder mixture of ipecac and opium with milk sugar, came in later life to be nicknamed "Dr. Quicksilver" because of his advocacy of metallic mercury for syphilis and other things. He published a book on the subject in 1732, tracing the history of the therapeutic use of raw mercury back to Paracelsus. We have seen reason to believe that mercury, probably as one of its ores (like cinnabar), was used to treat syphilis much earlier, perhaps as far back as the time of the ancient Chinese. As for Dr. Dover, he had opponents even in his own time, among them Daniel Turner, who insisted that raw mercury was useless in the treatment of syphilis.

The modern era of so-called chemotherapy dates from the announcement of Salvarsan—Ehrlich's No. 606—as a specific for syphilis. Ehrlich had won a Nobel Prize (with Metchnikoff) two years before for his studies of immunity. In 1909 his young Japanese assistant, Sahachiro Hata, who had learned how to work with syphilis in rabbits, retested two of Ehrlich's organic arsenical compounds ("arsphenamines"), numbered 418 and 606; earlier tests by another assistant had shown promise for the first but not for the second. In Hata's competent hands the reverse proved true, and 606, Salvarsan or arsphenamine, was announced as the first specific remedy for syphilis. But arsphenamine was soon found to have unpleasant side effects, which were modified but never entirely eliminated in successive years by synthesis of variants with improved properties. Among these, arsenoxides (such as Mapharsen) came to supplant the earlier compounds; but toxic effects and the need for prolonged treatment continued until penicillin displaced the arsenical drugs entirely.

In the meantime compounds of bismuth were introduced (first in 1921), and although they are again somewhat dangerous, their use as adjuncts in the treatment of late syphilis has not entirely disappeared today.

The status of the treatment of syphilis in the heyday of the arsenical drugs (1936) is suggested in these comments by a syphilologist, J. E. Klein:

> For proof of the eradication of the spirochete it is necessary to present a convincing series of careful necropsy [autopsy] studies on patients known to have had syphilis which was thoroughly treated. Thus far there has been no such proof. . . . It is . . . illogical to set a time limit, such as from three to five years, after which a patient may marry presumably with assurance of safety. From an ideal eugenic standpoint the syphilitic person is undesirable marriage material. . . . Modern syphilographers . . . recommend continuous treatment until the disease is clinically and serologically "cured," and then a lifetime of medical supervision. . . . At best there may be offered a prospect of a reasonable span of life with a minimum of complications and assurance of arresting the infection if it is properly treated in time.

In those days the treatment of syphilis was largely in the hands of dermatologists, who took Klein's "lifetime of medical supervision" seriously. There was a standing joke: "The syphilologist may be dying, but syphilis is not." Klein's viewpoint, however extreme, was medical rather than moral. In itself it suggests that little progress had been made since the time of Brieux's doctor a generation earlier. At most it seems that arsphenamines helped individual patients but hardly touched the problem of syphilis.

At the very time that Dr. Klein was making his gloomy pronouncement, the new age of chemotherapy was being born, first in the laboratories of the German dye trust where Gerhard Domagk found as early as 1932 that a sulfur-containing dye called prontosil could prevent otherwise fatal streptococcal infections in mice. Even before publication of this work in 1935, clinical trials were confirming the effects in man. By 1936 it became clear as a result of studies in France and England that the active component of prontosil was a rather simple benzene (or benzoic acid) derivative, sulfanilamide, and in succeeding years this and similar compounds called, as a class, sulfonamides (or sulfa drugs), proved dramatically effective in a range of bacterial diseases including gonorrhea. But within a few years the gonococcus developed resistance to the sulfonamides to the point where they became useless against it. The advent of penicillin saved the day and held it longer; but the same problem has since come up again.

Even earlier, in 1929, Alexander Fleming had noticed that a soluble product of a *Penicillium* mold which he called penicillin had valuable "antiseptic" properties and seemed entirely harmless to man. This fact did not bear fruit until 1940–1941, when, partly under the stress of war, Chain, Florey, and their associates in England were able to show how to produce penicillin in usable quantities. Within a short time penicillin had been tried and shown to be effective against a wide range of diseases, conspicuous among them both gonorrhea and syphilis. At first the method of treatment followed one that had just been worked out for the arsphenamines, based on findings with the sulfonamides. A series of injections was given every few hours over a period of days, so as to maintain an effective concentration of the drug in the blood. (This is the kind of treatment Burns describes in *The Gallery*—see Chapter 11). But as early as 1945, while distrust of penicillin for syphilis was still present, so that it was often used in combination with arsenoxide and bismuth, a method permitting a single dose of penicillin had been suggested. Several such drugs have been made—"repository" penicillins, from which the active material is released slowly after they are injected into a muscle (usually of the buttock). The first contained beeswax and oil. The two in widest use today are benzathine penicillin, called "Bicillin" and by other names, which is especially suited to the single-dose method, and a compound including penicillin in an insoluble soap, aluminum monostearate, known as PAM. While multiple injections have continued to be used, field conditions often dictate a single-injection treatment (or several injections made together), not only for syphilis but on a world-wide scale for the nonvenereal treponematoses, for which penicillin is equally effective.

Success with penicillin followed not only for early infectious syphilis but also for late syphilis, which had been refractory to the arsphenamine drugs. In 1923 a somewhat heroic method of treating neurosyphilis had been introduced: The patient was deliberately inoculated with malaria so that the resulting fever would kill the spirochetes. Later, noninfectious and more easily controlled means of raising body temperature came into use and were credited with helping to bring the syphilis rate in the United States down after Surgeon General Parran's control program was instituted in 1938, and *before* penicillin became available. But by 1954, ten years after the first wide-scale use of penicillin, all authorities in the United States agreed that penicillin alone was more effective than anything ever tried before, and that it worked in late as well as in early syphilis.

Europe lagged behind the United States in the exclusive use of penicillin, with reservations lingering there which, as we will see, were not altogether unjustified. In the Soviet Union arsphenamines and bismuth were still being used as adjuncts to penicillin treatment, at least until recently. In 1968 a German report mentioned that fever therapy was still being used with penicillin in some cases of syphilitic paralysis. But by 1962 penicillin was being used alone in many other countries as well as in the United States for all stages of syphilis. Results have been nearly completely successful, with important exceptions to be noted.

Treatment of syphilis is not entirely free from problems and difficulties, but no serious infectious disease can be treated more simply or with more complete success.

The first problem is allergy to penicillin, which has increased somewhat with increasing use of the drug; but serious allergic reactions have never been common. Allergy tends to develop in persons in whom a drug has been used before and is accordingly more common in wealthier than in poorer patients, and more common with multiple injections than with single ones. It is almost unknown in treatment of treponematosis among Africans and others not previously exposed to penicillin. Where a history of allergy to penicillin exists, other antibiotics can be used effectively.

R. R. Willcox published some interesting statistics in 1964 on the prevalence of allergy to penicillin, based on experiences in England and Wales during the year 1960. With a single injection allergy appeared in less than 1 per cent of 74,000 cases treated for venereal disease, but the figure rose to 10.2 per cent for multiple injections. Fatal reactions—known as anaphylaxis —occurred at the rate of one in 78,002 patients treated. Willcox remarks that this rate, applied to cases of syphilis and gonorrhea reported in the United States in 1952–1961, would give an expected total of 47 deaths in ten years, which is approximately one-fifth the mortality from playing "American football" in an equivalent period. He goes on to make the following comparison of penicillin deaths in VD clinics in England and Wales with deaths from other causes, all in 1960:

Penicillin in VD clinics	1
Gout	36
Aircraft accidents	96
Water-transport accidents	352
Homicide and injury inflicted by others	468
Railway accidents	508
Accidental poisoning	3,000
Suicide	10,236
Road vehicle accidents	13,480

Anaphylactic death is more likely to follow injection into a vein than into a muscle, and is less likely the more slowly the drug is absorbed, so that repository penicillins are safer than penicillin in water solution given by injection. Skin allergies, furthermore, are known to have a complex basis, often including emotional factors. A news item in the A.M.A. *Journal* (Nov. 17, 1969) is headed "The Average Penicillin Allergy is Not an Allergy"—and goes on to say that even when skin allergy to penicillin was recorded (in children with "strep throats") benzathine penicillin could usually be given without adverse effect.

Which is not to say that allergy to penicillin does not exist, or
that anaphylactic death never happens, but only that the risks
are smaller than is commonly supposed.

Another problem in the treatment of syphilis is the development of fever, occasionally as high as 104°, sometimes accompanied by a temporary *increase* in the severity of the lesions, following a few hours after the first injection of the drug. This
so-called "therapeutic shock," or Herxheimer reaction, occurred
with the arsphenamines as well as with penicillin, and is probably due to rapid destruction of spirochetes and release of their
irritating ingredients into the tissues in larger than ordinary
amounts. In other words, it may be taken as an indication that
the treatment is working. In early syphilis this shock reaction is
rare if it ever happens and is never harmful; but in neurosyphilis the symptoms may be alarming and are occasionally serious, and in syphilis of the heart and blood vessels such reactions
in very rare instances have been serious and even fatal.

Another problem, which is sometimes too lightly dismissed, is
that of so-called relapse, that is, of apparent failure of treatment
as indicated by reappearance of symptoms some time after presumably complete cure. From the patient's point of view this is
obviously an important matter. It has several aspects which we
had better look into one by one.

There is no doubt that early infectious syphilis—primary and
secondary syphilis—when treated with adequate amounts of
penicillin, in nearly all cases becomes noninfectious in a matter
of days after treatment is completed, leaving the patient, once
the sores have healed and disappeared, literally as good as new,
which is to say, completely cured. The earlier the treatment is
given in the course of the disease, the faster this curative process operates. If reagin-type blood tests have not yet become
positive, they may stay negative, or if positive they revert back
to negative. But for a variety of reasons doctors advise fairly
long follow-up periods. Dr. Pariser, for instance, advises blood
tests every month for six or nine months after treatment and

every three months after that for "at least two years." The U.S. Public Health Service suggests discharge at the end of one year in treated early infectious syphilis, with blood tests at intervals of one, three, six, and twelve months. When treatment is started during latency, either early or late, or in late syphilis, the follow-up period is longer; but even so the U.S.P.H.S. permits discharge two years after treatment. The same rules are applied to syphilis in pregnancy and to congenital syphilis, the follow-up period depending on whether the disease is treated in the early infectious stage or later.

Assuming that these rules are based on a proper caution alone, there is little doubt that they complicate the treatment problem from the social point of view, that they help to frighten people away from VD treatment. The rules are, to be sure, intended for the private doctor, who presumably has and can hold his patient's confidence, rather than for the public clinic, which often counts itself lucky if it can hold a patient long enough to confirm the diagnosis and give single-shot treatment. Nevertheless there are reasons for the caution, although, curiously enough, relapse following adequate treatment of early syphilis is almost certainly not one of them.

We need to anticipate a little at this point to recognize that immunity in syphilis, such as it is, develops very slowly. The details must wait for our examination of the possibility of making a vaccine. Slow development means that when syphilis is completely cured in its early stages there is no immunity at all. One of the peculiar things about syphilis is that the *untreated* syphilitic has an odd kind of immunity to a new infection, odd because it doesn't do him much good, since he is sick anyway. But the fact is that if he has a chancre, or has once had one and has not been treated, he does not develop another no matter how often or how massively he may be re-exposed. But once completely cured of early syphilis he can be reinfected and have another chancre and all its sequels. As a result, if syphilis is treated in only one of a pair of sexually active partners, the treated partner may develop new chancres once, twice, or many times. This repeating pattern had never been seen before the introduction of penicillin. It was quickly called "ping-pong" syphilis.

Such "reinfection" has often been mistaken for relapse, and it has taken some years and many pages of type to reorder our thinking away from the pessimism of the quotation from Klein we saw a few pages back. Penicillin, it was becoming clear, was giving fast and full cures such as had never been known before. Arsphenamines may have cured completely, but cure was so slow that a certain immunity always had time to develop, and second chancres were unknown. With penicillin it was reinfection, not relapse.

Usually. Relapse certainly happened with penicillin—sometimes—when the drug was started in later stages or when not enough was given. A common difficulty arose when gonorrhea and syphilis were present together, especially during the 1940s and 1950s, when gonorrhea was treatable with smaller doses of penicillin than were needed for syphilis. The gonorrhea, with its shorter incubation period, showed up first, and treatment aimed at it alone could merely mask the chancre so that it failed to appear or went unnoticed; but blood reactions and secondaries appeared later. Evan Thomas says,

> . . . patients may have infectious relapses and later may develop serious late lesions of syphilis, if the relapse was undetected. This fact explains the old dictum that inadequate therapy of early syphilis may do more harm than good, and also explains why it is so essential to keep patients under observation for long periods after treatment is completed.

But that was said in 1949, and ought to be thought of as the opinion of an older clinician still steeped in the old pessimism. Caution is a virtue; but if you have ever walked across traffic with somebody holding your arm who had the virtue a little too highly developed I needn't push the point that there can be too much of a good thing. Anticipating one small part of the large question we must face later—the question of control of VD—it seems plain that we must not unduly prolong the agony and uncertainty of treatment. In syphilis treatment can be done and done with: delay may spoil its value.

But finally—to finish the subject of treatment of syphilis in the only way the whole story allows, which is on a note of foreboding—we must face the truth that there are no absolutes in biology, and no disease is less absolute than syphilis. If the treatment of *early* syphilis approaches the ideal, so far, at all events—and it does!—the treatment of late syphilis falls short of it. There is a story to be told here that has been unfolding only in the last few years. Its full significance has come to be accepted in responsible quarters only with the greatest reluctance.

Beginning in 1962 Pierre Collart and his group at the Fournier Institute in Paris stirred up a small hornets' nest—not many people seem to have been interested at the time—when they announced that active spirochetes may persist in the tissues after apparently satisfactory treatment of late syphilis. Since that time Collart's work has been confirmed in at least three laboratories in this country, and also in Italy and in England. It was my good fortune to be able to spend several hours with Dr. Collart and his colleagues in his laboratories on the Boulevard Saint-Jacques, in April, 1970. They have been studying an important biological problem with appropriate objectivity, uncovering startling information and not worrying too much about all its implications. Being myself no longer a working scientist, I have allowed myself to brood a little on their discoveries.

Two points seem to me to need emphasis here. The first is that even massive and prolonged penicillin treatment of *late* syphilis sometimes fails to cure it, in the sense that spirochetes persist in the tissues, alive and still virulent for rabbits. This may well be the reason for persistently positive TPI tests in such patients. What it means in terms of actual progress of the disease in these late syphilitics is not yet clear and may not be known for some years. N. S. C. Rice and his English colleagues, who have confirmed some of Collart's work, make this encouraging comment:

> the findings do not alter the fully-substantiated facts that the clinical results of treatment of early syphilis are excellent and that it is only the moist lesions of early syphilis that are infectious by sexual contact.

The second point is the one that really disturbs me. Dr. Collart showed me some syphilitic rabbits and the fully active spirochetes taken from them, and brought out notebooks with details of his more recent work. *He has been able to make these spirochetes resistant to 2.4 million units of penicillin* (the common single curative dose for man). Penicillin resistance, a bugbear in gonorrhea, as we will see, has not yet been reported for syphilis—outside of Collart's rabbits—with a single possible exception. A group of workers at Johns Hopkins University, inheritors of one of the most distinguished traditions of syphilis research, reported in May, 1970, that a baby girl with congenital syphilis died 22 days after birth despite massive penicillin treatment. Penicillin had been given ten days before delivery and for seventeen days after birth. Live and virulent spirochetes were recovered from the infant at autopsy. The case is represented as the first on record in which adequate penicillin treatment failed to halt the progress of *early* syphilis. That the treatment was adequate by the usual standards became clear when blood samples from both mother and child taken at birth, ten days after the earlier penicillin treatment, showed enough penicillin still in the serum to kill the usual spirochetes. The authors do not speculate on the possible reasons for this baby's death: "Regardless of how *T. pallidum* survived in this infant, survive it did." They relate their observations to those of Collart and his followers, and mention the possibility of penicillin resistance.

There is reason to believe that our troubles in treating gonorrhea are due at least partly to negligence and delay: we might have scotched it if we had acted more quickly. Now it looks as though syphilis, in which we have faced pretty much the same set of problems *except* penicillin resistance, is capable of following gonorrhea into the same predicament.

But if penicillin resistance of the spirochete is what killed the Johns Hopkins baby, it is the only case of such resistance reported thus far for early syphilis. It is obviously important to treat syphilis in its early stages. It would be vastly better to prevent it outright. The problem, for this and other reasons to be seen in later chapters, is sure to get worse before it can get better. One of the further complications is an apparently increasing prevalence of *early latent* syphilis, possibly resulting from inadequate treatment. In the words of the reporters of this increase, Pereyra and Voller, "the ominous prospect of a widespread resurgence of the disease in its tertiary form looms ahead."

As we turn now from syphilis to gonorrhea, we meet the problem of penicillin resistance head on. While penicillin dosage has been increased for treatment of syphilis, the increase has been made not because of a change in the spirochetes but rather to be sure that the initial treatment would be sufficient to prevent relapse. But the gonococcus has been changing in its resistance to drugs from the start, first to sulfonamides and more slowly to penicillin and other antibiotics. The resistance of gonococci to sulfonamides developed rapidly. As many as 10 per cent were resistant from the start, and by 1943 cure rates were as low as 25 per cent among troops in Italy. A year later resistant strains of gonococci were even more common. The sulfonamides, moreover, were not always well tolerated, and reactions were sometimes severe. Penicillin, introduced in 1944, was therefore "providential," and in adequate dosage was found uniformly effective for more than a decade. But by the late 1950s penicillin resistance of the gonococcus was being reported all over the world. Yet resistance has developed slowly and in stages, so that increasing dosage could usually overcome it; and even today, in most parts of the world, penicillin in high dosage is preferred to any other antibiotic, although a wide range of other antibiotics is also effective.

A World Health Organization study from Copenhagen in 1969 found the highest proportion of resistant gonococci in 1967–1968 in Thailand, Taiwan, Vietnam, and Hong Kong. Other reports had noticed a high rate of failure in treatment in South Korea, as well as in Japan and on the west coast of the United States. These are all zones of war or military occupation or embarkation. In other world areas, including the rest of the United States itself, the failure rate with adequate penicillin dosage has been little more than 5 per cent; and in northern Europe a reversion of gonococci to "normal" penicillin susceptibility has been described. But increased penicillin resistance of gonococci has been found in other places, including Toronto, Canada; Sydney, Australia; and Helsinki, Finland. Nevertheless, and while a wide range of other antibiotics and other drugs (including a new sulfonamide in combination with another agent) continue to be tested with varying success, penicillin is still listed as the best of the lot.

Again in contrast to the syphilis problem, it has been reported that treatment of gonorrhea with penicillin tends to be more effective when a quickly absorbed water-soluble preparation is given (still as a single dose) instead of one of the slow-acting repository drugs. The idea is to build up the level of penicillin in the blood as high and as fast as possible. Certain other drugs have been used along with the penicillin to enhance the effect by slowing excretion of the penicillin through the kidneys. The fact is that in spite of resistance of gonococci to penicillin—and developing resistance to other antibiotics as well—up to now either penicillin itself in sufficient dosage, or one of the newer modified penicillins or another antibiotic, can always be found, by testing a culture from the patient, which can be used effectively in treatment. This has been true up to now; but there is evidently a race going on between increasing drug resistance of the gonococcus and the ingenuity of chemists in making new or modified drugs, with continuing war or military activity clearly acting on the side of the gonococcus.

The minor venereal diseases are all adequately treatable. Penicillin is not used for any of them, but sulfonamides have been found effective for both LGV and chancroid. Tetracycline or one of its variants has been used successfully for LGV, chancroid, and granuloma inguinale. Chancroid has also been treated successfully with streptomycin.

❧ 18 ❧

The Dimensions of VD

A FEW YEARS after the end of World War II we seemed to be in a position to solve the VD problem once and for all. On top of all we had before, there was penicillin inspiring a growing confidence that it would wipe out both syphilis and gonorrhea; and there were all sorts of new and encouraging bits of technology, among which the TPI test promised to do away with the nagging false positive blood test problem in syphilis. Money was pouring into science, and science could work wonders. Even then there were voices raised in warning; but medical Cassandras were no novelty, especially in the long war with syphilis. The prevailing theme was one of optimism.

For a few years the vital statistics tended to encourage the optimism; but by the time we were well into the 1950s the wind shifted. The incidence curves that had been going down so gratifyingly stopped and started up again. The syphilis line seemed to have more or less leveled out or even gone down a little until a year or so ago, but more recently it has started up again, alarmingly. Gonorrhea has been rising steadily, and fast. The United States figures for 1968 and 1969, which became available early in 1970, showed gonorrhea at the top of the list of reportable infectious diseases; and it began to be spoken of in terms of "epidemic proportions" and even as "out of control." Nor is any relief in sight or promised, although we have no reason to doubt that research and public health people are working to the limit of their resources. The problem persists or gets worse in the United States, and for its citizens scattered all over the world, especially those in uniform. Other countries have the problem, too.

The increase in VD is, of course, the principal reason for this book. With gonorrhea this increase has been going on long enough to be far beyond any chance of error or excuse; and as the same thing seems to be happening with syphilis, the danger signals are getting too loud and insistent to be ignored. This is news: every few weeks the daily press headlines "A New Epidemic in U.S.: Venereal Disease"; "Venereal Disease Rate Rising in U.S.; Many Youngsters Afflicted; Alarming Rise in VD Rate Told"; "Frightening Rise in V.D."; "Syphilis Cases Are Up Sharply, Reversing Trend in Last Decade"—all these are headlines in mid-1970.

We must take a close look at the figures, but we run into difficulties at once. I would have liked to give you the world picture, and in fact I have been trying hard to boil down a veritable ocean of world statistics to no more than a cupful of reasonably clear and palatable juice. But in the course of doing so I decided to go to Geneva and speak to Dr. Thorstein Guthe, the chief of the department of the World Health Organization called VDT, or Venereal Diseases and Treponematoses. Dr. Guthe is at the hub of the problem of world statistics on VD. His department is the clearing house for all countries that are members of WHO. His breadth of interests is by no means limited to statistics, but his grasp of this particular matter is no less than I would have expected from his position. Yet what he told me—I was not altogether unprepared for it, although I may have hoped for something else—was that current world statistics on VD for developed countries are generally quite unreliable.

He was explicit and emphatic about it, but he allowed three qualified exceptions which I will explain: Denmark, Poland, and the United States have usable statistics.

The reasons for this sad state of affairs are important. They bear on the whole VD problem in an intimate and revealing way. The problem is that the statistics are all based on cases of disease *reported* to local public health authorities, and by them, through national agencies, to the WHO. The number of *reported* cases usually bears no known relation to the *actual* number of cases: Denmark, Poland, and the United States are exceptions. The first two, in different ways, manage to compile statistics which pass Dr. Guthe's critical standards. The United States, with statistics as unreliable as any, has made two serious attempts *to measure the error,* so that a projection can be made which Dr. Guthe thinks is pretty good. Details will come later.

All reported disease statistics are subject to error, but VD statistics suffer more than others. People with reportable diseases do not always reach a doctor or a clinic, or may go undiagnosed or misdiagnosed. There is both underreporting (cases missed) and overreporting (mistaken diagnoses). The first group is usually larger than the second, and the statistics are therefore usually too low. The error tends to get smaller as the disease gets more severe; mild cases are least likely to be seen by a doctor, while fatal illness is hardly ever missed. Special efforts are made to spot highly communicable diseases, and everybody concerned usually cooperates in the public interest. There are exceptions. When bubonic plague appeared among Chinese immigrants in San Francisco in 1900, strenuous efforts were made by the local authorities to hide the fact—it was bad for business; and in the 1970 cholera outbreak in the Middle East and Africa there were charges that cases were unreported, presumably because the epidemic was bad for tourism. But statistical reports give us complete confidence that polio has almost disappeared from the United States, that malaria is coming in from overseas, and that diphtheria is kicking up again in areas where immunization of children has been neglected. Today when sporadic cases of bubonic plague appear, as they have been doing in New Mexico, or when a few people come down with botulism, as happened not long ago in Illinois, they are unlikely to go un-recognized or unreported.

The VD problem has always been and still is more like plague among the San Francisco Chinese in 1900 and cholera in Africa, and for reasons more complex and devious. An aroma still clings to VD which, though a long way from being the same, yet brooks comparison with that which emanated from leprosy in the Middle Ages. As the smog of today's cities chokes up the air passages of sensitive people, so does this stink of VD clog the channels of statistical communication.

For one thing there is an indeterminate number, presumably relatively small, of cases falsely reported as positive, especially for gonorrhea: instances reported without adequate diagnostic tests among sexual partners or assumed partners of known cases, or on the basis of clinical or technical errors. There is probably a good deal of gratuitous assumption of gonorrhea among pros-titutes and female prisoners. But the total of such false positives is offset many times over by failure to report confirmed cases of both gonorrhea and syphilis. On top of this we have people with VD who go untreated or are treated by quacks, as well as pa-tients, especially women with gonorrhea, whose illness is simply not detected. Most observers hold that failure to report known cases is the largest source of error in the statistics, and it is this error that the United States authorities have attempted to mea-sure. The nonreporters are, of course, private physicians protect-ing their patients against disclosure of what is treated by society as a crime.

Two reports have appeared in the *Journal of the American Medical Association,* one in 1963 and another in 1970, which un-dertook to measure the extent of underreporting of VD by pri-vate physicians. Both were made by the American Social Health Association, the first in cooperation with the A.M.A. and other medical groups, the second with the VD branch of the U.S. Public Health Service. In the earlier study (Curtis, 1963) we read that the reporting problem was made worse by the introduction of penicillin, which shifted much of the treatment from clinics to private physicians because of its simplicity. A questionnaire had been sent to 184,500 physicians, of whom 70 per cent, or 131,-245, replied. Of the total, 45,016, or 34 per cent, acknowledged that they had treated syphilis or gonorrhea during the three-month period April 1 through June 30, 1962. The following figures give the story of reporting as it was stated by these doctors:

	NUMBER OF PHYSICIANS	NUMBER OF PATIENTS	PER CENT REPORTED
Early infectious syphilis	7,082	13,930	11.3
Late syphilis	14,949	34,069	37.5
Gonorrhea	37,335	156,515	10.8

The second study was parallel with the first in covering the same three months of a later year, 1968. It was based on a somewhat improved questionnaire and included an attempt to allow for the physicians who *did not* respond. Corrected estimates of the percentage of reporting physicians were based on the total number of cases that had been reported to the public health authorities by private physicians during the whole year 1968. At the same time the figures from the earlier report were reviewed and a similar set of corrected estimates arrived at. We need give only these estimates for the two periods, repeating the last column of the table above (see table on page 232).

These estimates suggest that reporting was a little more complete in 1968 than in 1962. Taking the "projected" percentages as more nearly correct, reporting of infectious syphilis improved from something like 1 case in 12 to 1 case in 8, and of gonorrhea from 1 in 13 to 1 in 9. Official United States figures indicate that most VD reporting comes from public clinics; in 1969, more

PER CENT REPORTED

	1968		1962	
	FROM THE RETURNS	PRO-JECTED	FROM THE RETURNS	PRO-JECTED
Infectious syphilis	18.7	12.0	11.3	8.1
Other syphilis	51.2	33.1	37.5	26.9
Gonorrhea	16.9	10.9	10.8	7.7

than 65 per cent of cases of primary and secondary syphilis were public clinic cases. Although VD is now widespread among all classes of the population, there is a good deal of evidence that the mass of both syphilis and gonorrhea is still found among the poor, in ghetto and inner-city slums. It is from such areas that public clinics draw most of their patients. All such cases are assumed to be reported, but what proportion of the actual VD in these areas is never seen in the clinics? These are the populations most subject to ignorance of VD, and the clinic facilities are both inadequate and often unattractive. Whether this part of what the Chief of VD at the U.S. Center for Disease Control in Atlanta, Dr. William J. Brown, speaks of as the VD "iceberg" is greater or less than the group seen but unreported by private physicians is not known. It is obvious that our efforts to measure the error in reporting VD amount to little more than guesswork.

But let us do the best we can. The first thing to look at is the trend of VD in this country and elsewhere in so far as we can make it out. Our information on this score is all recent. Mortality statistics began to be published in the United States only in 1900, and included deaths from syphilis. Figures for illness as well as for death were published earlier for members of the U.S. Army as well as for military groups in other countries; but reporting of syphilis as illness in the civilian population of the United States began consistently only after Surgeon General

Parran's campaign was under way, in the year 1940–41. So our first national figures for syphilis and other venereal diseases are hardly thirty years old as I write.

Official United States statistics made available by the VD branch of the Center for Disease Control, U.S. Public Health Service, in early November, 1970, selected and summarized, tell us that between fiscal 1941 and 1970:

1. Primary and secondary (infectious) syphilis rates per 100,-000 nonmilitary persons rose from 51.7 to a peak in 1947 of 75.6 and then fell steadily to 3.8 in 1957. After that the curve rose again, reaching 12.3 in 1965, whereafter it fell off to 9.3 in 1969 and rose again to 10.0 in 1970. The total number of reported cases of primary and secondary syphilis for fiscal 1969 was 18,679 and for 1970 was 20,186. The official estimate of actual cases of primary and secondary syphilis in fiscal 1970 was 75,000, about 3.6 times the number reported. Taking into account the unknown as well as the known errors, the true factor may be ten or more. A somewhat lower correction may apply to the number of cases of syphilis reported in "all stages" including "stage of syphilis not stated." This rate has tended to fall from a peak of 575,593 in 1943 to 87,934 in 1970.

2. Comparable figures for gonorrhea show a rise in rate from 146.7 in 1941 to 284.2 in 1947, then a steady decline to 129.3 in 1958 followed by an uninterrupted rise to 245.9 in 1969 and 285.2 in 1970. The number of cases reported in 1969 was 494,-227, an all-time high figure which went even higher in 1970, to 573,200. These figures may be subject to considerably more than a tenfold correction, although again the official estimate assumes a factor of only about 3.5.

3. The rates for late syphilis (including late latent syphilis) and congenital syphilis have been falling steadily; but there were 49,537 of the former and 1903 cases of congenital syphilis reported in 1970. These figures were included within the "all stages" total given in paragraph 1. It may be taken as a portent that within the declining total of cases of congenital syphilis

those reported at 0–1 years of age have *risen* from 180 in 1957 to 300 in 1970, representing percentages of the total number of cases of congenital syphilis of 3.3 and 15.8, respectively. The declining total is found in the cases five years old and older; most new cases are adults. But it is still doubtful that there has been a real increase: the *rate* of congenital syphilis under one year of age per 10,000 live births rose from 1957 to 1965 but has since leveled off; so that the increased *total* in later years seems to reflect a rising birth rate rather than a rising rate of congenital syphilis itself.

4. The number of deaths attributed to syphilis fell steadily from 14,064 in 1940 to 2193 in 1966 and then rose to 2381 in 1967. In 1968 and 1969 there have been fewer deaths. The mortality is more than twice as high among nonwhites as among whites. The document from which this information comes remarks that "since deaths from syphilis represent casefinding and treatment failures, mortality due to syphilis may be considered an inverse measure of the success of the syphilis control program." The statement implies that although the control program has been getting better, it is still scandalously short of being good. Remember that even when it goes entirely untreated, syphilis is infrequently fatal, and that treatment can arrest its progress and prevent death at any stage before the fatal accident takes place. Nevertheless the most recent data I have seen, issued by the U.S. Public Health Service in December, 1969, list only tuberculosis among reportable infectious diseases as exceeding syphilis in mortality, the former with 6910 deaths in 1967 as compared with the 2381 for syphilis. During the same year, however, there were 55,417 deaths recorded as due to pneumonia (not a reportable disease), while 19,700 deaths in the United States were associated with the Hong Kong influenza epidemic of the winter of 1968–1969.

Official United States statistics for fiscal 1969 showed the highest incidence of both gonorrhea and early syphilis in the most populous areas, especially the big cities, and in the southern states (see Notes). For primary and secondary syphilis the states and territories showing the highest levels were the entire east-west belt of southern states except California (the only one somewhat below the average), plus New York, Maryland, and Illinois. For gonorrhea the above-average rates applied to California, Missouri, Arkansas, Tennessee, and Virginia as well as to the southernmost states; but Arizona, New Mexico, Oklahoma, Louisiana, Alabama, and North Carolina had rates somewhat lower than the national average. The Canal Zone and the Virgin Islands showed high rates for both diseases; Puerto Rico had a low rate for gonorrhea but a very high one for early syphilis, while the opposite was true for Alaska. Some of these differences may reflect different patterns of reporting and different availability of clinical facilities; but a detailed sociological-medical study would be needed to explain them and would probably be rewarding.

A similar point is illustrated by the most recent rates (issued under date of August, 1970) for a sampling of our largest cities, which are all high but have curious variations:

RATES PER 100,000 FOR JANUARY–MARCH 1970

	PRIMARY AND SECONDARY SYPHILIS	GONORRHEA
Boston	32.7	708.0
Newark	65.2	1505.1
New York	41.6	401.3
Philadelphia	8.6	480.8
Baltimore	36.2	1074.9
Washington, D.C.	54.6	1571.4
Atlanta	64.5	2359.1
Chicago	24.1	1179.6
Cleveland	19.4	1219.4
St. Louis	19.9	987.7
Los Angeles	13.0	633.1
San Francisco	47.5	1910.5

Another pattern for the United States, relating both to early infectious syphilis and to gonorrhea, is the distribution of new cases by age, sex, and skin color. Divided into the four groups, white and non-white for both male and female, and distributed by age, we find the incidence much higher for nonwhites and higher for males, with the curve beginning below age 10 and reaching peak incidence in the age group 20–24, but continuing well beyond age 50. The high rates for nonwhites are doubtless determined by economic rather than by racial factors, with their roots, as I said before, in the relative inaccessibility or inadequacy of clinics, the lack of VD education (as well as other kinds) and other offshoots of poverty. The data show clearly that although both absolute numbers and rates have been advancing more slowly among nonwhites for gonorrhea and actually going down for syphilis, the great bulk of both diseases is still found in this portion of the population. Sex differences are more marked for gonorrhea than for syphilis, as we would expect from the diagnostic problem in women; yet curiously enough, while the ratio of male to female at all ages among reported cases for the calendar year 1969 was approximately 3:1 for gonorrhea, it was still as high as 1.9:1 for primary and secondary syphilis.

A curious inference can be drawn from the most recent statistics which is contrary to widespread belief: the rising incidence of VD in the United States does *not* seem to be more marked among the younger age groups than the others. An increasing incidence of VD among teen-agers in Sweden was shown by a Swedish study in which careful mapping of annual case rates of gonorrhea by age group from 1916 to 1959 resulted in roughly but acceptably parallel curves for all groups, with similar peaks and valleys, except for the age group 15–19, in which a rise unmistakably greater than that in the other age groups appeared after World War II. But United States figures show no such trend. Figures given in a U.S. Public Health Service document dated August, 1970, for the calendar years 1956 and 1966–1969,

with case rates per 100,000 by age groups, show no age differences for gonorrhea in the ratios of the lowest year (1956) to the
highest (1969); while for primary and secondary syphilis the
highest ratios—that is, the most marked increases—appear in
the age group 30–39. In fact, the increase in the 40–49 age
group has been greater than those in either the 20–24 or the
15–19 group. Increases appear in all the groups, but these statistics lend no support to the idea that young people can be given
special responsibility for today's VD problem.

But although neither the peak incidence nor the highest increases in rates of VD are found among teen-agers, there is nevertheless a scandalous amount of VD among them and among
children as well. In a report from the Los Angeles City Health
Department in 1965, of one thousand case histories of males
with gonorrhea aged 15 to 60, all from the poorer part of the
city population, the *average* age of first sexual intercourse was
said to be 13, and more than half of the group had contracted
gonorrhea for the first time by age 16. Boston claims a 6-year-
old boy thought to be the youngest male with sexually acquired
gonorrhea ever reported in the literature. But as we have
seen before, gonorrheal vulvovaginitis in young girls, now regarded as caused mainly by sexual molestation by older male
partners, reaches down to even more tender years. In recent reports, gonococcal *arthritis*—a late symptom—has been found in
little girls aged as young as 2! and in a boy of 7.

At the other end of the scale is a report dated 1968 of early
infectious syphilis in patients aged over 60. Dr. Willcox, when I
saw him in London in April, 1970, told me of a reported chancre
in an 81-year-old man; and one of my hosts soon afterward at
the Fournier Institute in Paris, as little astonished by such an
event as one would expect a Parisian to be, countered with
mention of a similar record in a 91-year-old!

As I said at the beginning of this chapter, my hope of present-
ing a reasonably accurate summary of the world incidence of
VD was scotched by Dr. Guthe's authoritative comments. I

thought something useful might come out of comparing national figures with the corresponding practices: has any country been able to stem the tide of VD? The limited comparison we can make of the three countries with good statistics does not lead us very close to an answer to such a question. Denmark had a considerably better record than Poland or the United States for syphilis (in 1967), but was just about as bad as the others for gonorrhea. The simplest way of putting the essential facts of this matter is that so far as we can tell, all developed countries—the Soviet Union may be excepted for the moment—have serious VD problems. As nearly as one can tell, the United States is close to the bottom of the heap; our corrected figures would make our record much blacker than that of either Denmark or Poland. But for other countries we simply do not know. All that can be said with certainty is that the record of the United States is certainly nothing to be complacent about.

Something can still be gained, I think, by certain other comparisons, even though we may be treading on thin statistical ice in the effort to make them. There is some information worth looking into on VD in newly developing countries, especially of Africa; and a few words can be said about Greenland. Three Communist countries—the Soviet Union, China, and Cuba—are worth looking at separately.

Sketchy information for some of the tropical African countries comes from a paper by Dr. Guthe dated 1961, and gives curves for gonorrhea and syphilis that begin in 1946 or later and end in 1957 or 1959. In the careful language of the report, the pattern for this region is described as "somewhat different" from that of most other countries:

> There is no indication of a downward trend in syphilis, while the long-term component for gonorrhea shows a decided upward tendency.

Both in terms of trend and even more clearly in terms of actual rates, the facts are alarming, the most recent levels (per 100,000) for early syphilis ranging from more than 300 (Swaziland) to about 3000 (French West Africa, 1958, before independence), and for gonorrhea from more than 1000 (Basutoland) to some 2500 (Bechuanaland). A more recent paper by Guthe and Grab dated 1968, on control of yaws, which has been highly success-ful, gives no statistics for syphilis, but comments as follows:

> Following penicillin mass campaigns the age groups now attain-ing puberty are without the relative cross-immunity from yaws against venereal syphilis which was present in the previous genera-tion. The increasing number of susceptibles to this adult treponema-tosis may thus represent an epidemiological factor of some impor-tance to be taken into account, in conjunction with other recent ecological changes, which favour national and international spread of venereal syphilis.

The nature of the "other recent ecological changes"—and the word is surely used here in the limited sense of relations be-tween *human beings* and their environment—may be suggested by reports going back to 1952 and 1953 of an "epidemic" of syphilis among the Bantu of South Africa as they had migrated during the preceding forty years into the country's newly estab-lished industry, where they met social and economic problems "that fall largely outside the concern of existing health services." The notorious doctrine of *apartheid* has become widely known since that time.

In conversation with me in 1970, Dr. Guthe went much fur-ther than the 1968 statement. In areas from which yaws and bejel have been cleared through WHO efforts, he said, including Bosnia (Yugoslavia) as well as parts of Africa and elsewhere, syphilis is currently appearing and increasing. The prediction that this would happen has come true.

A group of papers on Greenland all dated 1965 indicated ex-tensive VD among Eskimos there: 40 per cent of both males and females had had gonorrhea on more than three occasions; a quarter of the unmarried population had been infected during the preceding six months. Of 52 young women aged 16 to 19, only 5 had not had gonorrhea.

Let us see now what can be said of VD in the Soviet Union and China, which together account for something like one-quarter of the population of the earth. I have no very recent figures for the Soviet Union, but it is worth while to give what is available. There is a WHO report, prepared by a traveling seminar of twenty-two physicians from nineteen countries who visited Moscow, Leningrad, Kharkov, Kiev, and the Uzbek S.S.R. under the leadership of the British venereologist R. R. Willcox. The report is dated 1964. The statistical material in this report is summarized as follows, using again rates per 100,000 of population:

	1913	1950	1960
Syphilis (active)		24.6	1.4
towns	180.3		
villages	53.7		
Gonorrhea		81.6	57.2
towns	126.2		
villages	13.7		

The report mentions that the early figures, for Czarist Russia, are doubtless low because of much unregistered VD treated in private practice, and points up the evident deficiency of gonorrhea control as shown not only by the figures but by the overall ratio of males to females (3.5:1) which suggests that much gonorrhea in women was undiagnosed.

Nor can we tell from these figures whether there has been a rise in VD in recent years, as has occurred in other advanced countries. If the 1960 figures are compared with the low figures for Western countries, the record of the Soviet Union would be no more than average for both diseases. But if these levels have been maintained, the Soviet Union would be in the lead for syphilis control and only a little lower for gonorrhea.

Another index of syphilis in the U.S.S.R. is given in two reports from the Soviet literature, one cited in a WHO paper, the other in a German report. Both give results of tests for antibodies of the reagin (Wassermann) type, the first in 1,560,000 pregnant women tested in the U.S.S.R. between 1958 and 1968, the second for the general population between 1955 and 1963. In the first set the figure given is 0.0013 per cent, the lowest by far in a tabulation including, for the same period, in increasing order, Denmark (0.01–0.08), England and Wales (0.08–0.43), France (0.4–0.5), Norway (0.78) and the U.S.A. (0.8–1.2). The second Soviet figure, for the general population, is 0.0032 to 0.02 per cent. Some figures for positive blood tests among national populations, given in the WHO report, may be compared: in West Germany, 1957–1963, estimated as 0.20; in Switzerland for 1963, 0.04 among 95,000 blood donors; and in France for 1958, 1960, and 1963, 0.30. Again the Soviet percentages are the lowest of the lot. The Willcox committee report, beyond making it evident that syphilis has not been abolished in the Soviet Union, emphasizes gonorrhea:

> The opinion has been expressed that in the world as a whole the methods so far available have failed to control gonorrhea and that new techniques (for example, immunization, if that can be achieved) are required.

Reports on clinical aspects of both syphilis and gonorrhea continue to appear in the Soviet technical literature. This fact supports the general impression to be drawn from what I have said —namely, that the U.S.S.R. may now be somewhat, perhaps considerably, ahead of the rest of us in VD control, but has not yet come close to abolishing either disease.

As for China, we have, of course, no WHO data at all. But there is information available, including some statistical data for syphilis. The testimony of several observers seems to me tantalizing.

Thanks especially to Buret, and in spite of Astruc (or if we accept Astruc's information and merely reject his interpretation of it), it appears that all the commoner forms of VD existed in China from very ancient times. There is every reason to believe that syphilis and gonorrhea flourished there before the Revolution, probably especially in the coastal cities, where prostitution was rife, but also in the interior—as may be judged, for instance, from casual references in William Hinton's story of a Chinese village, *Fanshen*. But we are told by two independent Western observers, Edgar Snow and Felix Greene, that by 1957–1960 or so VD had been virtually conquered in China. Both Snow and Greene tell us of an American doctor born in Buffalo of Syrian descent, Dr. George Hatem, who has lived permanently in China since the 1930s, and who has apparently been largely responsible for the campaign there to eradicate VD. Snow says that Dr. Hatem, whose Chinese name is Ma Hai-teh, and who had been chief of the Institute of Venereology and Skin Diseases in Peking, occupied this post "during a successful national war against syphilis and gonorrhea"—but, with that campaign presumably finished, thereafter became a deputy director and concentrated on skin diseases and malaria. The war against VD, Snow says, began soon after the Revolution in 1949. The details of the campaign must wait until later. But Snow tells us:

> Within two years most of urban China was cleansed of the chief carriers. Work was extended to the rural towns and then to the whole country.

Felix Greene adds some details:

> Perhaps one of the most spectacular public health victories achieved by the new regime has been the virtual wiping out of venereal disease. I visited, in all, ten hospitals in China—city and country, old and new. In each one I asked about the incidence of syphilis. In each it drew a similar response: "None for two years," "None for a long time," etc. Wassermann tests are required from both partners before a marriage certificate is granted.

Greene met Dr. Ma and speaks of him cordially:

. . . but it was from others that I learned about Dr. Ma's remarkable achievements, and these were confirmed from various sources. It appears that in the past five years [up to 1960 or 1961] only four fresh cases of syphilis have been diagnosed in Peking, a city of four million people. Two of the four cases involved a man and his wife who had come in from an outlying province. One was a baby, born to a woman previously infected, who had neglected her pregnancy blood test. Thus only one of the four represented an actual new case in Peking. . . . Most venereal disease work is now in distant areas, among the national minorities. The doctors go out to clean up localities where there still remains some infection—and to obtain specimens for slides at medical schools. At the Research Institute in Peking, most graduates during the past five years have never seen an active case of syphilis or gonorrhea. Dr. Ma reported that in his last three trips to Inner Mongolia, which used to be a sinkhole of venereal disease, he had not found a single case.

More recently an English surgeon, Dr. Joshua S. Horn, has written of his fifteen years' experience as a doctor in China (1969), with a chapter on "the conquest of syphilis." Dr. Horn is avowedly partisan to the Chinese cause. Perhaps his medical training compensates in part for a lack of the neutrality or impartiality to which the two journalists, Edgar Snow and Felix Greene, aspire. It is, of course, unavoidable that anything written about China today is sure to provoke a charge of bias on one side or the other. Dr. Horn gives evidence that he knows what he is talking about and that he saw most of what he describes with his own eyes. His chapter, nevertheless, has the defect of concentrating on syphilis at the expense of gonorrhea, which he mentions principally in order to point up how great a problem it is in other countries. I counted it an additional defect that Dr. Horn unhesitatingly accepts a corollary of the Columbian story, evidently because it fits his preconceptions in a curious reversal of what I have suggested may have been the basis of the European fallacy. Horn says:

> Until 1504, venereal disease was unknown in China, and this was not because it had not yet been correctly diagnosed, for at that time Chinese Traditional Medicine [capitalized thus in the origi-

nal] was already well advanced and hundreds of diseases had been accurately described in manuscripts which are still extant.

In that year, the old colonialists introduced syphilis into Canton and it soon spread widely throughout the whole land.

Dr. Horn speaks of his "friend Dr. Ma Hai-teh," and credits him with much of the material he presents. He states categorically that "active venereal disease [in the context, syphilis] has been completely eradicated from most areas and completely controlled throughout China." He adds this comment:

> The criteria for community cure were strict. They included the finding and treatment of all existing cases, a total absence of new cases appearing in the community, disappearance of congenital syphilis in new-born babies, and normal pregnancies and pregnancy outcomes in previously treated mothers. When these criteria had been fulfilled and maintained for five years, the community was considered to be cured.

Dr. Horn includes the following statistical information:

> In Peking it is impossible to find active syphilitic lesions to demonstrate to medical students. A generation of doctors is growing up in China with no direct experience of syphilis but this is of little consequence for the disease will never return.
>
> At a conference held in the Research Institute of Dermatology and Venereal Disease of the Chinese Academy of Medical Sciences in January 1956, specialists from eight major cities reported that a total of only twenty-eight cases of infectious syphilis had been discovered in their areas in the four years 1952–55. An investigation of infectious syphilis in seven major cities between 1960 and 1964 showed that by the end of this period, the early syphilis rate was less than twenty cases per hundred million of population per year [sic]; that is, it had very nearly reached the point of extinction.
>
> In the National Minority areas, especially those where the syphilis rate had been highest, a striking fall occurred in the ten years between 1951 and 1960. In the Wulatechien Banner of Inner Mongolia, where the syphilis rate had been nearly fifty per cent in 1952, not a single case of infectious syphilis was found among 3,158 persons examined at random in 1962. In the Jerimu Banner of the Djarod League, which had shown a sero-positivity rate of thirty-five per cent in 1952, ninety-seven per cent of the whole pop-

ulation was tested for syphilis and not a single new, infectious or congenital case was found.

The meager statistical information I have been able to gather about Cuba comes from a report by an American physician living in Hawaii, Dr. Willis P. Butler, who has been to Cuba and written about its medicine and public health. His statistics are taken from *Metas Directrices*, MINISAP 1968–1970 (p. 28), and give the rates for 1967 per 100,000 population, for syphilis of 12.9 and for gonorrhea of 4.5. Presumably new cases are implied, but we are not told whether the first figure refers to early syphilis or all stages; nor do I have earlier figures for comparison, although there is reason to believe that the prerevolutionary levels were high. Let us compare these rates with those given for the same year (1967) by WHO for the two countries for which, following Dr. Guthe, little or no correction is required:

CASES PER 100,000 POPULATION, 1967

	SYPHILIS	GONORRHEA
Cuba	12.9	4.5
Denmark	6.5	179.0
Poland	40.2	145.1

For Denmark and Poland the rates in the first column are for early syphilis. If the same is true of the Cuban figure, it is relatively high and calls for no comment until more information is available. But the gonorrhea rate for Cuba is not merely much lower than those for the two other countries; it is also lower than the *uncorrected* 1967 rates for any country in the WHO ambit—low enough, if true, to be phenomenal. Since Cuba is a UN member, perhaps a WHO team study made there like the one in the U.S.S.R. would tell us whether or not something is happening ninety miles from our shores that we ought to know about.

I will have more to say about VD control in Communist countries in Chapter 23. Considering Poland, it is clear that they have not all been successful in their control efforts.

The minor venereal diseases have declined sharply in the United States since the war years. Rates for 1969, the lowest on record up to that time, were, for chancroid, 0.5, for granuloma, 0.1, and for LGV, 0.3 (per 100,000 of population). These diseases are still prevalent in undeveloped countries. Willcox reported as examples in 1967 that of 1000 VD patients in East Africa there were 99 with chancroid, and in a later paper that 164 cases of LGV had been reported in Jamaica in 1965 together with 163 of granuloma and 75 of chancroid. But in developed countries, including, in addition to those of Europe, New Zealand, Czechoslovakia, and the Soviet Union (and doubtless others for which I have no figures), the minor venereal diseases appear to have become rare.

PART IV

CONTROL: PAST, PRESENT, FUTURE

☙ 19 ☙

Before Penicillin: Futility

WE THINK of "control" of infectious diseases at several levels. In the United States, cholera, smallpox, yellow fever, and epidemic typhus fever no longer exist at all, although they are still present elsewhere in the world. Polio and typhoid fever, bubonic plague and diphtheria, all continue in this country, but at varying low levels. Compared with their depredations in the past, they are effectively under control. The term does not imply that efforts to keep them so can be relaxed or abandoned; on the contrary, it is fully recognized that any of them can come back as soon as carelessness creeps in. Nor is this merely an abstract principle, as recent outbreaks of cholera in southern Russia, the Middle East, and Africa, and of diphtheria in Texas, remind us.

Control, then, does not necessarily mean elimination of a disease, even though elimination may remain as the ultimate goal. The control of VD would not necessarily entail disappearance of the last instance of infection. It might call for reduction down to very low levels of prevalence with effective surveillance of the few remaining patients with gonorrhea and infectious syphilis, much as typhoid carriers have been kept under observation since epidemics were controlled by purification of drinking water. Today when typhoid fever shows itself, it is always as a small outbreak caused by contamination of food by a carrier. We might set our sights provisionally at a similar level of VD control.

Effective control measures for infectious diseases fall generally into two groups: sanitation and immunization. Sanitation—meaning, broadly, destruction of the agent of the disease in the environment—is the means used against cholera, yellow fever, typhus fever, typhoid fever, and bubonic plague, among the examples already mentioned. Immunization has been responsible for control of the others, and for an assist in some of the members of the first group. Sanitation is the more positive of the two measures where it can be applied. It eliminates the microbe or virus before it can reach its human host. Immunization, apart from its accessory role in cholera, typhus and typhoid fever, and plague—all microbic diseases—is most dependable in virus diseases—smallpox, yellow fever, and polio—or in the few diseases due principally to bacterial toxins, of which diphtheria is the single example in our group. Yellow fever actually belongs equally in the sanitation and immunization categories. In more developed parts of the world it is spread by easily controlled mosquitoes, and sanitation—in this instance, elimination of the mosquito—is therefore the mainstay of control. In tropical forests and areas adjacent to them, other mosquitoes, much more difficult to deal with, carry the disease; and for control in such places a first-rate vaccine is available.

Vaccines for microbic diseases not due primarily to toxins tend to be second-rate: useful, but far short of absolute in protective value. Venereal diseases fall into this group. So far we have no vaccines against them at all; and as we will see, it is unlikely that vaccines can ever have the degree of effectiveness against them that they have against virus diseases or those due primarily to toxins (a group which includes tetanus as well as diphtheria). Sanitation is simply not available for control of venereal diseases: their agents pass directly from person to person, and are not in the environment long enough to give us any chance of scotching them there.

A third means for control of infectious disease is effective treatment, which, in the absence of the other two, has been the basis of modern efforts to control VD. Treatment has worked well for control of the nonvenereal treponematoses, but it obviously has not worked with VD. This is true despite the fact that gonorrhea has been, and syphilis still is, easily curable; both, in fact, notwithstanding all the exceptions of which I have already spoken, are among the most easily cured of all infectious diseases.

I think this point can't be emphasized too often or too strongly: VD can be cured. This is still true of gonorrhea as well as of syphilis, in spite of the recalcitrance of the gonococcus. If a given dose of penicillin doesn't work, a larger dose usually will; and in the individual case there are always alternative drugs. I emphasize this point to make it clear that failure of control is not simply failure of treatment. Anyone who has any of the venereal diseases can get rid of it. Doing so at the earliest moment, before the infection is passed on to others, is an essential ingredient of control. If we could find a way to get every person with early infectious VD into a treatment center before he or she could have passed the disease on to somebody else, we would have the problem cleaned up just like that. But it was, perhaps, precisely because we thought this would be easy, back in the late 1940s, that we failed.

Let us take one more look at history.

The story of attempts to control venereal diseases can begin only as their venereal nature came to be recognized; and as we have seen, this recognition was a gradual, stumbling, two-steps-forward-and-one-step-backward process down to modern times, forming one strand of the tangled web of ideas about contagion. As the particular web of contagion became disentangled, which happened only at the beginning of the twentieth century, we were able to start effective machinery for control of diseases *other than* VD; but the VD problem seemed to remain in a separate snarl.

Before the advent of penicillin it was difficult to think of controlling VD by treatment, although Surgeon General Parran did think in such terms, the sulfonamide drugs having added a means of approaching gonorrhea to the use of arsphenamines for syphilis. But penicillin introduced a prospective means into the control scheme so strikingly new that it seemed to change the whole picture. There was also, at the same time, the historical dividing line of World War II. Accordingly the period before the war and before penicillin is a separate chapter. This early period, as we look back at it now, is one in which we could hardly have hoped for success in VD control.

The early history of control measures resolves itself into two lines of endeavor, intertwining into the snarl I have mentioned; we must do our best to disentangle them. The first is made up of attempts to control prostitution, which was recognized from very early times as a major source of venereal infection, as it still is. The second consists of efforts at VD control by various local, national, and international bodies, culminating in the United States in the efforts spearheaded by Dr. Parran as the pre-penicillin era closed.

A French doctor, E. Lancereaux, in a two-volume *Treatise on Syphilis* published in 1869, gives us details of early attempts to control prostitution. He says that in ancient Rome, with its "unbridled libertinism," nothing was done "to prevent the effects of debauchery," there being concern only "to watch over the cleanliness and dress of prostitutes, and over the luxurious and comfortable fitting up of the privileged houses." But by the time of the emperor Constantine, in the early fourth century, there were introduced harsh, punitive, or "draconic" measures to restrict prostitution, including confiscation of furniture, clothing, and houses, whipping, and banishment. These measures were continued under Charlemagne (eighth to ninth century) but, evidently proving ineffectual, were abandoned during the four following

centuries "despite the greatest immorality." From the time of
Louis IX (Saint Louis), in the thirteenth century, who saw the
failure of an attempt to prohibit prostitution, efforts were made
to tolerate and regulate the practice. Since that time,

> special neighborhoods have been allotted to prostitutes. Avignon,
> Toulouse, and many other towns had, like Paris, Venice, and Lon-
> don, their prostitution districts and special laws in reference to
> prostitutes.

Astruc quotes from the Rules and Ordinances of the Stews of
Southwark in London of about 1430, which mention the occurrence of VD among the women (see the first paragraph in Figure 1).

At the time of the fifteenth-century epidemic—to continue
Lancereaux's account—

> The sequestration of syphilitics was the law of that period. The rich
> were compelled to remain in their houses, the poor were driven
> away and threatened with death, and abandoned even by the phy-
> sicians, who felt themselves unable to combat the disease. . . .

A severe measure was adopted at Strasbourg in 1495 and sanc-
tioned by the Parliament of Paris on March 6, 1496, which ban-
ished all foreigners affected with the great pox. James IV of
Scotland, in 1497, also ruled that syphilitics must leave Edinburgh or be branded on the cheek with a hot iron.

In the same year of the Southwark ordinances, 1430, Lancereaux tells us, regulations were also in force in London affecting
men who frequented licensed houses of prostitution; and at
some unspecified but still early date similar measures seem to
have been applied in Hamburg. But although suggestions of
medical or sanitary regulations of such houses date in Paris from
as early as 1714, the same author gives them more explicitly as
beginning half a century later:

> In 1762, Aulas required that the persons who kept tolerated houses
> should be made responsible for the sanitary condition of their
> women, and that all, without exception, should be subjected to

constant visits made by surgeons attached to the police and under
the direction of a head-surgeon. Gardane in 1770, and Bourru in
1771, each expressed a wish for the establishment of public offices,
or of special hospitals, for the treatment of venereal diseases.

It was during this period, according to Dickson Wright
(Chapter 13) that Catherine the Great of Russia established the
first VD hospital, a fifty-bed institution in St. Petersburg.

We learn from Parran that in Denmark as early as 1788 an attempt was made to provide *free* medical service for VD. He
quotes this regulation issued by the diocese of Aarhus:

> Every person, rich or poor, suffering from a venereal disease
> should receive free medical advice, free medicine, together with
> free nursing when infirmaries or premises were equipped for the pa-
> tient's treatment; that patients must agree to take treatment; that
> those who failed to do so should be punished; that priests should
> notify persons known or suspected of being infected and that ex-
> penses should be defrayed by the whole diocese.

But in the same year, Parran continues, another document states
that an attempt to implement this regulation was met with this
response:

> We were faced by more than a hundred men, armed with heavy
> flails, foaming with rage and threatening us; if we did not leave
> their women and children alone, they told us, they would do viol-
> ence to us. So we had to content ourselves with those who submit-
> ted to the treatment of their own free will. *In this way the disease
> will never be eradicated.*

So the regulation was amended to provide that the first efforts
were to be made by means of "gentleness and reasoning," but—
quoting from the same document:

> *If the means be not sufficient, however, the diocesan governor is to
> provide the required police or military protection for those who
> perform the visitation.* [Italics in original]

Parran gives the Danes credit for sweet reasonableness. Even so,
he says, the Danish penal law as late as 1866

provided that those who "practice sexual intercourse, knowing or supposing themselves to be infected, may be punished by imprisonment, even with hard labor."

The first dispensary for prostitutes seems to have been established (in Paris) no earlier than 1802, and was reorganized in 1811, leading, according to Lancereaux, to benefits such that similar centers were set up in other French cities. But the major emphasis was on women, and—as we need not doubt—the measures were nearly always punitive, often severely so. Around this time Belgium initiated a system in which

> inspection of prostitutes, of servant-women, and of matrons, was made there twice a week and entrusted to a controlling inspector for the purpose of preventing the propagation of syphilis in the army.

Each soldier with VD was required to go to the dispensary and "point out the woman who had infected him." As a result, we are told, in 1846 only 1 soldier in 190 was syphilitic, whereas in Strasbourg the proportion was 1 in 33, and in Lyons 1 in 40, with the familiar suggestion that the actual rates were higher because of soldiers treated privately.

Lancereaux says "sanitary visits and punishment" were the means available to the "intelligent administration" of the period. Fournier is quoted from his thesis, dated 1860, as advising, for prostitutes,

> either to keep in hospital and treat every syphilitic prostitute during a time sufficiently long to ensure a cure within the limits of possibility, or, after a longer or shorter time, to place her at liberty, but to keep her under special observation. This . . . would necessitate the attendance of the woman every second or third day at a dispensary, after which, if she was found to be again affected she would be sent into hospital again.

Lancereaux adds:

> As regards workwomen and married women, there are great difficulties; but it suffices to meet the evil at its source, that is to say, in

the houses of prostitution. Moreover, punishment of the man who willingly transmits syphilis to a poor workwoman, would be a powerful adjuvant.

I am charmed by the "would be." The effects of punishment are always in the future conditional. They are still in the same place today, expected to be effective tomorrow, or if not, it is assumed to be only because not enough was applied.

Lancereaux has some advice about the handling of nursing infants and their wet nurses. He wants both of them carefully and thoroughly examined and medically certified. He traces the idea back to 1775, when

> the Faculty of Medicine of Paris proposed to impose upon accoucheurs and midwives the obligation to signalise syphilitic children, and to fasten to their arms, before giving them up to the nurses, a ticket which would show their condition as well as that of their parents. . . . [It is] advised that the state of health of soldiers' children should be ascertained before they were put out to nurse . . . [and] to subject new-born children to medical examination, either at the time of registering the birth, or two or three months later . . .

and more to similar effect.

International control measures for infectious disease generally date from the mid-nineteenth century. We have nothing but the occasional word of contemporary doctors that such measures did any appreciable good; in the beginning, at least, efforts at control over the whole field could have had little more effect than King Canute had on the sea. In these earlier years there is no reason to think that control of VD was even considered seriously among the other problems, except through a Victorian veil of affluent respectability tinged with distaste. But let us see what was attempted.

A First International Sanitary Conference, to deal mainly with cholera and plague, was called by France as early as 1851—before much was known about sanitation in any true sense. This was three years before John Snow had pointed to the Broad Street pump as the source of cholera in London—the first important landmark in modern sanitation—and before anything useful was known about the transmission of plague; so it seems unlikely that the conference could have accomplished much. But the idea of such international conferences caught on, doubtless because epidemic disease was raging in Europe's growing colonial empire; and it probably seemed a good idea to talk about the problem even if that was all that could be done. In 1907 an "Office Internationale d'Hygiène Publique" was set up as a permanent center to try to revise and enforce such international sanitary regulations as there were.

According to Theodore J. Bauer, an early director of the VD division of the U.S. Public Health Service, the whole worldwide approach to VD before World War I tended to be "identified with broad social issues rather than with health," a phrase I interpret as a euphemism for attempts at repression, or meaning little more than a polite turning away from the facts. Yet as early as 1899, and again in 1902, there were international conferences "on the prophylaxis of syphilis" in Brussels, and it is of interest that in addition to recommending "distribution of leaflets emphasizing its dangers to persons entering the armed forces" the conferees did come out in favor of free treatment for all VD patients, more than a century after the same idea had been suggested in Denmark.

The need to do something about VD must have become inescapable during World War I, but the difficulties then were greater than they are now. The new diagnostic methods were revealing the extent of gonorrhea and syphilis. Nevertheless effective treatment for gonorrhea was totally lacking, and the sustained therapy with arsenical drugs required for syphilis was clearly unsuitable for mass use by the military.

Establishment of the League of Nations brought its Health Organization into being, forerunner of today's WHO. For the first time the urgent job was begun of setting up international standards for biological products and tests, and an effort was made to bring order out of the growing confusion in treatment. At that time, every VD specialist had his own way of using the arsphenamines. The Health Organization arranged working laboratory conferences of experts in 1921, 1922, 1923, and again in 1928 and 1930. Its world-wide study of the treatment of syphilis with arsenical drugs was reported in 1934. Its greatest accomplishment in the VD field was the international Brussels Agreement of 1924, providing treatment of VD for merchant seamen in the ports of all subscribing nations, of which there were 56 by 1938. The United States, steeped at the time in "isolationism," had not been one of them—we were not a member of the League of Nations—but we have cooperated since 1938. The Brussels Agreement was revised by the WHO in 1960, but more recently the rapid growth of sea traffic, especially in Asia and Africa, seems to have outdated it again.

Certain specialized organizations cooperated with the Health Organization to help apply the Brussels Agreement. In addition to the Office Internationale d'Hygiène Publique there was the International Labor Office, which received a Nobel Peace Prize in 1969, in its fiftieth year. There is also a nongovernmental group, the International Union Against the Venereal Diseases and Treponematoses (IUVDT), which grew up between the two world wars. Founded in 1923, the IUVDT was subscribed to by nineteen countries at first and had headquarters in Paris. It has continued to function, having been reorganized after World War II. By 1953 its member countries numbered thirty-six. Its headquarters were moved to Rome, with regional offices elsewhere, including one for Europe in Copenhagen and one for the Americas in New York. This last is affiliated with the American Social Health Association, formerly the American Social Hygiene Association, which makes the problem of VD control its special province.

The early history of VD control in the United States is given authoritatively by Parran, who in fact himself *made* the first definitive history. Before his time, as he explains it, there was officially no VD in this country; the American Medical Association's first recorded address on VD was given in 1874 with apologies for bringing up so unpleasant a subject, and in Parran's own time a dinner guest whom he calls Mr. Blank admonished him for "stirring up a fuss" about syphilis and continued,

> "There may be a good deal of it as you say, but take my word, you'll find these filthy Europeans brought it over, along with communism. Now my great-great-grandfather fought on the *Constitution;* able-bodied seaman, died of his wounds after the battle with the *Guerrière.* Line comes right on down. Clean American stock. Why should my wife and daughter have to listen to nauseating details about this horrible disease and why should I shell out good tax money to take care of the reprobates who have it? Ship 'em back to Europe where they belong!"

And Parran goes on to say that

> one of the names on the list of the *Constitution's* ship's surgeons was that of great-great-grandfather Blank, who had required treatment for a particularly wicked syphilitic ulcer!

Under Parran's influence while he was Surgeon General of the U.S. Public Health Service, the National Venereal Disease Control Act was passed on May 24, 1938. Federal funds budgeted for VD control rose each year from 1939 to 1944, and after a small cut during the war continued up to a peak in 1948, at which time over-optimism, doubtless abetted by the postwar change of federal policy, cut them back. State funds continued to rise until 1951.

We can hardly do better than look to Parran for an enlightened view of the VD control problem just before the penicillin era. He wrote, in 1937, specifically of syphilis. He asserted that although there were great unsolved scientific problems,

> we know enough now to save from the consequences of the disease both its victim and the society which now is burdened by him.

He proposed a triple attack for the control of syphilis, which he summarized in these words:

First, every early case must be located, reported, its source ascertained, and all contacts followed up to find possible infection. Second, enough money, drugs, and doctors must be secured to make treatment possible for all cases; it is not in the public interest for treatment, which is our most practical means of control, to be retarded or precluded by cost. Third, both public health agencies and private physicians throughout the country must be re-aligned to form a united front and re-educated to use scientific modern methods in their joint fight against syphilis. In addition, citizens must be informed as to the means and methods required for individual and public protection.

Elaborating, Parran remarked that the early symptoms were often so subtle, or so like those of common minor illness, that the patient might dismiss them and the doctor overlook them, circumstances aggravated by the prevalence of quacks and patent medicines and the fact that the early symptoms tend to go away by themselves. Laboratory diagnostic tests are therefore indispensable; and Parran recommended

a blood test whenever and wherever physical examinations are given, as routinely as the doctor now takes pulse and blood pressure and listens to the heart action.

And so blood tests before marriage came to be universal in the United States.

Parran also asked for preservation of the confidential rights of the patient,

the name of the patient need not be reported; his initials, his date of birth, or a serial number are sufficient for purposes of record so long as he and his infected contacts continue to take treatment.

And the only suggested penalty for failure to continue with treatment is loss of "the privilege of privacy." This, remember, was in the days of arsenical drugs, when treatment usually took at least eighteen months. Parran's thesis was based on the capacity of these drugs to bring about "temporary non-infectiousness" after only a few doses, so that the chain of infection might thus be broken.

He asked for reporting to facilitate tracing of contacts, and emphasized the need for trained investigators who must be "scrupulously careful to protect the co-operative patient." And treatment "must be medically efficient for every patient, rich and poor." He went into details of costs, which were higher in 1937 than they are now despite intervening inflation. They ranged in clinics from $30 to $165 per patient, not including overhead, and were still higher for private physicians. Hence the need for public funds to assure treatment for the poor, with federal and state agencies cooperating.

And Parran closes his "Platform for Action" with appeals to physicians for improved competence in handling syphilis and greater willingness to do so, to public health officers to eschew politics, and to all these and citizens as well to

> learn to think of syphilis scientifically as a dangerous communicable disease, which it is; rather than moralistically as a punishment for sin, which it often [!] is not. Also we must learn that this is everybody's business. That everybody is endangered by the present status; that everybody pays for it, whether or not afflicted by the disease; that no one agency is big enough or clever enough to do everybody's job alone.

Dr. Parran was, to my knowledge, as forthright and free from sham as any government official, as any official doctor, has ever been, anywhere. His views have left a legacy of frankness and candor in that part of the U.S. Public Health Service which deals with VD and other communicable diseases. His program was set back by World War II but enormously facilitated by the advent of penicillin.

But it failed, and we are trying to find out why.

❧ 20 ❧

After Penicillin: Failure

D R. PARRAN SPOKE with a good deal of admiration of attempts
that had been made to control VD in the Scandinavian
countries before he started on his own campaign in the United
States. All these efforts were begun before World War II and
before penicillin. Although they have not been completely ineffectual, we know now that they have failed. Even with penicillin and with the many other advances that have been made
in the great scientific upsurge since 1945, efforts at VD control
in all these places have still failed.

The way Parran framed the problem in 1937 is still valid today, and it can hardly be doubted that if his program could
have been made fully effective, especially with the addition of
penicillin, it would have worked. Failure of VD control must
have resulted from failure to implement his plan.

The first step toward control of VD—the key step, and the
one in which we can at once see persistent and significant
failure—is to find people who have VD and to bring them in for
diagnosis and treatment. "Case-finding" is what we call it. The
major stumbling block in control is the patient who runs away,
or treats himself, or goes to quacks or inadequate doctors. The
three elements here, which are still as Parran saw them, are get-

ting the patient to go, having adequate diagnostic and treatment centers available, and teaching doctors to think of VD and to recognize it when they see it.

We will have to face later the question, why do patients run away? to the degree that the answer may not be obvious. For the moment, the fact that they do leads to the next tactic: to try to find them whether or not they want to be found, and then to try to persuade them to be treated. While "education" intended to get them to come in voluntarily limps along, and often seems to go backward instead of forward, most of the people immediately concerned with control, the public health VD people, do the best they can. In the modern period, in the United States, among civilians, the basis of the approach is persuasion, persistent but not punitive. Local exceptions occur, especially among prison or other institutional populations. Much effort is spent to avoid moralistic or puritanical methods; it is not to be expected that it often succeeds. But the purpose of the approach is to have each patient with VD lead to others: to interrogate, to persuade, to cajole.

If the initial patient comes to a VD clinic, the operation begins there at once. If his illness is reported by a physician, the public health personnel take over for the search. The people who do the tracing are nonmedical workers with special training, often nurses or social workers. An attempt is made to respect the patient's anonymity, but the results are not always convincing to suspicious patients, and in fact the attempt itself is not always successful. Other means, sometimes skillful, sometimes clumsy, are used to gain his confidence.

The search for contacts has to be made quickly, partly because people often move considerable distances in brief periods, partly in the effort to find them all before each one has been able to infect so many others that the job may become overwhelming. Dr. James K. Shafer, another former VD chief of the U.S. Public Health Service, called this fast operation "speed-zone epidemiology"; and his workers nicknamed it "peppy epi."

This was in 1954 and was especially intended for gonorrhea, in which the incubation period is usually less than six days. Dr. Shafer says,

> Consequently, the speed-zone program concentrates upon female contacts of the male gonorrhea patient within a period beginning six days before the onset of his clinical symptoms and ending at the time of his appearance in the clinic.

At that time the search was made principally by telegraph, but by 1965 the telephone was being used, all confidential information being sent, however, in code. But it is unavoidable that identification of cases cannot preserve the strict anonymity intended; it may be only in the final record that names are omitted.

Even so gonorrhea, with its short incubation period, tends to move too fast, although its rising incidence is forcing new efforts at this "cluster testing." But for a time the practice was limited to the more leisurely syphilis. And we have a new nickname, maybe with military activities again in fashion, namely "blitz." The RPR card test helps.

Sometimes the results have been spectacular. A report by R. W. Ball of South Carolina covered a five-month period beginning in January, 1964. It began with a case of primary syphilis in a man thirty-seven years old, reported by a private physician with a request for the contact investigation, for which the doctor had evidently cleared the way. This particular blitz involved 263 persons, 225 of whom were contacts. Of these contacts 207, or 92 per cent, were examined, and an additional 44 infectious cases of syphilis—primary, secondary, and early latent—were found and brought to treatment. Most of these patients lived in a single manufacturing town of 10,000-odd population, but there were named contacts in eight other states as far away as Washington. The patients ranged from an unemployed high-school dropout to prominent citizens of the community. All were white, most of them middle-class. Four were under twenty, the youngest a fifteen-year-old girl.

The average number of sex contacts per patient interviewed was five. Every patient named more than one different sexual contact. In one instance a 16-year-old girl admitted to having sex relations with 13 different men during a six-month period, six of whom were found to be infected with primary or secondary syphilis.

Contacts with no clinical signs of syphilis and with a negative blood test were given a single curative dose of benzathine penicillin as a prophylactic. A noteworthy feature of this outbreak was the active cooperation during its course of fifteen physicians and of the twenty-six patients they reported.

Another blitz was reported more recently from Alabama by W. H. Y. Smith and J. J. Hill. The rising prevalence of syphilis was beginning to get the state VD people badly scared when more cases of primary and secondary syphilis were reported in 1965 than in any of the preceding sixteen years. The "epidemic" described occurred in Talladega County, beginning in September, 1967, and reached a peak early in 1968. It involved 92 persons with infectious syphilis, an additional 801 known or suspected contacts who were given prophylactic treatment with penicillin, and 239 others examined but not treated, making a total of 1040 persons examined out of 1283 who had been named. This outbreak began with a woman twenty-nine years old who infected a man of thirty-six who, in turn, infected eight females. The authors find it

interesting to note that a 15 year old female with secondaries infected an 11 year old male with a primary. He in turn infected the 15 year old's sister who was nine years of age. This nine year old child infected an eight year old male and in addition named a total of 19 contacts. It is also interesting that the 15 year old girl named 43 contacts.

The report contains no information on the skin color or economic status of the people involved in this outbreak. But the following note, which follows the brief description of the outbreak and concludes the report, is worth giving in full:

Controlling syphilis in the free populations is much more difficult than in the confined captive group. In a southern prison of 1,076 prisoners there were found 66 primaries, 14 secondaries, and two each early latents [*sic*]. These named 209 contacts and all cases and contacts were given 2.4 million units of penicillin. In addition all the other prisoners were given 2.4 million units of penicillin and each new inmate was given 2.4 million units of penicillin. As a result not a single case of syphilis has occurred in this prison since June 1965.

That's one way to do it!

Another search with unusual if not unique aspects was reported in *The Wall Street Journal* for March 30, 1970, from the VD center in Atlanta. This incident involved a single prostitute near Los Angeles who, for one thing, had a clientele made up entirely of truck drivers and, in addition, kept a diary in which she recorded the names and "home bases" of 310 customers who had seen her from early September, 1969, to mid-February, 1970. The men's movements following their contact spread over thirty-eight states, Canada, Mexico, and Germany (to which one driver's Army reserve unit was sent). As it turned out, of 168 of these men who were found with the aid of the diary, only seven needed treatment for syphilis. Evidently the chance of contracting syphilis by a single sexual contact is sometimes small. The woman had secondary syphilis—a highly infectious stage; yet only some 4 per cent of the men examined were found to have been infected. Nor is there a suggestion that they had spread the disease further; it is noted that the wives of the married truck drivers were examined, but it is not recorded that any of them were infected. Willcox, in 1958, cited a study in which L. M. Ram interviewed 194 men infected by prostitutes in Singapore in 1950. Three-quarters of these prostitutes were known to have VD. Of these 194 men,

> 19.5 per cent exposed themselves on the average of once a month, 29 per cent twice a month, and 20.5 per cent more than twice a month. Of 154 [additional] men, *only 3 per cent were infected following the first exposure,* 15 per cent in less than ten exposures,

40 per cent so late as the fortieth exposure, and up to one hundred exposures were achieved with impunity by 33 per cent [italics added].

Willcox points out that these figures do not take into account men who may not have been aware that they had syphilis when they were questioned. Nevertheless exposure to VD does not necessarily lead to infection, and the fact ought to be entered on the credit side of the control ledger.

Something like the control method used in the southern prison, as mentioned before, but without the use of force, has been the basis of the WHO campaign of mass eradication of the treponematoses in many parts of the world. Attempts had in fact been started along these lines even in the days of arsenical drugs; but the introduction of single-dose penicillin preparations after World War II led, with the support of UNICEF, to a massive campaign. Up to 1965 it had involved 363 million people, of whom 46,117,000 active and latent cases and contacts had been treated, at a cost of $50 million. Some forty-five developing countries and areas were included, in Africa, the Americas, the Eastern Mediterranean, Europe, Southeast Asia, and the Western Pacific. As a result, original incidences such as 18 per cent of the population in parts of Indonesia (yaws) and 5 per cent in parts of Yugoslavia (bejel) were reduced to levels of the order of 0.1 per cent; while in Bosnia (Yugoslavia) complete eradication was reported.

If we could apply the "blitz" approach universally, would it work? The question is not so simple as it may seem, since all the factors in the control problem are wrapped up in it, many of them hidden, some of them no doubt still unclear to anybody. But without assuming—for the moment—anything different from what we now have, say, in the United States, except for virtually unlimited resources: if every case of infectious VD that came to notice could be given the full epidemiological shock treatment, could we expect to reverse the present trend? If we could simplify the question down to a matter of *finding every*

case of infectious VD and administering treatment sufficient to
make the case noninfectious—as I have said before in other
words—the answer would be "yes." And if we could have done
something of this kind with gonorrhea before the gonococcus
began acting up, we would certainly be in a better position than
we are today. If the Chinese and the Cubans have really done
what our meager information suggests, the key to their success
must be some such operation. We will look into this as far as we
can a little later on.

Here in the United States whatever part of the problem is
technical ought to be subject to control. Included are better diagnostic methods for gonorrhea, more easily available diagnostic and treatment facilities, and perhaps most important, better
VD education of physicians. We no longer have a journal in this
country devoted to VD; the goodly output of VD research going
on at Atlanta and in a few centers elsewhere (supported largely
through the Center for Disease Control in Atlanta) is published
for the most part in a British journal or in publications of the
WHO. Now that the specialty of dermatology has largely given
up VD, as it has done since penicillin made treatment easy (and
relatively unprofitable?), VD practice, except for local and federal public health services, has reverted to its ancient status as
an outcast.

I am under the impression that public clinics in this country
are better than private doctors in the handling of VD, which is
not to suggest that they even come close to being as good as
they might be, or that there are enough of them to meet the
needs especially of the poor. Public clinics and general hospital
outpatient services even in matters more socially acceptable
have not altogether outgrown the aroma and chill of the charity
ward. Conditions in some of them are still little better than medieval. What has been accomplished in the effort to improve
them has been offset, or more than offset, by shortages of medical and paramedical personnel and by accumulating illness especially as the average age of the population increases, and as

expanding technology introduces new diseases and aggravates old ones. In hospitals and clinics as well as in private practice, the "interesting" patient, the one who feeds the growing need of medicine as a self-styled science (or promises to help out with research grants and potential prizes) is likely to be greeted with more enthusiasm (although not always with better results) than the one with problems banal, disagreeable, and dirty. And of these last, VD is still in the position it has always had, at the bottom. Nevertheless, if you have or think you might have VD, you are still likely to do better in a public clinic than with a private doctor.

So there are factors in our failure to control VD that are due to *professional* ignorance, carelessness, lack of interest, negligence, and similar vices that public awareness and pressure might conceivably correct. To correct such things was part of Dr. Parran's objective. If we could make full use of the resources we have, we could accomplish something. But again, if we assume that Sweden, Denmark, and some other countries are better in these respects than we are—and there is reason to believe they are, although they too might be still further improved—we glimpse the idea that such failure is no more than part of the problem.

As for technical deficiencies themselves, they are a significant but probably even smaller segment of the whole difficulty. The painless vaginal chancre, and the existence in women of a mild but infectious gonorrhea, also have their counterparts among males, especially homosexuals; here it appears to be syphilis (with a rectal chancre) more than gonorrhea that is likely to go undetected. Syphilis, as I mentioned before, can be diagnosed in the primary stage if the patient suspects it and has himself examined. Untreated, it will show up later in the blood test—by which time it may, of course, have been passed on. So in part this is a problem of public education and cooperation of the patient, actual and prospective. But the difficulty in detecting gonorrhea in women is technical. Thayer and Moore reported in

1964 that the best available tests had been negative in nearly half of a group of "bona fide female contacts." Thayer and Martin subsequently improved a culture medium for the gonococcus that has come to be used all over the world. One recent paper by the Atlanta group reports that the use of this medium with cultures from several sites in the vagina and from the rectum cut the number of failures to 6–8 per cent and suggests that the figure could be reduced further by repeated tests. Studies reported in 1969 from Denmark give reason to expect that the failure rate could be reduced even further with additional technical refinements, including a combination of cultures on Thayer's medium with a fluorescent-antibody method of identifying gonococci taken directly from the patient. Meanwhile work continues on a blood test for the gonococcus. Problems of this kind can be expected to crack open if given enough of the combination of time and pressure, the latter meaning money for research.

Penicillin resistance is another technical problem. It applies up to the present only to gonorrhea and mainly to war areas, notably the American zone in Vietnam. At its worst it is not—or not yet—an insurmountable obstacle. It can be overcome by increasing penicillin dosage, with improved penicillin preparations and associated drugs, or where necessary by switching to other antibiotics. There may be a time limit for all this. If the race between the gonococcus and the chemists is to be won by our side, it may be necessary for us to stop wasting time and get to work on other aspects of the problem. I have mentioned before that a similar warning signal for syphilis may be just beyond the horizon. It may well be that the problem will not wait.

❧ 2 I ❧

The "Social Diseases"

Admittedly, then, there are technical deficiencies in VD control; but few VD experts, if any, doubt that the non-technical problems are more serious. And one of the toughest is to decide just what they are. This part of the problem is social, economic, even possibly political; but sociologists, economists, and political scientists do not concern themselves with it, and very likely ought not to. Here is the opinion of a social worker, Celia Deschin, who has had many years' experience with VD problems, much of it in cooperation with the American Social Health Association and the New York City Health Department:

> At present, the only effective prevention of VD is through changes in sexual behavior, increased understanding of the diseases, and establishment of goals that make possible postponement of premarital and extramarital sexual experimentation.

What Mrs. Deschin means in this context by "increased understanding of the diseases, and establishment of goals . . ." is not clear to me; but her intent in the passage is made quite plain in the rest of her book, which she calls *The Teenager and VD* (1969): no sexual intercourse before marriage, and no playing around afterward. Here again is a statement by a social worker from the famous Department of Venereology in St. Mary's Hospital, London, J. O'Hare, quoted from another recent popular treatment of the subject, *Venereal Diseases*, by R. S. Morton:

> The promiscuous [girls] spring from every class of society and every type of home. Lack of an intelligent and affectionate approach by the parents is a predisposing factor. Society in general, by refraining from moral sanctions, has smoothed the path which is made more attractive and brought forcibly and persistently to notice, by business interests. Films, the Press, dress and cosmetic firms all concentrate on the importance of sexual attraction. But for every girl impelled to promiscuity by these external factors a girl can be found in precisely similar circumstances who has resisted them, the individual character and psychological make-up being the final determining factor.

Dr. Morton, himself a venereologist, includes the foregoing in a chapter entitled "Venereal Diseases as a Social Problem," which is an earnest and learned statement by an evidently sober and scholarly man, who, however, seems to take conventional notions of sin completely for granted.

I discussed this question with Dr. Richard R. Willcox, the venereologist of St. Mary's, in his pleasant home close to the south bank of the Thames just west of the Hammersmith bridge. Dr. Willcox is an affable, jolly man who showed no penchant for moralizing. He said nothing to me of virginity, abstinence, unwavering monogamy, or original sin. Not that I could pin him down to anything like a prescription for VD control. He did suggest that we have failed to achieve control because we haven't wanted to achieve it, that we haven't tried hard enough, that—if I understood him correctly—we have not made as much use of the resources we have available as we could if we really wanted to control VD.

We might try to approach this question of nontechnical aspects of VD control by going back briefly to something I said in Chapter 8. We saw the theory put forward there, especially by Hackett, that syphilis may have emerged as the venereal form of treponematosis as people came together in the first cities. As they changed their way of life from nomadic and rural to settled and urban in more northern and colder climates, people needed clothing and adopted other new customs and habits which tended to block all the direct-contact routes for the exchange of spirochetes except the sexual one. And even earlier, in Chapter 6, it appeared that we might explain the great epidemic at the beginning of the sixteenth century in terms of the movement and interchange of populations associated with war and commerce and other aspects of the burgeoning Renaissance. Now let us grant to the moralists only this much: that a certain fraction of man's total sexual activity is abnormal or pathological in the sense that it would be socially destructive even apart from VD. We may then be able to put puritanism and prudery aside and find the reasons for our failure to control VD somewhere other than in the healthy sexual behavior that remains, whether Mrs. Grundy approves of it or not. It may then appear that VD developed out of the circumstances of man's progress on the earth; that what happened in the earliest times and flourished in the Renaissance has gone on happening and become more marked, more exaggerated, especially in recent times. VD is one of so many problems we face today, consequences of man's ingenuity and ruthlessness, that we can probably agree readily to accept as a sort of working hypothesis the idea that VD belongs with war, pollution, racism, starvation with abundance, and whatever else you may wish to include among the great problems of our day.

The following statement, made by Drs. Guthe and Idsöe of the WHO's VD division at a meeting in Manila in December, 1968, comes nearer than any other expert statement I have seen to expressing what I have in mind. It is phrased for a technical audience, and you must remember that the WHO has to be more concerned than you or I need be about offending Powerful People. But the message is clear enough. It needs to be studied

with a properly critical eye. I omit only some statistics at the
end which amplify the last point made; and I include the diagram referred to in the text:

> The intensity of the epidemiological processes in infections ac-
> quired by sexual activity depends to a greater extent than in any
> other group of diseases on the *balance* between the complex eco-
> logical, human and environmental forces which facilitate or restrain
> the spread of disease. We have attempted to visualize these multi-
> ple interdependent forces [Figure 11]. Their shifting aggregate
> weight may in one period drive the epidemiological pendulum in
> one direction—which facilitates spread and high incidence of
> disease—and in another period in the direction which favours con-
> trol and possible "eradication."
>
> The rising world trend in incidence of early syphilis and of gon-
> orrhoea in the last decade has occurred during a period charac-
> terized by:
>
> (i) unprecedented demographic and economic changes, tech-
> nological developments, industrialization and urbanization, move-
> ments of civilian and military personnel in all regions;
>
> (ii) psychological and social changes, permissive male and fe-
> male patterns in sexual life and new attitudes to prostitution and
> homosexuality; and
>
> (iii) medical and public health developments—particularly easily
> applied and effective antibiotic treatment in syphilis and gon-
> orrhoea, which have led to unconcern in regard to these infections
> among the public, health administrations and doctors.
>
> These developments have all contributed to increasing sexual
> activity and added to the probability of acquiring venereal in-
> fections. The economic, social and sexual emancipation which has
> taken place has particularly favoured women and it is therefore
> not surprising that there is evidence in several countries of in-
> creasing VD rates among females as compared with the situation
> a few years ago. . . .

VD tends to be concentrated in cities and to follow people's
movements; it is aggravated by war, poverty, ignorance, and
lack of public health and medical facilities. Being spread by sexual contact, it is increased as sexual intercourse increases in the
population, with promiscuity an essential factor in the process,

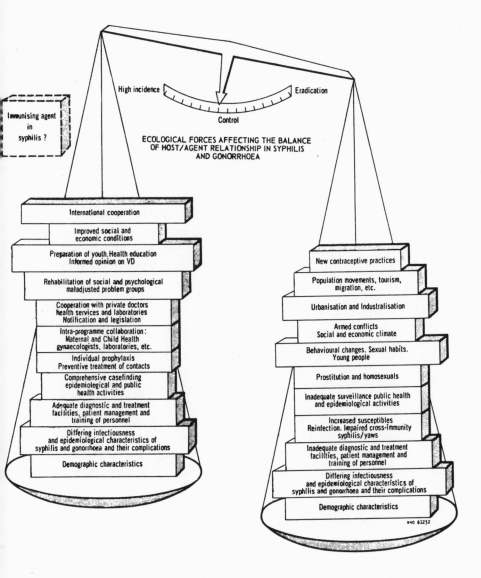

Figure 11. The Guthe-Idsöe diagram on the VD problem. (WHO 81232)

since it is the mechanism whereby the infected individual is introduced into the group. The poverty factor operates in part by encouraging ignorance, in part by limiting access to treatment facilities. It is true, although it seems to be less so than in the past, that there is more VD among the poor than among the rich. But there is plenty at all levels of society. A notion advanced by some advocates of sexual freedom seems to me as mischievous as any that come from the other side—that you can avoid VD by choosing sex partners from the apparently clean and well-dressed members of the well-heeled. The only difference between the aristocrats of today and the kings of old—as far as VD is concerned—is that today they have effective diagnosis and treatment available to them. And it is still true that such things are more available to the rich than to the poor. But the generally middle-class population concerned in the South Carolina "blitz" described in Chapter 20 seems to me enough to warn against any simple rule for the guidance of one's sex life.

After writing the preceding words I talked with Dr. Guthe in his spanking modern office on the sixth floor of the WHO building in Geneva. I have mentioned his comments on world statistics before, and some of his other remarks on technical matters find their places elsewhere in this book. I was interested in getting from him an overall view of the VD problem from his position at the center of the global situation. But while he affirmed what emerges from his chart and the words previously quoted —that VD has intrinsic social ramifications—his main emphasis seemed to me to be technical. Syphilis needs a vaccine, gonorrhea needs a blood test. And mathematical: as world population rises at an ever-increasing (exponential) rate, contacts between people, including sex contacts, rise even faster, very much faster; this is one reason for the increase in VD. Dr. Guthe is Norwegian, the model of a diplomat, suave, affable, with fluent and flawless English. He was entirely cheerful, but I was a bit gloomy as I left him; of course we must keep doing the best we can, but there is no certainty that the road we are traveling actually leads anywhere. Possibly there was a distant echo in his words of the terrible dilemmas faced by the more political center of the UN in New York.

But the whole UN, including the WHO, can do little more than serve its member states as gatherer and assembler of information, caller of and presider over meetings, mediator, referee. Its officers are likely to be observers of the great battle, not participants in it. WHO and some other specialized UN agencies can sometimes get out into the field and do something actively, as WHO has done with the nonvenereal treponematoses; but there may be frustration in being so close to such problems as war and VD and being able to do so little about them. Dr. Guthe did not say anything like this: the thoughts are mine alone. He may not even have any such ideas; but they came into my head as we talked. It occurred to me, too, that if we are to solve this problem—and by "we" I mean you and me—we may have to do it ourselves.

So let us get back to it, taking up the remaining specific social factors in the VD problem. They are, in order, sex education; the special problems of seafaring men and soldiers; prostitution and homosexuality; and the question, why do people fail to go for treatment, or run away?

On sex education, which has its own vast literature, a few words should suffice, as unequivocal as I can make them. There is no serious disagreement today that greater knowledge of VD is one of the essential elements of any control scheme, and that it must come early to do the most good. If one is to know what VD is about, one must first know what sex is about; so sex education must come even earlier. Sex education begins with anatomy, physiology, embryology, and genetics, scaled to meet the natural curiosity of children about themselves and their playmates, helped by examples with animals, growing in detail and complexity as increasing understanding permits, leading progressively to an undistorted picture of conception, embryonic and fetal development, and birth as part of the preparation of children for the stresses of puberty. That the process has the intrinsic beauty of life, but that the course of life meets problems, can become the kind of introduction to VD that might eliminate the smirking, the false modesty, the hypocrisy, which are close to the root of the whole nontechnical side of the VD problem. Somewhere along the line the questions that come up about homosexuality, as well as about contraception and abortion, must be dealt with as directly, with as little sugar-coated duplicity, as all the rest. Yes, we all know it is not easy. But the heart of the problem of sex education is not with the children but with the adults around them. The role of adults in sex education ought to be essentially passive, following the leads and the pace set by the children themselves. Let them learn, and help them to learn, and help them to teach one another, as they do anyway. Help to immunize them against the hucksters, and against the ugliness and cruelty that are inescapable in our world.

The merchant seaman has a special VD problem. Although his lot has improved since the days of sailing vessels, with voyages tending to be shorter and ships better supplied with medical facilities, the basic problem has hardly been touched. Men are without women for abnormally long intervals, often under conditions of stress. Their urge to seek female companionship in port is as normal as sex itself. A report in 1964 by Guthe and Idsöe tells us that while VD is coming to be treated extensively aboard ships as well as in the ports, the minimum requirements established for treatment under the Brussels Agreement are seldom met. The rising trends in VD affect especially small seafaring countries like Norway, Sweden, and Denmark as well as Finland and Poland. The problem is of course associated with that of prostitution in port towns.

But commercial navigation has been increasing at a rapid rate in all parts of the world, and no area is exempt from the problem. The same report alludes to high rates of VD among floating populations in Antwerp, Liverpool, London, and New York, but only as examples; elsewhere there is reference to the growing problem in the developing Asian and African countries.

A brief story in the *New York Times* of May 5, 1969, notes that medical care aboard American ships compares unfavorably with that provided by major foreign-flag merchant marines; British, French, Dutch, and Danish ships are mentioned specifically; their seamen "receive far superior shipboard medical care than American seamen." An unrelated story in the same newspaper of April 13, 1969, tells us that in Britain, as an experiment, wives are being allowed to accompany seamen on voyages. Neither of these stories deals specifically with VD. With improving mechanization, with the muscular strength of men getting less important in the performance of work, would it be possible to limit crews to married couples? No doubt such a notion is against all tradition, and I can picture the maritime unions, among others, objecting vociferously. But it's an idea.

Something like this idea has been suggested for another group, but not seriously. It is becoming a major scandal, although the facts usually appear only in small items in the papers, that the gonorrhea rate among United States troops in Vietnam is reaching record-breaking levels. I have seen the figure of 70 per cent per year, which for comparison with earlier figures is 70,000 per 100,000, even higher than the incidence in Greenland Eskimos (Chapter 18). According to *Time* (November 21, 1969), Brigadier General David Thomas, top medical officer of the U.S. Army in the war zone there, has gone so far as to suggest Army-operated brothels. Shades of Saint Louis (the king, not the city)! But the idea was countered by a Baptist weekly in California, which called it "government-sponsored moral collapse," with the even wilder suggestion that only married men be sent to war, *with* their wives, who would stay near but behind the battle zones. I have heard some of the young people who oppose the Vietnam war suggest that the old folks who started it ought to do the fighting themselves; but even so

the suggestion did not, within my hearing, include the old men's
wives. Yet we know that, given a war young people can believe
in, the women are as ready as the men to fight it—and the children, too, down to a tender age. Now that civilians cannot escape the line of fire, they pitch in and do their best. Our own
women and children would do the same, I think, under similar
circumstances. But I do not mean to turn the Baptist weekly's
suggestion into something serious. I hold only that women can
do nearly everything men can, and no less well; just as, conversely, men can do nearly everything women can. I think
women could help operate ships. And I would suggest that their
full and equal cooperation with men in controlling VD will be
found indispensable.

The soldier's VD problem is like the merchant sailor's, exaggerated by the even greater need for release when opportunity
offers, as well as by pressures of another kind: from his buddies,
to "be a man"; from his situation, which makes his life forfeit
anyway. In modern armies he has the advantages of efficient
medical care. In Vietnam the gonococcus counters with advantages of its own.

Some comments on prostitution are in order here because of
the obviously great importance of the practice in the spread of
VD, and of the evident need to control or eliminate one in
order to do the same for the other. But it is easy to oversimplify
this relationship, and difficult to speak of it without moralizing.
I will try to avoid doing either.

One of the reports Dr. Willcox gave me when I saw him at
his home in April, 1970, is a UN (not WHO) document of 184
pages entitled *International Review of Criminal Policy* (No. 13,
October, 1958) which is devoted entirely to prostitution, and
contains among other things a detailed review by Dr. Willcox
himself entitled "Prostitution and Venereal Disease." The name
of the document is revealing: prostitution has come to be
thought of as mainly a police problem. Part of the problem, of
course, overlapping with, and extending beyond the police area,

is thought of as a moral problem; it is extraordinary to me that some of the papers in the volume (not Dr. Willcox's) take it for granted unblinkingly that the field is made up entirely of crime and sin.

I would argue that the point does not follow from any sort of logic or necessity, and that part of the control problem—of prostitution and VD, both—may require that we think of prostitution in other terms. We saw in Chapter 8 that prostitution may have originated in relation to the earliest settlements of man, perhaps at roughly the same time that treponematosis was becoming venereal. Since then it has taken virtually every imaginable form, not all of which have been regarded as either illegal or immoral. Some have had religious sanction; and one has only to think of the hetaerae of the Greeks, the concubines of the Romans, and the geishas of Japan to recognize that there is nothing new in the widespread and persistent tendency to accept prostitution as inevitable or even socially beneficial. I have heard men of my generation with a central European background look back on the local prostitutes of small towns wistfully and with nothing but friendly memories. Examples of this attitude could be multiplied; it is expressed, for instance, in some of the stories by Colette.

But to object to the idea that prostitution is necessarily criminal or sinful is not to approve of it: I think, in fact, that the practice needs to be thought of as abnormal or pathological, much like VD itself. In our culture, at all events, prostitution can be traced back to the earliest patrilineal family groups, to the emergence of male dominance and private property which made the indisputable assignment of parentage essential—in short, to the beginnings of what sociologists call civilization. In the context of the total history of man as the archeologist sees it, these are all relatively recent developments; and it may be important to recognize that none of them need be considered immutable.

Prostitution is usually defined as promiscuous sex activity that is paid for or practiced as a means of livelihood. Both elements, the economic and the fact of promiscuity, contribute their share to the VD problem, the first by sustaining it, the second as the means whereby infection is introduced into the population. Or to put the matter in different words, promiscuity starts the mischief and money keeps it going. If a mistress or a gigolo were as faithful as a wife or a husband, he or she would contribute little to the VD problem: money alone, in short, is not enough. Conversely, the "amateur"—the unpaid casual mate—can spread as much disease without financial catalysis as the professional. Let us recognize that both prostitutes and promiscuous amateurs can be of either sex; it is only because most of the literature is written by men that it tends to concentrate on women. The male prostitute, usually a passive homosexual, has been the subject of a considerable literature in recent years. But he is mentioned by Juvenal in the poet's sixth satire. If there is anything new about any aspect of this part of our problem it is a matter of its visibility.

As for homosexual practices, aside from their lack of novelty, there are two particular features that show up in the literature. It is male relationships rather than female that tend to be promiscuous (lesbians generally pair off in what amounts to marriage without legal sanction, and tend to maintain stable relationships; but men usually do not); accordingly, it is the male rather than the female homosexual who is significant in the VD problem. Secondly, the male relationship generally involves pederasty, so that the lesions and symptoms in the passive member of the pair are usually found in the rectum, where they may show some of the diagnostic difficulties otherwise peculiar to women. This applies more to the painless primary sore of syphilis than to gonorrhea, which is more likely to be painful in men whether it be urethral or rectal, and so draws the patient's attention to it.

Prostitutes are, of course, traditionally female; and I find it curious that conventional English seems to lack a separate word

for the heterosexual male prostitute—"gigolo" comes closest but
may also mean only a professional dancing partner. Presumably
the reason for this is related to the male dominance characteristic of most advanced societies, and to the consequence that the
heterosexual male prostitute is typically restricted to the relatively affluent, so that we are dealing with the sexual opposite of
"mistress" rather than of "prostitute." Generally the male prostitute at lower levels is a homosexual, a "hustler" as he calls himself, but as only one of many slang meanings of the latter word.

Basically, then, this part of the VD problem comes down to
the two elements, promiscuity and the forces that encourage or
sustain it, which in turn fall into the two groups, professional
and amateur, or free-enterprise and just free. Back in Chapter 14
I gave you a quotation which alluded to an idea that was developed in many papers of the period (1955), that prostitution was
decreasing while amateur promiscuity (especially among young
girls) was increasing. Willcox, in his review of prostitution and
VD, in the 1958 UN Report, put the point this way:

> In a prosperous economy, the bulk of women work and provide
> for themselves, living alone if necessary. Many, if not the majority,
> have sexual intercourse before marriage, some with a number of
> men. The more promiscuous no longer require money for rent and
> food but still crave for luxuries—which their wage cannot provide
> —from men who are attracted to them by the possibility of sexual
> intercourse. Many girls, too, are promiscuous because they like to
> be, although few writers say so. Thus the demand for prostitution
> decreases. The prostitute now has a competitor and she ceases to
> be the major factor in the spread of venereal disease. Such is the
> state of affairs in Canada, the United States and, to a varying de-
> gree, in a number of countries of western Europe today.

As late as 1961 a paper from Finland cited the general opinion voiced in Sweden and the United States, and also by the
WHO, that the significance of prostitution in the spread of VD
had declined. There was the suggestion that this might not have
been true for seaport towns. But even so there is reason to believe that what had been happening in those years was not so

much a decrease of prostitution as a change in its form, with a diminution or disappearance of the old traditional whorehouses and red-light districts, and an emergence of one or more different types of organized operation.

An example relates to New York City, where the Health Department, on June 30, 1967, closed its Criminal Court clinic, where accused prostitutes had been examined and treated for VD, substituting a pledge that they submit to examination within forty-eight hours either by a private doctor or at a public VD clinic. This action was taken in the belief that prostitutes had become less important than formerly in spreading VD. Then, in September of the same year, a law calling for up to one year in jail for convicted streetwalkers was "liberalized"; the maximum penalty became fifteen days in jail and a fine of $250. It had been argued that the longer jail term had not been effective, and that prostitution, in any event, was a "social" rather than a "criminal" problem(!). It then appeared that the lenient new law encouraged and in effect *caused* the proliferation of a variant of the old practice. Pimps, each with a coterie of whores, began to infest New York's midtown area of theaters, restaurants, flashy shops, and hotels; the girls solicited in traditional fashion and used the hotels as their base of operations; the pimps took care of the legal side of the transaction and pocketed most of the take. Judges and police had no doubt that the lenient law was the cause of the increased activity, forgetting that the harsher earlier law had been admittedly ineffectual.

By February, 1969, the operation had apparently become so scandalous—or could the media merely have discovered something they considered spectacular?—that a six-part TV report was broadcast. The TV report, according to Jack Gould in the *New York Times* of February 26, 1969,

> said there were 25,000 prostitutes in New York and that the lenient 15-day sentence for conviction had led to an invasion of the city by girls from as far away as Alaska and Hawaii.

So, at the end of March, 1969, Governor Rockefeller of New York State signed a bill increasing the penalty to ninety days and the maximum fine to $500. The law went into effect September 1; and a Criminal Court judge was quoted on August 31 in the *New York Times* as saying that the new law "may end this business. . . . It may cut street crime. . . ." A year later in the same newspaper (September 10, 1970) a small news item mentioned that there had been a decrease of 18.2 per cent in arrests for prostitution in New York during the first seven months of 1970 as compared with the same period of 1969: 4092 as compared with 4838 arrests. Increased penalties are likely to evoke sharpened means of evasion; it does not follow that a decrease in *arrests* means a decrease in prostitution. During the same interval, we know, the VD rate was rising.

Here are a few scattered items on prostitution in other countries in recent years. A Reuters dispatch from Bonn, Germany, datelined December 1, 1968, reported that the city had legalized prostitution "in the hope it would help to bring street prostitution under control." About fifty prostitutes moved into a new "Eros Center," where each woman was to pay rent for her one-room apartment. It is mentioned that a similar brothel, one of the largest in Europe, had existed in Hamburg for years; and a later dispatch by the same news agency (March 23, 1969) gave some details of the clubs along the neon-lighted Reeperbahn of West Germany's biggest port city. It appears that sailors are no longer the main customers, who have now come to include businessmen, tourists, mainly American and Scandinavian, and troops, both American and British. The troops are said to be the biggest spenders, but some of the establishments have achieved such world-wide renown that South African and Australian businessmen have sought them out by name. The Hamburg city fathers have plans to clean up the city eventually, but "are not rushing ahead . . . because of the tremendous tourist profits based on Hamburg's 'wicked' reputation."

In Japan, the traditional brothel system in effect for centuries was officially dissolved by law in 1958 at the urging of women who had gained the suffrage in 1946. Prostitution had been active there for the "benefit" of United States troops, and has evidently not disappeared. An AP dispatch in the *New York Times* on March 12, 1969, reported that brothel operators in Amagasaki, a suburb of the industrial city of Osaka, site of "Expo 70," had been discouraged by police raids which embarrassed the customers so much that many never returned. The police estimated that 800 prostitutes worked in Amagasaki, and one raid netted 280 arrests.

According to another newspaper story, some 1400 legally registered prostitutes ply their trade in the red-light district of Juarez, Mexico, where the girls are supposed to have daily inspections and one-dollar penicillin shots before going to work. This operation evidently depends largely for customers on American troops stationed just over the border. Juarez "businessmen" are worried because the United States has barred servicemen from similar facilities in Tijuana; but the Pentagon seemed to be more concerned about the exposure of troops to marijuana than about VD. A more recent note (AP, January 4, 1970) mentioned that perhaps as many as 300,000 South Vietnamese women are living as prostitutes, bar girls, and "temporary wives" of American troops there. The details are similar to those reported from Japan. The girls earn much more by this means than they could by any other. In Vietnam, the *New York Times* reported on September 7, 1969,

> where the average farmer's annual income is about $240 . . . "it will be difficult for the girls to return to farm life after living on $400 or $500 a month."

In Vienna, a new cleanup drive forced prostitutes off the main thoroughfares but did not attempt to stop their practice. The new regulations were said to be a compromise between the harsher measures asked for by legislators and police, and "business interests that argued that some prostitution there was desirable for tourism." Vienna's leading newspaper, *Die Presse*, scornfully termed this "a typically Austrian solution"; but on reading further one finds that the newspaper meant to advocate licensing brothels which, although prohibited in Vienna, are tolerated in some of the provincial Austrian cities. It cited a recent opinion poll which found that among Viennese who were asked, 75 per cent favored such licensing.

Clearly, professional promiscuity is not disappearing. But Lancereaux's idea that VD could be controlled if we were to "meet the evil at its source, that is, in the houses of prostitution" (Chapter 18), must have been as much of an oversimplification in his time as it is today. Nor is amateur promiscuity a new phenomenon, as many alarmists would have us believe. There would be no difficulty in establishing this point for the upper and lower classes, if only from the poetry of all periods; and nobody doubts that it has always existed among middle-class *men*, who have made use of female prostitutes or lower-class amateurs. The question then remains, has there been an emergence or a marked increase in promiscuity among middle-class *women?* Again the question might be narrowed further. The seemingly greater promiscuous sexual activity of suburban housewives today is probably, like the apparent increase in homosexual practices, a matter of visibility rather than of any significantly increased activity. I cannot prove this, but I suggest that the burden of proof rests with those who argue that puritan repression has ever done more than drive sexual activity into hiding. But has there not been a significant increase of promiscuous sex among younger middle-class women, especially teen-age girls? Margaret Mead, as I have heard her speak several times on television, seems to think not, and I am not disposed to dismiss her opinion lightly. But our times have seen the emergence of this group of girls and young women into school and college and the business and professional world, where they are appearing in unprecedented numbers in increasingly open competition and cooperation with boys and men. Feminism is demolishing the old double standard, and freedom for women has come to mean, in part, freedom for the premarital sexual experimentation that has always been considered normal in men. Men in their turn are finding what appear to be new possibilities for experimentation with women of their own social class. The ready availability of new means of contraception, and of abortion as well as knowledge of the increased ease of treating VD, are thought to have removed the last barriers to young female sexual freedom.

But the question is in fact a good deal more complicated than this restricted matter of middle-class teen-age female sexual activity. Young people all over the world, people born since the end of the second World War, have found themselves in a world beset with extraordinary new problems. The problems are not peculiar to any country, and although they are more acute in some places than in others, it is unlikely that any corner of the earth remains untouched by them. The two major components of these new problems, as I see them, are the enormous technological advances made in the period and the persistent strife between the two major economic systems, capitalism and communism. Each is, of course, in part a product of the other. The consequences include unprecedented affluence (side by side with persistent widespread poverty), an accelerating rate of population growth (and the still greater rate of contacts, as Dr. Guthe said), widespread pollution of the environment and ecological damage, advancing militarization and continuous warfare, and other great problems of our day. Today's youth, faced with staggering new problems, hardly needs the further supplement from its elders of an alleged "permissiveness" to move it into turmoil beyond anything those elders could ever have experienced.

And if by any chance I am wrong in this assessment, be it noted that the root of the problem, in any event, is to be found in the older generation rather than in the young. I find the notion of "permissiveness" trivial if not absurd in view of the confusion of repression on the one hand and stimulation on the other. Repression persists, as the vestige of puritanism that is dying but not dead, and by efforts of adults to control this and related problems by force; stimulation operates by example (what is new is the *display* of sex by adults) and in the exploitation for profit of every aspect of sex.

A change in the pattern of sexual behavior and in common attitudes toward sex is illustrated by a pair of two-page advertisements by a single drug manufacturer, which appeared in a professional magazine at the beginning and at the end of 1969. They advertised the same product—a single-dose penicillin preparation for treatment of syphilis. The theme of both is, doctor, you had better use a single-dose treatment, she (the patient) may not be back. A picture covers one full page of each set. The earlier picture shows a full face, over a turtleneck, with a half-burned cigarette dangling from the lips, dark glasses reflecting a kiss in one glass and in the other a night-life scene of bar and marquee showing a movie "for adults." No caption is needed. The later picture—has the advertiser learned something?—shows a pretty, nicely dressed teen-age girl with an expression matching the caption, "She's stunned, incredulous, and mortified."

Which brings us to the last point of this chapter: Why does she (or he) run away? Why do they not come in for diagnosis and treatment in the first place? Why all the elaborate detective work of the blitz, the searching out of patients and contacts, the cajolery, the specially trained investigators? The questions almost seem to answer themselves, and a good deal of the answer is so obvious that we needn't waste time on it. VD is shameful, and no matter how much we try to make it less so or avoid the fact that it is so, the penalties associated with its presence remain; and retribution looms larger than any benefit to be hoped for in what amounts to confession. Again, we are told that ignorance is rampant: sick people would go for treatment if they knew they were sick, or if they suspected what it was they had. But to the degree that ignorance makes up a significant part of the problem, it is itself a reflection of the shame. Nice People don't talk about the whole subject, or if they do, it is with mincing and blushing or with a phony solicitude, under which finger-shaking is more plainly visible than the Nice People can imagine.

Dr. Parran urged us to deal with VD as a problem of disease, not as punishment for sin, and his principle is supposed to be the basis of modern practice. Yet we have not been able to give his principle force in the more than thirty years since he stated it.

Nevertheless the situation is changing under our eyes. For centuries we have made each sex hide parts of its anatomy from the other, with consequences we are only beginning to think about now that the curtain is being raised. Nudity has become commonplace today, not only in the theater but in the daily life of tens or hundreds of thousands of young people as well. More and more young men and women—witness the enormous rock music festivals in the open air that have been a feature of recent years—simply take off their clothes and mingle with one another as though they were back in Eden. Older people are either appalled or fascinated (or both); their own morbid curiosity matches or exceeds their impulse to put the practice down by force. A United States presidential commission (appointed by President Johnson) issued a detailed study indicating that pornography doesn't harm adults, based on several sociological studies and quickly confirmed by others. But this majority observation was countered vociferously by that of an outraged minority; and on October 25, 1970, the commission's report was rejected (I think one might fairly say "denounced") by President Nixon, who said he had "evaluated" it but did not say he had read it. The notion that nudity and even a display of sexual activity, normal or otherwise, can have any effect other than to bring damnation down upon us at once—or that it might have no significant effect at all—is to millions of staid citizens utterly outside the pale of belief and beyond endurance.

I found more nudity in London in early 1970 than I had seen in any American city. Anyone who thought of associating nudity with the word "dirty" might have been struck by the contrasting fact that London, as I saw it, was physically clean at a time when garbage was piling up in New York and air pollution in all our cities was becoming almost palpable. London's buildings and streets were clean, pollution had been markedly reduced, and it seemed to me that even traffic noise had been cut down. But as compared with Times Square, where one has to go *inside* the pornography shops to see the displays, in Soho it is in the shop windows. All over London I found stores with contraceptive devices and sex literature set out in plain view from the street; and although books on sex are no novelty in this country, it seemed to me that there were more of them on London bookracks everywhere. The "microskirt," barely covering the buttocks, seemed to be standard on young women despite cold, wet weather. Advertising placards parading along the walls of the Underground escalators showed female underwear and bikinis in flagrantly seductive postures; and similar full color posters alternated with cigarette ads among the six-by-twelve-foot posters behind the tracks. An English friend suggested that all this is better than the open solicitation on New York streets; and it is true that I saw no such solicitation in London; although Piccadilly was full of long-haired boys and jeaned girls, often standing together, boy kissing girl without shyness or ostentation on streets or Underground platforms.

I found this freedom of public endearment among young couples an even more striking feature of Paris. Pairs seemingly oblivious of anything or anybody but one another were everywhere on the streets, in the parks, and especially (I thought) in the Métro, where they seemed glad to stand together whether or not there were empty seats. I thought—but the idea may be colored by an impression Paris gives me but London doesn't—that the couples in Paris were ever so slightly more tender, more convincingly loving, than those in London. The fact is that couples kissing unashamedly in public were common in Paris when I was there in 1962; but I didn't see them then in London. Paris, in sharp contrast to London in 1970, had no sexy posters. I missed Montmartre on this trip but was in several other parts of the city on both sides of the Seine. In passageways leading off the Place de la Concorde and the Champs Elysées there are shop windows displaying full-color nudity that seemed to me franker but somehow less seductive than those in London. Elsewhere all the displays were sexless: posters in the Métro were devoted exclusively to health foods, cooking appliances, and similar nonepidermal objects.

I have not seen Copenhagen or Stockholm in recent years, but they are of course known as the world centers of pornography. When I mentioned the results of my London researches in this field to Dr. Willcox, he suggested blandly that London may be halfway between New York and the Scandinavian cities.

London seemed to me more frank and open, less hypocritical, than New York; and Paris in some ways gave me the impression of still greater frankness. I had a chance to talk with three young woman students, daughters of friends in London and Paris. They were much interested in my book on VD, and could talk and listen without mincing or blushing. I do not think this would have been true ten years ago or so. These girls added their young voices to those of Dr. Willcox and Dr. Collart and his colleagues in assuring me that there is no longer any shame about VD in London or in Paris. Yet one of Dr. Collart's clinical associates mentioned that reluctance to come in for treatment of syphilis has not disappeared in Paris, and that one finds less of it among prostitutes than among others. Blood testing for syphilis is universal in Paris among employed people and students. One of my young informants there, to whom I put the direct question, replied without blinking that if her test turned up positive she would certainly go for treatment.

Denmark and Sweden, evidently more than other places, are currently making serious efforts to break down taboos against nudity and sexual display. Although many horrified observers seem to have decided firmly what the outcome of these efforts will be, I consider it too early as yet to decide whether the result will be an increase or a decrease in prostitution and VD, or whether there will be no effect on either; there are many indications that the immediate effect has been boredom. But these great national experiments on the effects of open pornography will be worth watching; and Denmark's reputation for accurate VD statistics will make its example especially informative.

Whatever we may eventually find to be the relationship between nudity, sexual display, prostitution, and venereal disease, it ought to be clear that the use of force will not alter the first two or correct the others. The VD problem is a problem of disease, as Dr. Parran said, and we must find a way to get at it as we do with other diseases. We can hardly hope for success in this undertaking until we have divorced the VD problem from the traces of original sin which still cling to our approach to it. There is a possibility of technical control which we have not yet explored in detail—the use of vaccines; but I have warned you not to expect too much in that quarter. If by some chance we could vaccinate against VD, we might forget all the other troublesome areas of the problem. If not, or if the vaccines take too long in becoming available, we shall need to return to this social heart of the question and see whether anything can be done about it.

❧ 22 ❧

The Chance for Vaccines

THE DEVELOPMENT of effective vaccines holds out the most immediate hope for the future to the scientist whose job it is to discover new knowledge about VD, who has accepted the fact of failure of control by all means now available, and who feels incapable of dealing with the "social factors," whose importance he fully recognizes. So work on vaccines goes forward, but there are formidable obstacles. Technical difficulties peculiar to gonorrhea and syphilis, different for the two, make the prospect of success for either disease less than dazzling. The unpleasantness and unpopularity of the VD problem make it unlikely that the resources of a crash program, including the required funds, will be focused on it. And for reasons parallel with both of these difficulties—for both technical and nontechnical reasons—there is some doubt that we could make use of effective immunizing agents even if we had them.

To understand the general outlines of the problem of vaccines for VD, we had better begin with a few principles as they apply to the general subject of immunization. Before the great victory over polio in the mid-1950s there were only a few really effective vaccines. For general domestic human use in this country we could have begun and ended the list with vaccines against smallpox, diphtheria, tetanus, and whooping cough. For use in special circumstances, including foreign travel, occupational hazards, and other things, there were several others, among which only yellow fever vaccine compared in value with the first three. But since the success with polio vaccines several additional ones have emerged, nearly all the strikingly effective ones being for virus diseases, including measles, rubella, and mumps. Be it noted that some other vaccines—against the typhus group of fevers, and against typhoid and related diseases, cholera, and plague, none of which are new, and all of which have been improved in some degree—do not rank in effectiveness with those listed. They have value and are recommended for use under appropriate circumstances; but control of the disease in each instance is based mainly on something other than immunization, like destruction of insects or purification of water supplies. On the other hand, control of diphtheria, tetanus, smallpox, polio, and whooping cough, as well as of yellow fever among travelers, is squarely based on immunization.

Vaccines contain antigenic materials; they stimulate the production by the body of antibodies that react specifically with the antigens. If the antibody is to be effective in preventing disease, it must match a particular antigenic component of the disease agent which is responsible for the symptoms. There must be enough of the antibody to do this, and it must be present in the right part of the body at the right time. Whether recovery from the natural disease leaves immunity or not is less important to the success of a vaccine than one would expect it to be. We could have good vaccines against diseases due to streptococci (sore throat, scarlet fever, and others) and pneumococci (lobar pneumonia), except that there are so many different varieties or types of each of these bacteria, each of which immunizes only against itself, that one can have streptococcal or pneumococcal disease repeatedly, and effective vaccines seem impractical. The same seems to be true of the common cold group of viruses: there are just too many of them. With influenza there is a related but distinct problem: the two main types of influenza virus are subject to mutation which alters them antigenically; a vaccine can be effective only if it matches the genetic type involved in an outbreak.

The most effective vaccines are those prepared against viruses or what are called "toxins" in a restricted sense; and they are most effective when the virus or toxin is present in the circulating blood at some time *before* the most serious symptoms of the disease appear. Viruses are the smallest infectious agents, being in effect single molecules, huge as such but very much smaller than bacteria. True toxins—of which diphtheria and tetanus are the most important examples—are also single molecules. As such, both viruses and toxins are *neutralized* by antibodies specific for them: the virus becomes noninfectious, the toxin nonpoisonous. The viruses of smallpox and polio, and the toxins of diphtheria and tetanus, do most of their damage after being distributed by the bloodstream. If enough antibody to neutralize the virus or the toxin is present in the blood before this happens, the serious symptoms do not develop.

Cellular agents of disease, including the bacteria, are, compared with viruses and toxins, huge and chemically extremely complex. When the whole cell, killed or otherwise made harmless, is injected as a vaccine, the antibodies formed against the mass of antigenic material hardly ever kill or inactivate living virulent cells. They may nevertheless act in various ways by helping the body's phagocytes take up the bacteria and destroy them; but generally speaking, they are less effective immunizing agents than those for viruses and toxins.

Just the same, whooping cough is caused by a bacillus which does not form a significant toxin, and neither bacillus nor its products are distributed through the bloodstream. The fact that immunity can nevertheless be produced by inoculation of killed pertussis bacilli shows that these rules are not fixed, and gives us some hope for gonorrhea and syphilis where, for the most part, the rules also do not apply.

The characteristics of gonorrhea, in fact, make it a pretty unlikely candidate for a good vaccine. The gonococcus has all the
typical complexity of bacteria as a class, and more. It is not
transported through the blood until late in the disease, whereas
it is of course the early infectious part of gonorrhea that we
need to prevent. The natural disease leaves no recognizable immunity, nor does the lack of immunity seem to be related to antigenic type variation. Possibly this lack of natural immunity is
associated with the characteristic pattern of growth of gonococci
inside of phagocytic cells, which, instead of destroying them as
we ordinarily expect, provide nests for them and help to carry
them around!

The possibility of a vaccine for gonorrhea is nevertheless
being explored—especially recently, as the statistics have been
mounting alarmingly. The same kind of work that is being done
primarily in the hope of developing a blood test for gonorrhea
also has, as a by-product, the aim of producing an immunizing
agent. The gonococcus can be grown in culture, and in recent
years studies by the VD research group at Atlanta have been
successful in maintaining a culture that is fully virulent. Another
important recent advance made by the same workers has been
to produce experimental gonorrhea in chimpanzees, where here-
tofore no experimental animal was available other than man
himself. It will now be possible to test experimental vaccines in
chimpanzees before trying them in human volunteers.

A ray of hope for an eventual gonorrhea vaccine slants in
from an unexpected source. The bacterium of cerebrospinal
meningitis—the "meningococcus"—is a close relative of the gonococcus, although the two diseases are very different. Both are
problems among the military, but meningitis is a "nice," respect-
able, but terribly fatal, epidemic disease. More significant is the
fact that the meningococcus tends to live harmlessly in the
throat, and only occasionally breaks through into the blood, and
after that to the lining tissues of the brain called meninges. So
there may be a natural immunity against it resulting from its so-

journ in the throat; and a vaccine leading to antibodies in the blood might prevent it from passing from throat to meninges. Such a vaccine (for one of three existing types of meningococci) has recently been developed by a group at the Walter Reed Army Institute in Washington. The meningococcus still has no experimental animal except man, as was true until recently for the gonococcus, so that the tests of the Walter Reed vaccine could be conducted only on human subjects. Extensive preliminary tests on volunteers have been encouraging. Hope is held out for a triple vaccine (for all three types) in a few years. Some of the hope is reflected onto the gonococcus.

More work is going into a syphilis vaccine than into one against gonorrhea, but, as Dr. John Knox put it in 1969, "more money is being spent to eliminate athlete's foot than syphilis." The technical difficulties are not the same as for gonorrhea. The spirochete of syphilis, as you know, cannot be cultured predictably or in virulent form either by methods used for bacteria, in soups or jellies, or in developing hens' eggs or the tissue cultures —cultures-in-glass of cells from man or animals—used for viruses. *Treponema pallidum* grows only in the tissues of man or of a few species of living animals. Lack of the usual culture methods is a serious drawback to vaccine development. Just the same you may remember that the very word, *vaccine* (Latin *vaccus,* "cow") relates back to the use by Edward Jenner in the last years of the eighteenth century of cowpox material for inoculation against smallpox, long before cultures were dreamt of. So, while the hope of growing the spirochetes in culture has not been abandoned, work toward a vaccine goes forward mainly along other lines, using spirochetes from experimental animals.

One of the advantages of cultures is that they can provide large quantities of the bacterium. Large quantities are needed to separate the bacterial substance—the intended antigens—from contaminating antigens that might cause allergies and other unintended effects. But other ways can be found to accomplish these ends. Members of the VD research group in Atlanta have been cooperating with workers at the atomic energy laboratories at Oak Ridge, and by using newly developed special large-scale equipment have been able to prepare a sizable batch (13 liters, which is nearly 3½ gallons) of extract of spirochetes from rabbit testicles, from which they made a purified immunizing agent for rabbits.

In one respect syphilis conforms to the disease pattern which encourages an effective vaccine: the spirochetes are in the blood very early in the course of the disease, possibly early enough to prevent even the chancre if the effective antibody level were high enough.

Before I tell you about other work with animals looking toward a syphilis vaccine, we had better go into the question of the peculiar immunity that develops in syphilis as a result of infection. It is necessary to emphasize that it is peculiar. Usually we think of immunity against infectious disease as something that follows recovery from the disease. But in syphilis, although recovery without treatment may happen in something like one out of four cases (Chapter 7), it is unpredictable in the individual patient. We usually expect somebody with an infectious disease either to get well or to die; but the latent syphilitic can live for many years without knowing that the disease will not reappear.

Certain things happen in syphilis that are explained by most experts in terms of immunity, although others, accepting the facts, explain them in different terms and argue that there is no true immunity to this disease. The argument has been going on since the prebacteriologic era and has never been completely resolved. It has generated an enormous literature and a lot of ingenious research. If we ever do have a syphilis vaccine it will have grown out of this argument. But this is not the place for the details: let me try to give you the essentials as simply as I can.

In untreated syphilis, or in syphilis that is not treated until several months or more have elapsed after the first appearance of symptoms, another exposure usually does not renew the disease. In the untreated syphilitic this is obviously not immunity, since he is still infected. When he is treated late in the disease and cured, he seems to be immune; but as we saw in chapter 17, there is a residual doubt as to whether the cure is complete.

The same picture is seen in experimental syphilis in rabbits, and has in fact been confirmed in experiments on human volunteers. In both man and rabbit, when the disease is cured in the early infectious stage, reinfection can take place with a new chancre. Repeated reinfections were first seen in 1943, soon after the introduction of penicillin, especially when only one sex partner was treated. The result, as I have mentioned earlier, was given the name "ping-pong" syphilis. At that time the occurrence of such new chancres, or reinfections, was accepted as evidence of complete cure, something which had otherwise been thought by many to be impossible. In short, everyone was agreed that reinfection did not happen while the old infection was present. The controversy centered on the question, did the absence of reinfection after late cure mean immunity, or did it mean persistence of infection, even though the infection might prove permanently latent?

What resolved this question for most people, in favor of a true immunity, was the demonstration of antibodies against the spirochetes, culminating in the TPI test (Chapter 16). These antibodies abolish the virulence of the spirochetes even before they stop their movements. They seem, accordingly, to be a factor in immunity to syphilis, although they are evidently not the only one. But the fact that they actually kill the spirochetes is a focal point of hope for an eventual vaccine.

Syphilis is unusual in that its immunity—if we assume there is such a thing—develops very slowly and is not directly measurable in terms of antibodies. But if the fact of immunity be accepted, the search for a vaccine becomes the more promising.

Another aspect of immunity in syphilis relates to the other treponematoses, yaws, bejel, and pinta. Any one of these diseases protects in some degree against the others, in much the same way, although usually less effectively, that each protects against itself. This fact fits the pattern we saw in Chapter 7, being offered by Hudson as evidence for his contention that the four treponematoses, including syphilis, are all variations of one disease. This "cross-immunity" bears on the vaccine problem.

An effective vaccine must contain the particular antigen or antigens of the virus, cell, or toxin that give rise to the protective antibodies, treated if necessary so as to be harmless. The ideal vaccine would contain nothing else; but no vaccine has as yet achieved such ideal purity. Toxins are treated with formalin to make them nontoxic ("toxoid"); viruses, and bacteria and other cells, are killed or inactivated, or otherwise modified so that at worst they produce a mild, localized, but immunizing infection—as does cowpox virus, which is used as the live agent, producing the vaccination sore and scar most people still remember, normally a small price to pay for protection against smallpox. With syphilis it is unlikely that any comparable price would be tolerable. If a vaccine against syphilis could not be made harmless, the response to it, at the very least, would have to be mild and unquestionably self-limiting, entirely distinct from syphilis and incapable of turning into syphilis.

There are two general approaches to such an objective. The first and more popular attempts to modify virulent spirochetes, taken either from rabbits or via continuing efforts to grow them in glass cultures. The second would approach the problem of reducing the virulence of the spirochetes by starting with the one from the mildest of the natural treponematoses—pinta—or possibly from one of the newly discovered African simian treponematoses. Let us look at these two in reverse order; the second, although potentially important, does not yet have much to be said for it.

The second approach is based in part on a finding reported in October, 1968, that the pinta spirochete, *Treponema carateum*, is sometimes infectious for chimpanzees. This spirochete, which

Hackett (Chapter 8) thinks to be the most ancient and most
highly adapted of the agents of treponematoses, had not previously been found infectious for rabbits or other animals, so
that no basis was available for accumulating enough spirochetes
for study, and especially for use as a vaccine. The 1968 report,
by a cooperative team of workers from the VD laboratories in
Atlanta and the Mexican Institute of Health and Tropical Diseases, is a brief preliminary statement dealing with only a few
animals, and promising further details later. Whether this spirochete would be used directly to immunize human beings, or
whether attempts would be made to modify it so as to result in
something less than naturally occurring pinta, has not been
mentioned, although the author of a separate discussion of the
subject hints at the second of these alternatives. Pinta is not a
serious disease, but its bleached lesions are regarded as disfiguring, especially by dark-skinned peoples, and might not be accepted as a satisfactory price for preventing syphilis by anybody
but an albino. But there are at least two other difficulties in the
path of the pinta vaccine for syphilis. One, shown in another
brief report in 1970 by the same group but giving little new information, reveals that of three chimpanzees inoculated one was
completely negative, another developed a darkfield positive lesion but no positive blood tests, while only one had both of
these things but still failed to show any TPI antibodies—
presumably the important ones—183 days after inoculation. The
second difficulty is that natural pinta is a disease of such slow
development, and presumably manifests immunity, if at all, so
much more slowly than does syphilis, that the prospect of using
it to immunize against syphilis seems extremely dim. But this is
an assessment and not a prediction; there were many who
doubted that a polio vaccine could be developed.

Dr. Guthe, when I spoke with him, suggested that the new African monkey spirochete (see Chapter 7) is a more hopeful basis
for a syphilis vaccine than that of pinta. This monkey spirochete

has been found closely related to the spirochete of yaws, but very little is known as yet about its behavior in animals other than monkeys. All that can be said of it here is that a possibility of an eventual vaccine is associated with it. The same may be said of the spirochete of the disease of dog-faced baboons mentioned in Chapter 8; but the first announcement of this one appeared only as I was completing the manuscript of this book, and it will be some time before we know more about it.

As for the other approach, different methods are being tried in the attempt to make rabbit-virulent *Treponema pallidum* harmless but still immunizing. James N. Miller in Los Angeles, working partly in collaboration with a group in the Netherlands, uses irradiation with gamma-rays, which destroys the virulence of the spirochetes without stopping their movement. Rabbits inoculated with such irradiated treponemes developed both reagin-type and immobilizing antibodies without showing symptoms. When virulent spirochetes were later injected into their skin these animals appeared in preliminary tests to be immune, and sensitive tests for virulent spirochetes in their tissues failed to reveal any. These are the most promising studies so far, but application to man is a long way off. In other experiments of this sort, not as well along as those of Miller, efforts are being made to alter spirochetes from rabbit testicles by chemical means; and in still others, the idea is to alter the virulent spirochete genetically so that it may retain its virulence and yet be cultivable. The interesting method being used in this last instance involves what amounts to a shotgun wedding of virulent spirochetes and Reiter culture treponemes, inoculated together into the testicles of rabbits. Up to 1968—the date of the most recent report—these attempts had not yet succeeded.

Success in developing a vaccine for syphilis is obviously not in sight, and whether it is just around the corner is not to be guessed by anyone who hasn't been there. But even if it should succeed in its first phase—even if a safe and effective immunizing agent could be developed, as I said at the beginning of this chapter, serious obstacles both technical and nontechnical still lie in the road.

The technical obstacle inherent in all work on a syphilis vaccine is that antibodies to antigens in the vaccine will foul up the blood tests on which diagnosis of syphilis depends—both reagin or Wassermann antibodies and those to the spirochetes themselves. Vaccines based on virulent spirochetes, or spirochetes that had been virulent before their treatment for vaccine purposes, whether they came from chimpanzees, monkeys, baboons, or rabbits, are likely to elicit both types of antibodies and, accordingly, if used at all widely, would make all the recipients Wassermann-positive and TPI-positive and so make diagnosis by blood tests impossible. We seem to face the extraordinary dilemma that, if we succeed in solving the major technical problem of syphilis control—preparation of an effective vaccine—we may receive in exchange the major technical problem of gonorrhea control—lack of a satisfactory blood test!

But suppose the seemingly impossible proves no more than difficult, and only takes a little longer to get itself solved. Imagine materials and methods developed, with all the technical problems taken care of. Safe, effective vaccines, with no unpleasant or undesirable technical side effects. Even so, could they be used? Among the military and in prisons, there might be no problem. But it is hard to conceive of the use of such preparations among the general public, among the boys and girls of elementary- and high-school age—which is where they would have to be used if they are to accomplish their purpose—without the serious objection that is, in brief, the nontechnical side of our problem, and the subject of my next chapter.

❧ 23 ❧

Beyond Technology

EVER SINCE Dr. Thomas Parran's time we have known what we
need to do to control VD. We have no reason to doubt that
he was right in what he said. Our difficulty is not lack of information or lack of means, but an inability to apply what we
know, to do for all who need it what we can do for any individual. I may have seemed to emphasize our technical deficiencies,
but it was in an effort not to gloss over them. They are not to be
blamed for failure of control. These deficiencies, moreover, are
all being looked into. Each of them—diagnostic problems with
gonorrhea, much more subtle ones with syphilis, the problem of
penicillin resistance of the gonococcus—is more than likely to
be minimized if not abolished before many more years have
passed. I do not say this of vaccines. They represent an attempt
to circumvent the intrinsic obstacles on the road to control.
The outlook for effective vaccines in the near future is not bright
for syphilis, and it is a good deal dimmer for gonorrhea.

What is to be done? I have made it plain from the start that I
don't know. Nor, so far as I have been able to find out, does
anybody else. Dr. R. R. Willcox of St. Mary's Hospital in London
suggested to me that we could solve the problem if we really
wanted to, that we need to put our shoulders to the wheel and

push. This is in effect what Dr. Parran said, and what I said my-self just a paragraph back. It implies, again, that it is not means we lack but will, or perhaps power. Dr. T. Guthe, chief of the division of venereal diseases of the World Health Organization, seemed to me to be a bit gloomy about the prospects for control. His focus is on the immediate goals of a vaccine for syphilis and a blood test for gonorrhea, and he holds out promise for both. When I suggested that the whole problem may have no *techni-cal* solution (I emphasized the word), he replied with something like, "Yes, you may be right; the problem may have no solution."

We are slowly getting used to the idea that some of the world's worst problems have no technical solution, among them disarmament and population overgrowth. Both, like VD, have technical *aspects;* and it is likely that technology will play a part in a solution of any of them if we ever find it. But concen-tration on technical aspects of the question to the exclusion of others was, in my opinion, a principal reason for the failure of efforts toward disarmament after World War II. VD is not, of course, a closely parallel problem. Technology is *relatively* more important in VD control, but it is still far from being the whole story.

If I may define the second term in the title of this book as "habits of life or modes of conduct" with the fewest possible overtones, we may say that VD control must emphasize *morals* more than microbes. But it is hard to escape those overtones; and it may be less ambiguous to repeat the definition rather than to use the word. However we speak of it, this is the subject we have come to.

VD is certainly a product of our habits of life and modes of conduct, and its control is likely to require that such habits and modes be changed. This seems to me self-evident. The question is not whether the change is needed but what the nature of the change is to be. Nor am I concerned with how difficult it may be to make the needed change, although it seems obvious to me that it will not be easy. If we are to control VD, we must change our habits of life and modes of conduct. The question is, in what respects, and how?

A good way to search for clues that might lead to an answer to such a question would be to compare national differences in VD rates with variations in habits of life and modes of conduct in the same countries. But we lack the statistics. Some of the differences look as though they ought to be important, but we have no good basis for being sure that they are or, if they are, for measuring the degree of their importance. When I spoke of the sex display in London and its relative absence in Paris to Dr. Collart's group at the Fournier Institute, one of the group offered the rejoinder that as compared with the French and other Latins, the British, after all, need the stimulation. Others have suggested that this may be even more true of the Scandinavians. The same commentator at the Fournier Institute assured me that Latins are acknowledged masters of "la poésie de l'amour"; Dr. Guthe, when I passed this thought on to him later in Geneva, suggested that the Japanese are a step further advanced in this art. I think other national groups, for example the Hindus, might vie for the same prize. But they all have high VD rates.

We might draw some tentative *negative* conclusions from this otherwise fruitless quest. Spirochetes and gonococci know nothing of poetry. Profound differences in religion and politics, as well as differences in climate and all the social and cultural habits of life and modes of conduct that are associated with all three of these things, do not necessarily have anything to do with differences in VD rates. Within the group of developed countries, moreover, variations in the quality or availability of medical care are also evidently without significance, at least to a degree we can recognize. Health service is excellent in Finland and especially in Sweden, which has the lowest infant mortality rate in the world, an accepted index of first-rate health care; but both have high VD rates. There are high rates in countries which depend heavily on seafaring, which in turn encourages prostitution and the importation of VD; but official Czechoslovakian statistics admit rather high VD rates for that landlocked country. The statistics on prostitution in different countries that have been collected by Willcox tend to support the truism that the practice encourages VD, but they do not reveal any enlightening differences among the countries we are speaking of. A painstaking analysis of laws governing VD in some twenty-three European countries, published in 1964 by two specialists in health legislation, showed wide variation which, once more, revealed no clear bearing on the VD rate. All of which is not to dismiss these matters. If we had good VD statistics I think we would probably be able to point to some of them as factors in the overall pattern of VD; yet their importance can be no more than relative, since all of the countries I have been speaking of have high VD rates.

It remains to look at some Communist countries other than those on the eastern fringe of Europe, among which, as we saw in Chapter 18, there is tantalizing evidence of VD control surpassing that of the rest of the world. I have some information on our present subject, which is habits of life and modes of conduct, gleaned from various sources that look reasonably authentic. We saw before that the U.S.S.R. seems to have had some success in control of syphilis, but less with gonorrhea; that Cuba, for which our information is meager—but we are in a position to snatch at straws—is reputed to have done well with gonorrhea but not with syphilis; and that China may have been so successful in controlling both diseases that Dr. Ma, who is given credit for the job, can now devote his energies to the control of other diseases.

Let us look first at the U.S.S.R., and begin with its health services, which have been well studied by Western experts and have been described in the United States over a period of many years in several books and in frequent articles.

In the Soviet Union today, medical care is widely available and free. I do not have information permitting a direct comparison with Sweden, which is generally credited with having the best medical care in the world; but there are many suggestions that Soviet citizens have as much access to medical care as Swedes do, although there are hints as well that Soviet medical techniques are not always quite so sophisticated. The U.S.S.R. makes wide use of partly trained or paramedical personnel ("feldshers") working under the supervision of physicians; these act, with local variations, as midwives, sanitarians, and pharmacists.

The U.S.S.R. has evidently taken strenuous measures to control VD, from its early years. Both Dr. Victor Heiser, whom I quoted earlier on leprosy, and Dr. Thomas Parran, in his *Shadow on the Land* (1937) were much impressed with early efforts to control VD in the Soviet Union. Heiser, who was there in 1929, spoke of the use of radio to reach illiterate persons in farthest Siberia, and of the handling of VD simply as infectious disease in great contrast to our "ostrich-like" attitude. Parran mentions that syphilis had been "pandemic" in many parts of the country before the Revolution, and that gonorrhea had become widespread with the return of the soldiers after World War I. Intensive anti-VD efforts were begun in 1922 after the hard early years, with widespread Wassermann tests and treatment by flying squadrons of doctors and assistants, spreading to the farthest reaches of the country. In the cities, he says, treatment was noncompulsive during that period;

the Russian with syphilis is treated with a delicacy and with a due regard for his sensibilities which is almost British [!]. . . . If a patient is examined and found to be infected, permission is asked to examine his whole household. . . . The effort is also made to trace all sources of infection; but the permissive attitude is emphasized in spite of the fact that in 1927, at about the same time as in Germany, a law was passed making treatment for syphilis compulsory. . . . There is no cost for treatment. There is no penalty, social or economic, attached to the disease. . . . The almost complete liquidation of the commercial prostitute has helped the problem greatly.

In the more than thirty years since those words were written, as we know, the U.S.S.R. has had its ups and downs, has been through another devastating war, and has emerged as a technological and industrial power rivaling the United States. We know that it has had problems of urbanization and restless youth somewhat like our own.

The VD situation in recent years has been something like this: syphilis and gonorrhea have been reportable in the U.S.S.R. since 1935. All cases of early infectious syphilis are hospitalized within twenty-four hours after diagnosis is made and must remain in the hospital for four to six weeks while contact investigation is undertaken. This would provide enough time to make the patient fully noninfectious. Similar measures are not routinely used with gonorrhea, but are enforced for uncooperative patients or defaulters. If these measures appear harsh, it is interesting to learn from the health legislation experts I spoke of before that eighteen of the twenty-three European countries they studied have some form of compulsion in their VD laws, with compulsory hospitalization in seventeen, including provision for the use of police in three (West Germany, Switzerland, and Turkey). (Available statistics, as I said before, point to high VD rates in all these countries.)

In the U.S.S.R., case-finding is said to be about 80 per cent effective, facilitated by intensive health education of both inpatients and outpatients and of the population in general. Routine blood tests are done on expectant mothers, food handlers, blood donors, applicants for work in children's institutions, and children entering boarding schools; they are voluntary for hospital inpatients generally, and, oddly enough, are not obligatory before marriage. Cities provide free prophylactic centers with no check on their users. The WHO commission that gives us this information says that penicillin is not used prophylactically except in Kiev—other cities have used somewhat antiquated drugs. The use of these prophylactic centers is said to be slight and waning.

In the handling of seafaring men there is a surprising *lack* of compulsion. Medical staff is provided for ships on the basis of length of voyage rather than size. Seamen are examined medically twice each year, but not routinely when leaving the ship or when returning to it after shore leave. All treatment is free to foreign seamen (and other foreigners).

We learn from the same source that prostitution, once rife, is now said not to be a problem, because of laws against it, improving social conditions, full employment, and absence of sexual discrimination. American newspaper correspondents in Moscow, however, have mentioned the existence of prostitution there. Soviet authorities told the WHO commission that there were at that time (1964) no significant VD problems concerned with male homosexuality, or in teen-agers, or in migrants, in spite of considerable population movement in connection with industrial development.

The Soviet Union is known to take a somewhat puritan view of sex activity, presumably unrelated to the doctrine of original sin. Perhaps "puritan" is the wrong word; and perhaps a foreign observer cannot avoid measuring what he sees and reads against his own prejudices. Soviet actors and dancers do not flaunt sex as ours do; their people, young or old, are not constantly stimulated by sex on television or in display advertising. We are inclined to accuse them of swinging too far in the other direction. It is difficult for us to take a balanced or sympathetic view of the remarks of Viktor Bolshakov, who charged in *Komsomolskaya Pravda* in 1969 that nudes and pornography were being used in Czechoslovakia to influence people toward *la dolce vita* instead of strengthening Communism, with the assertion, as quoted in the press here, that "the difference between art and pornography is completely obvious." And another press story quotes a Moscow monthly as saying:

> There is a new moral criterion for condemnation and approval of sex—the question is not whether it is marital or premarital but whether it was based on mutual love. . . .

Our sex differs greatly from simple sex attractions of the ancient people since it presupposes mutual affection and places women in a position equal to men, which was not the case in the times of ancient Eros.

The so-called sexual revolution in the West is weakening family ties, rejecting a number of traditional taboos on sex relations, meaning freedom of sexual intercourse. . . .

Something closer to my own conception of puritanism is implied, I think, in a press account of an article in *Literaturnaya Gazeta* by Professor Viktor N. Kolbanovsky of the Institute of Philosophy in Moscow, accusing the medical and teaching professions in the U.S.S.R. of failing to educate or help out young or old with sexual problems. Despite easily available medical service for everything else, he says, people with such problems have nowhere to turn. Even in medical schools students "are not acquainted with the ABC's of sex." Dr. Kolbanovsky wants more study of Freud, whose teachings have never been popular in the U.S.S.R. Further details suggest strongly that Soviet doctors and teachers foster widespread sexual ignorance with a Victorian flavor, leading to impotency in men and frigidity in women, and to similar problems only too familiar in our own culture. But Soviet youth, although itself straight-laced by our standards in its writings on sex matters, shows signs of breaking with the old traditions. A popular youth magazine, *Yunost*, has started giving advice to the lovelorn. The excessive consumption of vodka is beginning to alarm Soviet police officials. Increasing affluence seems to be infecting teen-agers, if not with VD, then with that other Western disease, an obsession with expensive gadgets and the same soft life of which they accuse the Czechoslovaks, at the expense of a proper interest in ideology and physical work.

The story for Cuba is a little different. Willis P. Butler, the American doctor from Hawaii, who was there for several weeks in 1968, reminds us that the Communist regime had been in existence less than a decade at the time of his visit; so that what progress had been made, allowing for an inevitable lag in the beginning, was very recent indeed.

> Prostitution [he says] has . . . been vastly reduced by elimination of organized gang-style operations, improved economic conditions at the lowest levels, and emigration. Probably 80 per cent of prostitutes over 25 years of age left the country . . . and 80 per cent of the younger ones remained. Almost all of those who stayed, it is claimed, have been rehabilitated, largely in farm work centers and trade training programs. Statistics on venereal disease . . . reflect this improvement in social conditions.

If the spectacularly low gonorrhea rate given us for 1967 is accurate, it is going to be of the greatest interest to watch the trend during coming years, and to see whether the high syphilis rate is also on the way down. Meanwhile it is to be noted that Cuba is a Latin land, and that Roman Catholicism (which traditionally treats sin more leniently than heresy) continues to have an influence there. The Church has begun to show sympathy for the Castro regime to the extent that not so long ago eight bishops in Havana formally petitioned the United States to lift its blockade.

Cuba, at all events, is not a puritan country. Its attitude toward sex seems to differ sharply from that of the U.S.S.R. (as well as of China). As we saw before, Havana, formerly a playground for rich libidinous Americans, has been largely freed from prostitution. An effort is evidently under way to deal with women as the equals of men, something particularly startling for Latin America. Butler comments parenthetically,

> The writer's wife and other female travelers fresh from other Latin American cities observed with some surprise that the Cuban male tends to look a woman "straight in the eyes, as though she were another human being."

In further comments, some of which, in my mind, cry for more clarifying detail, Dr. Butler tells us that the state of personal and social sex problems in Cuba would seem to rate as slightly better than average by middle class U.S. standards. Sex education in high schools is fair, with adequate mannequin demonstrations and physiology lectures. It is an interesting commentary on the common sense attitude toward sex that at least 95 per cent of the extensive artificial insemination work done in cattle is done by young women and teen age girls.

Birth control information and materials (an intrauterine device rather than pills, which were considered unsafe even in 1968) are freely available in hospitals and clinics, but there is no campaign to encourage their use. A sharp rise in the rate of infected abortions from 5.7 per 100,000 live births in 1959 to 30.7 in 1965 was explained "by a high-ranking Ministry official" on the ground that during the first few years of the Castro regime,

> as more and more pimps and profiteers of organized prostitution were detected and emigrated or were imprisoned increasing numbers of their victims came to the attention of authorities, women whose deaths would have passed unrecorded in previous eras.

By 1967 the septic abortion rate had fallen to 7.2. The problem had come under control the year before, with illegal abortion decreasing. Abortion is legal if the attending physician and one consultant certify that the operation is essential to safeguard the life or health of the mother or that a defective baby is probable, the decision being frequently left to medical opinion on the spot. Dr. Butler characterizes this practice as lying between the most restrictive and the most advanced United States practices; but in New York State especially these have advanced still further since his words were written.

Homosexuality, formerly treated with the utmost harshness, is beginning to be handled as a "medical problem," usually with "only violence or seduction of a minor" leading to police interference. The scarcity and high cost of alcohol limit its use; rum is for export, with each Cuban family allowed one bottle a year, at Christmas. Even beer is scarce. Illicit use of drugs is said to be minimal.

A sidelight on medicine in Cuba comes from the *Journal of the American Medical Association* (October 29, 1969) reporting as a news item from Soviet sources that the number of hospital beds has nearly doubled since 1959. There are now 180 hospitals, including 47 in outlying mountain areas, as well as 38 regional clinics and 232 outpatient stations, with over 7000 physicians. Dr. Butler had mentioned earlier that of about 7200 trained doctors before the Revolution, "2500 found the idea of moving to Florida between 1959 and 1965 irresistably attractive." There are still too few doctors in the country and too many in Havana, but

> with 2100 new graduates on deck for the coming three years (50 per cent are women) the picture looks bright.

Another note in the A.M.A. *Journal*, for June 15, 1970, mentions a Cuban report to the WHO that there had been no polio in Cuba since 1964 and that malaria had been completely eradicated there since June, 1967.

When he returned from a visit to North Vietnam in June, 1969, Henrik Beer, Secretary General of the League of Red Cross Societies with headquarters in Geneva, was reported in the press as having spoken highly of doctors and social workers there, and as having said that civilian health had improved despite wartime shortages. He spoke of measures for control of a number of epidemic diseases but said nothing of VD. I wrote him on June 9 and received a courteous reply dated June 24. Noting that he is not a physician but had seen something of VD especially in Poland and Germany after World War II, he offered the opinion, based on what he had seen in North Vietnam, that VD did not seem to be regarded as a major health problem there. According to his "very amateurish" observation, as he characterized it, he had seen no sign of public prostitution in Hanoi or Haiphong, and thought that night life was mostly forbidden and almost entirely absent in the northern cities. This would be in marked contrast to what we have seen reported of

South Vietnam under the influence of the United States (Chapter 21). Ngo Cong Duc, wealthy socialist opposition leader in the National Assembly of the Saigon government and editor of Saigon's principal newspaper, wrote in the *New York Times* of October 24, 1970:

> American political and economic aims have completely altered the nature of Vietnamese society. With their money the Americans are setting communities against one another, and destroying all the traditional spiritual and moral values. The number of prostitutes increases daily. More than 400,000 Vietnamese women are currently engaged in this wretched and humiliating profession.

As for China, if it is true that VD has been largely eliminated there, we have information that may help us understand why. To begin with, Edgar Snow, whom I cited before, gives us these details about the campaign waged against VD by Dr. Hatem or Ma Hai-teh, nicknamed "Shag." The story was told to Snow by one of Dr. Ma's associates, the Chinese doctor, Tai Ch'un-ch'i:

> "Our first goal was to eliminate the chief carriers, the prostitutes," said Shag. "We started off in the Peking-Tientsin area, with a team of about a hundred doctors and assistants. Women party workers first went into the brothels and explained the program. It wasn't hard to win support; most of the girls were slaves who had been sold into the houses. . . . No guilt was attached to anyone and no punishment involved.
>
> "When everything was prepared we closed down every brothel in Peking in one night. The women were taken to hostels specially set up for them, where they were thoroughly examined and treated. Most of the brothel owners and pimps had fled; a lot of them went on to Shanghai and later to Hongkong [*sic*]. Those who remained were rounded up and treated. About 80 per cent of the 70,000 whores in the Peking-Tientsin area were infected with V.D. My own team treated and cured as many as 1,200 cases every two weeks. That's about all it takes with penicillin; ten to fifteen million units does the job. The follow-up work took a lot longer, of course, but that wasn't our responsibility."
>
> "What did happen to all these Suzie Wongs?"
>
> "Some went back to their villages, some to work in factories,

quite a few were young enough to be sent to primary school. We made medical helpers out of the more intelligent. We produced several very able laboratory and research workers from among them. Nobody refers to their past and there's no stigma attached. Many of them have married."

The campaign was soon duplicated in Shanghai, Hankow, Canton and two dozen other cities. In the process medical assistants were trained in the techniques of diagnosing and treating syphilis and gonorrhea, and the anti-V.D. forces quickly expanded.

Additional information comes from sources that are likely to be trustworthy, especially since different observers are in pretty good agreement. For example, a report datelined March 2, 1969, by the Canadian journalist Colin McCullough, tells us that in 1949 there were eight medical schools in all of China, and only 20,000 doctors trained in Western medicine. By 1964 the number of schools had risen to eighty and there were 450,000 doctors, surgeons, dentists, nurses, and other medical personnel. In that year, 1964, there were 90,000 medical students. China continues to make use of partly trained "barefoot doctors" as well as of aspects of traditional or non-Western medicine; but according to this account, which was reprinted in the *New York Times,* they function mainly in the countryside and mainly in emergencies, and "probably confine their attention to relatively simple cases."

The English doctor, J. S. Horn, whose book *Away with All Pests* (1969) I have spoken of before, gives a good deal of space to the means used to extend health care to the farthest reaches of China. Although the number of physicians has been increasing there, it has remained far below the need. The Chinese have sought to meet this problem by giving brief but intensive training to very large numbers of auxiliary medical personnel. Dr. Horn calls these people "peasant doctors." After three years of secondary school they receive six months' training in the elements of medicine and surgery and are then sent back to work among their own people. They provide emergency services and, perhaps more important, they arrange for prompt attention by fully trained doctors when they meet problems that are too much for their small competence. Among Dr. Horn's many details, some that I found most fascinating point to a kind of medical practice oriented primarily toward the patient, whoever or wherever he may be, which is in marked contrast to the medical practice most of us know. Today's scientific medicine, which is undoubtedly far more advanced technically than China's— although Dr. Horn is convincing in assuring us that they are far from primitive—is admitted even by our doctors to be oriented primarily toward research or teaching. As patients, whether in hospital or clinic or the doctor's office, we are seldom encouraged to feel that we are being looked at as anything but problems rather than people. And so it is possible that the Chinese do not have as much as we do of that tendency to run away when the problem is a personal one.

Both Edgar Snow and Felix Greene, American and Canadian observers respectively, whom I have quoted before, speak of the sex practices of the Chinese and the attitudes they reflect. There is, on the one hand, a new equality of women, and on the other, a discouragement of premarital or extramarital sex. The care and education of children are given the highest priority, and in part the freedom of women to compete fully with men in field, office, and profession is compensated for by opportunities for communal care of children. Marriage in China is easy, while divorce, although granted "on demand," seems to be restricted by custom. Young people are encouraged to delay marriage; yet it appears that young marriages are not uncommon. Birth control information and materials are widely and easily available; in the back country, Edgar Snow says, there has been much resistance to their use. An item in the *New York Times* (March 20, 1970) datelined Hong Kong, attributes to visitors from Canton the statement that contraceptive pills, evidently made in China, are being sold there in the towns and villages.

In China as in the Soviet Union, in contrast with the West, there is none of the almost constant sexual stimulation we grow up with and become used to in the theater, in the movies, on television, and in advertising in all its pervading forms. I offer one of many paragraphs from Felix Greene on this subject:

> China is today an intensely, almost compulsively "moral" society. Of the many communes I visited, all except one denied any knowledge of children born out of wedlock. In the one exception, two cases were cited, both involving parents who were under the legal marriage age (twenty for boys and eighteen for girls). Both cases were resolved in the same way: by court orders permitting early marriage, "in the interest of the child."

An anonymous article in the *New York Times Sunday Magazine* for June 1, 1969, written by "a Westerner now resident in Peking," gives some further details. Late marriage is advocated, at the age of twenty-eight to thirty for men and a few years younger for women; but these suggestions are often ignored without penalty. The marriage procedure takes five minutes in the municipal registrar's office and "is very seldom denied to those who wish to avail themselves of it." This observer reports that unmarried young men and women are usually chaste, but when he says that "puritanism is the hallmark of Chinese society" he is using the word in a sense different from ours. He notes that men and women wear identical clothing in winter, and that otherwise women may use a little color but avoid jewelry even on festive occasions, and never use perfume. The press complains of the spreading, presumably Western, disease of "falling in love." According to this same account, however, young couples can be seen together in parks and secluded places; and although there is little ostentatious flirtation, there is much gaiety and liveliness, and little shyness or timidity.

But we need not assume that a state of perfection has been achieved in China, which has had its share of turbulence in recent years. Another *New York Times* news item, datelined Hong Kong, August 22, 1970, offers the information that in Canton, which had become "virtually a vice-free city" during the Communist regime, there has been a return of prostitution since 1966 in the wake of the Cultural Revolution. It appears that city girls who had been sent into the countryside had been coerced into having sexual intercourse with peasant farmers and sometimes forced to marry them. Some of the girls subsequently escaped and returned to the city; but lacking residence permits or ration cards, they turned to prostitution as a means of livelihood. The news item concludes by noting that stringent control measures were being instituted, with emphasis on prevention of marriage without consent. Although punishment is mentioned, it appears to be directed against the men rather than the girls. Chinese "puritanism" does not seem to be based on original sin.

Conclusion

Two claims of VD control have been described in these pages, one in an Alabama prison and one in China. The first is probably acceptable at face value but doesn't help us much. It related only to syphilis, and we could hardly think of applying the methods used to the whole population. The Chinese claim includes both gonorrhea and syphilis and cries for impartial assessment. With more and more countries of the Western bloc establishing diplomatic relations with China it may not be long before we have the truth, whatever it turns out to be. But even if their claim proves true we could hardly follow their example. If both claims are true, they tell us mainly that the problem can be solved. If there are two ways of solving it, there are doubtless more. To know beyond a reasonable doubt that the job has been done is to know that it can be done, and to stimulate us, or even to shame us, into doing it ourselves.

Nobody is closer to the control problem in the United States than the people at the Venereal Disease Branch of the Center for Disease Control (CDC) in Atlanta, part of the U.S. Public Health Service. Having written the preceding chapters of this book, I went to Atlanta and spent a few pleasant hours there with Dr. William J. Brown, chief of the Branch, and some of his lieutenants. The territory is familiar. A few years back I was a grantee of the VD Branch, having been one of many (the list includes some distinguished names) who tried and failed to grow cultures of *Treponema pallidum*. The group was gracious in giving me all I asked for in the way of stimulation toward writing this Conclusion.

All scientists know that face-to-face talk with colleagues generates something more than one can get either from reading or from one's own experience in laboratory and field. The questions I asked in Atlanta were, in the order in which I plan to deal with them, something like this: How did the whole problem stand as of the day of my visit, November 4, 1970? What does the immediate future hold in terms of research developments? More generally, how does it feel to be working on a problem that keeps getting worse, and that is widely thought of as the dirtiest subject of them all? And most important, what is their current opinion on the core question of control?

On the answers to the first two specific questions I can give the information as I got it. But even on these, and especially on the more general matters, I prefer—on my own responsibility, no restrictions having been put upon me—to offer what are in fact my own opinions, influenced by what I was told in Atlanta, but essentially as I had formed them before I went there.

On the current status of VD, I came away with the most recent statistics, which are compiled and issued from that very center; and these I have inserted in their proper places earlier in the book. The new statistics emphasized that gonorrhea is now the paramount VD problem, but that syphilis has moved up from fourth place to third among reportable diseases; that the increase in VD in the last few years has shown up in all age groups and is not primarily in teen-agers or other young people; and perhaps most important, that although there is a lot of VD all across the economic scale, the problem is still, as it has always been, principally among the poor, where it is aggravated if not generated by inadequate clinic facilities and lack of education.

Among pending research of greatest significance perhaps the first item is authoritative support for a prediction I made earlier: that a workable blood test for gonorrhea is likely to be available before very long. Several different methods are being explored in Atlanta under the direction of Dr. Douglas Kellogg, and one or more of them look promising. (Work along these lines is also going forward elsewhere in the world.)

The second item I found more surprising, and I am glad to transmit another optimistic note. The status of a gonorrhea vaccine is better than I had judged it to be from the published record. Not exactly bright yet, but better. The work on a meningogoccus vaccine at Walter Reed is taken very seriously in Atlanta, and the parallel to the gonococcus may be closer than I made it. An important new accomplishment which, perhaps alone among these developments, ought to be published by the time this book appears, is the transmission of gonorrhea to chimpanzees, the first experimental animal other than man. This, combined with intensive studies on gonococcus antigens, will make preliminary testing of vaccines easier than it would have been with only human beings to test them on. Anyway, there is a sharpened focus on the gonorrhea vaccine problem, and there are improved tools for working on it. The brightened prospect is blurred a bit by an emerging complication which might have been predicted: there are antigenic types among gonococci as there are among meningococci and most other bacteria; and it may be necessary to devise and test a separate vaccine for each type.

Vaccine work is going on in other places, too. A WHO report which reached me after I returned from Atlanta gives details of a vaccine actually developed at the Canadian CDC in Ottawa, and tested on fifty-eight human volunteers, most of whom responded by developing antibodies which prevented growth of the gonococcus in tissue culture. The report stresses the obstacles to a clinical trial which will have to be made to find out whether the vaccine can really prevent gonorrhea. Chimpanzees ought to help bridge the gap.

On the syphilis vaccine problem I talked directly with Dr. U. S. G. Kuhn, and got from him principally that he is still plugging away at his studies of pinta in chimpanzees and is anything but despondent about them. Dr. Kuhn also has his eye on the new treponematoses of monkeys and baboons. But the emphasis for vaccine development seems to have shifted somewhat from syphilis to gonorrhea. Gonorrhea lacks the peculiar immunity problem of the treponematoses, and for the present at least there is no threat that a vaccine would interfere with diagnosis of gonorrhea as it probably would with syphilis. This problem may arise if a blood test for gonorrhea comes into use, but it is not likely to be the same as in syphilis; and anyway, as we will see in a moment, means may be in the offing to sidestep this whole problem.

Dr. Leslie G. Norins, the young chief of the VD Research Laboratories, was trained in the flourishing field of immunology, which was born out of bacteriology but has developed its own family of subsciences ranging from the earliest applications of blood grouping and forensic blood tests to auto-immune diseases, organ transplantation, and a whole area of basic chemistry which both explores and uses the increasingly subtle and sensitive ramifications and devices of antigen-antibody reactions. One of the things we have known for some years is that antibodies begin to develop in man and animals within a day or so after the first antigenic stimulus, even though ordinary tests may not show them for three weeks or more. Sensitive methods are available to disclose and measure this early antibody response. The gap between science and its applications shows up in the fact that nobody seems to have thought of applying these relatively old techniques to so mundane and practical a matter as the diagnosis of disease. Dr. Norins is exploring this question.

He thinks it might be feasible to develop diagnostic (blood) tests for syphilis (and for gonorrhea, too) that would reveal incipient disease long before the first symptoms appeared. With such a test early treatment could scotch the disease before it started and obliterate the possibility of contagion. A person who thought he had been exposed to VD could then go for testing two or three days after exposure, before either the disease or most of its associated shame had developed.

Together with this fascinating idea is another: the ramifications of antigen-antibody subtlety are such as to raise the possibility of evading the bugbear that a vaccine would interfere with blood tests, if it can be shown that immunity and diagnosis are or can be based on different antibodies. I would not recommend putting any bets on this idea. But there it is.

How does it feel to be working on what people think of as a dirty subject and one that keeps getting worse? Maybe the question is already answered. The research people in Atlanta have the characteristic enthusiasm of all research people, growing out of the often tacit assumption that the problem can be solved and is worth solving. They are helped rather than hindered by knowing that they are, in Dr. Norins's phrase, "mission-oriented"; they are doing scientific work toward an important practical objective. It is my strong impression that there are not enough of them, and that they don't have the resources they and their problem deserve; but I found among them no hint of the pessimism that seemed to come to me from Dr. Guthe in Geneva. The same was true in Dr. Brown's immediate area. Venereal disease is disease and ought to be dealt with as such; dirtiness is an attribute applied by outsiders, strangers to the problem.

VD people do not forget that syphilis has a proud tradition as a subject of research and a field of medicine and public health. Some of the great names are in this book. When I spoke warmly of Dr. Thomas Parran in Dr. Brown's office I thought I saw his eyes light up. There is something here to counterbalance the low esteem in which VD has been held in other quarters through the ages. But with gonorrhea such low esteem has hardly ever been mitigated. Dr. Kellogg and I had both observed—as what VD person has not?—how the bacterial genus *Neisseria,* which contains as its two disease-producing species *N. meningitidis* and *N. gonorrhoeae,* is customarily treated in medical textbooks and in the lecture hall. It is a little like the traditional horse-and-rabbit stew, made with equal parts, or one horse and one rabbit, the meningococcus being, naturally, the horse. Nobody takes any satisfaction in seeing gonorrhea at the top of the list of reportable diseases; but there is a macabre justice about it, as though the bedraggled low man were way up there now, thumbing his nose at ùs.

And in fact it is gonorrhea that seems to be the main VD problem now. There is something of a consensus that syphilis could be controlled without new techniques, if only there could be more of what there already is. More and better clinics and facilities for diagnosis and treatment, including trained VD personnel; more VD education over the whole range from physicians to schoolchildren; more honest concern with the problem in the highest places; less nonsense about shame and punishment. All of this implies more money for VD control. This is another way of saying what Dr. Willcox said to me in London: we could solve the problem if we really wanted to.

Gonorrhea faces tougher sledding. One of the main resources of the syphilis control program, case finding by cluster testing, had been given up for gonorrhea because of its short incubation period; but efforts are under way to revive it. The two other main difficulties are, of course, the persisting diagnostic problem in women, and penicillin resistance. None of these obstacles is insurmountable; but when they are added to the difficulties gonorrhea shares with syphilis control, they could well account for the different incidence rates and the different emphasis that is coming to be placed on the two diseases. So hopes for control of gonorrhea cling to technical advances, especially to a workable blood test; but obviously also to a vaccine, which might sidestep the other roadblocks if we could get one.

What all this comes down to is that the core problem of VD control, allowing for technical elements with gonorrhea, entails mainly a change of attitude in the right places and the money and means such a change would provide. If the new weapons against gonorrhea now being worked on were available, they might help to change the attitude. But the change of attitude is basic, and it is no small thing.

Assuming that what they say about the Chinese turns out to be true, I suggest a race with them over VD control something like the race we had with the Russians over Sputnik. Let us turn shame back upon ourselves: what a terrible shame VD is to the United States! and get the appropriations rolling, and start keeping score.

NOTES, BIBLIOGRAPHY, AND INDEX

Notes

1. Some Background, and a Look Ahead

5. *"life on man."* In the book with that title by the author (T. Rosebury, *Life on Man.* New York: Viking Press, 1969) I use the phrase to refer to the microbes which live on the skin and all surfaces of healthy people, including the whole alimentary canal.

2. A Few Old Ideas and the Beginnings of Gonorrhea

15. *Astruc,* and Figures 3 and 4. The quack, "Boile" (Boyle), to whom reference begins in the last paragraph of Astruc's page 126, is not to be confused with the great Robert Boyle, who died in 1691. Astruc's author wrote a 34-page book which appeared in Paris in 1726, in which he claimed 92 animalcules as the causes of disease; and he did indeed have a trick microscope with which he perpetrated frauds much as Astruc says. Here, as in many other places, the great Astruc has the facts right enough but goes a little too far in interpreting them. See Bulloch.

4. *Syphilis or the French Disease,* by Fracastor

29. (In the quotation from Fracastor) *the Sickness of Maevius.* Mrs. Wright, the translator, appends a footnote here:

This form is a printer's error for the name of a saint who was associated with syphilis, i.e., Saint Minus, of Neufchatel, whose name is variously spelt in the early literature of syphilis as Meen, Mein, Main, Maenus, Menus, Maevius, Mevius. On a Nürnberg broadsheet is a picture of St. Minus, who had himself had the disease, blessing a sufferer from syphilis. . . . Syphilis was also associated with S. Roch, S. Sementius, and *Job who was thought to have had it.* (See Chapter 13.)

31. *St. Mevius.* See the foregoing note.

Fracastor's poem. Baumgartner and Fulton list complete English translations: by Nahum Tate (1688), reprinted in collections by John Dryden dated 1693, 1716, and 1828; by a surgeon, John Lewis Milton (1884); in prose by Martin (see bibliography); and again by William R. Riddell (1928) and W. Wynne-Finch (1935), as well as a translation into rhymed verse by William van Wyke (1934).

6. Exit Columbus

51. On leprosy in U.S. veterans, see Brubacker.

55. Congenital infection is reviewed by Barrett-Connor. Among rare transplacental bacterial infections, tuberculosis has been mentioned.

61. For references on *alleged syphilitic bones* see, in addition to Hackett, Willcox (1967).

62-63. The two quotations by Symonds are from the *Encyclopedia Brittanica,* 14th edition, article *Renaissance.*

7. Syphilis and the "Treponematoses"

72. On the treponematoses of monkey and baboon, see Sepetijian (b), and Baylet.

74. *250 pirochetes.* Cannefax cites experiments reported in 1956 by Magnuson and others in which eight human volunteers were given graded doses of rabbit-virulent *Treponema pallidum* injected into the skin of the arm. Rabbits were inoculated similarly for comparison. The dose required to infect 50 per cent of the men, calculated statistically, was 57 spirochetes; for the rabbits, 23; the difference was not thought to be significant.

77. For the Oslo study of untreated syphilis, see Clark; Thomas.

79. *A report from Boston.* See Fiumara and Lessell.

8. The Other Theory

88. On the treponematosis of African monkeys see Willcox (1968); Sepetjian (b). On that of the dog-faced baboon, see Baylet.

90. In the paper by Hudson (1963), Linton and Mumford are given as sources.

9. From the Bible to Rabelais

99-100. *Moses had forbidden them.* See, in order for this paragraph, Deut. 4:16; Levit. 26:1; Exod. 34:15; Judges 2:17; Exod. 32:18–25, 35.

The "running issue." See Levit. 15:2, 22:4; Numb. 5:2.

cleanliness. See Levit. 15:4–33.

copulation. See Levit. 15:16–17.

"one that hath the issue." See Levit. 22:4; Numbers 5:2; II Sam. 3:29.

". . . stones . . . broken." See Levit. 21:20.

101. *". . . the daughters of Moab."* See Numb. 25:1; Judges 2:17.

while they were copulating. See Numb. 25:8,9; Psalms 106:28–30.

". . . by lying with him." See Numb. 31:17.

hygiene and disinfection. See Numb. 31:19–24.

102. *the seduction of Bath-sheba.* See II Sam. 11:3, 4; 12:18, 24.

103. The following references to Job apply to the quotation in the sequence given, with the sentences of the paragraphs numbered in parentheses: (1) 16:13. (2) 2:7; 7:5; 10:16; 9:17; 16:14, 16. (3) 19:9; 30:17. (4) 7:7; 17:7; 17:1; 19:17. (5) 6:6; 17:7; 16:8; 19:20; 7:14, 3; 9:18; 30:30, 27; 32:19; 30:18. Paragraph 2, (6) 19:13–17. (7) 42:12–17.

104. *bowing down to images* (in the second quotation from Willcox). See Exod. 20:4, 5.

Miriam's "leprosy." See also Deut. 24:8, 9; Numb. 12:15.

11. From John Donne to Modern Times

123-24. My source for the quotations from John Donne is *The Complete Poetry of John Donne,* edited by John T. Shawcross (New York: Doubleday Anchor Books, 1967). In his footnotes the editor gives Galen's opinion that cocks and lions are vivacious after sexual intercourse; he also translates *makes botches poxe* as "makes syphilis from pustules," *By thee the seely Amorous* as "through perfume [the subject of the poem] the simple lover," and the allusion to quicksilver in various possible terms including treatment of syphilis.

12. VD in the Graphic Arts

133-44. Principal sources for Chapter 12 are Fleming; Knipping and Kenter; Kurth; Pusey; Rousselot; and Timken-Zinkann. The best reproduction I have seen of the Rivera mural, including a large detail in color, is in *Mural Painting of the Mexican Revolution, 1921–1960*, Vebustiano Carranza No. 32, Mexico, 1960. The opinion that Dürer's "The syphilitic" is uninspired (which I share) comes from Timken-Zinkann; doubt as to its authenticity is expressed by Kurth. Timken-Zinkann is also responsible for the opinion that the detail in "The temptation of St. Anthony" by Grünewald may represent syphilis. See also the note to page 29.

142. *a diligent search would be fruitful*. The point is exemplified, some of its difficulties are illustrated, and another item of alleged syphilis in art is turned up, in a recent review which reproduces the item in question. The English literary scholar Peter Quennell (*New York Times Book Review*, October 4, 1970) reviews a retranslation of Lichtenberg's "Commentaries" on Hogarth's *Marriage à la Mode* series of engravings (*Hogarth on High Life*, by A. S. Weinsinger and W. B. Coley, Wesleyan University Press, 1970). Lichtenberg was a German professor of physics; his commentaries were first published beginning in 1784, twenty years after the artist's death. The item is a detail of the last plate, showing a little girl being held up by her nurse to kiss her expiring mother, the Countess. The child is first described as "weak and rickety"; the detail shows her wearing an iron brace on her leg. But Lichtenberg is quoted as calling her a congenital syphilitic because of a black patch on her cheek about the size of the nurse's thumbnail. The reviewer tells us that such patches were often used to hide a syphilitic sore. This intelligence was new to me. I would not otherwise have recognized the lame little girl as syphilitic; and unless Hogarth himself indicated in some way that this was his intention I doubt that anyone else would have known it.

13. The Famous and the Infamous

161-64. The following additional famous persons are known or believed to have had VD: Louis XV of France (1710–1774) is thought to have had syphilis. He was Astruc's patient, but that great doctor is discreet on this point. Other sufferers among public figures during the period were King Christian of Denmark (1749–1808) and the French revolutionist Honoré de Mirabeau (1749–1791). Mirabeau is known to have ruined his health by "wild excesses" and appears to have died of syphilis, thereby perhaps saving his head from the guillotine. Another is Lord Cardigan (1797–1869), who led the disastrous charge of the Light Brigade at Balaklava in 1854, possibly unhinged at the time by reason of a severely painful gonorrhea; but if Lord Tennyson knew of this he kept quiet about it. Continuing down to modern times with political figures, Paul Deschanel, president of the French Republic in 1920, was forced to resign after a few months because of ill health and, according to Dickson Wright, died of syphilis. René Viviani (1863–1925), premier of France in 1914, suffered the same fate according to the same source. Lord Northcliffe (1865–1922), British journalist and famous owner of some of London's great newspapers, is said likewise to have died of general paresis. Alexander Protopopov (1866–1918), according to R. A. Massie in *Nicholas and Alexandria,* probably had tabes.

The list of nonpolitical figures to be added to those in the text is longer and, if anything, even more impressive. It includes the great operatic composer Christoph von Gluck (1714–1787), believed by Dickson Wright to have had general paresis; Lorenzo da Ponte (1749–1838), librettist for some of Mozart's greatest operas, who is known to have had severe secondary syphilis for which he received mercury treatments; the English poet Thomas Chatterton (1752–1770), who contracted syphilis at the age of sixteen and committed suicide two years later; Gaetano Donizetti (1797–1848), composer of operas including *Lucia di Lamermoor,* who died of cerebral syphilis; Robert Schumann (1810–1856), who died of paralysis and insanity thought to have been syphilitic; and William Makepeace Thackeray (1811–1863), who acquired gonorrhea while in Paris and was catheterized for urethral stricture. Dickson Wright, who contributes many of these details, also suggests that Walt Whitman (1819–1892), who is known to have become partially paralyzed in 1873, may have had syphilis.

I have searched for names of other famous Americans, since it is obvious that the list is sadly deficient on this score, but have come up with nothing authoritative. The question ought to be looked into further.

It is known that Charles Baudelaire (1821–1867) had syphilis. He said of himself in a letter, "Étant très jeune, j'ai eu une affection veriolique" (While I was very young I had a syphilitic infection). He died at the age of forty-two with symptoms of neurosyphilis. Gustave Flaubert (1821–1880) had a severe malady which may have been syphilis. Fyodor Dostoyevsky (1821–1881) appears to have had neuro-syphilis. George Meredith (1828–1909) is said by Dickson Wright to have had syphilis for many years, culminating in tabes. The painter Edouard Manet (1832–1883) died with syphilitic paralysis at the age of fifty-two. Alphonse Daudet (1840–1897) described his tabes in a sixty-page book, *La Doulou*. Dickson Wright says his illness was diagnosed by the great doctor Charcot. The composer Hugo Wolf (1860–1903) died in an insane asylum, presumably with syphilis. Henride Monfa, better known as Toulouse-Lautrec (1864–1901), whose more obvious deformity resulted from his having broken both legs while he was a child, admittedly lived "a life of extreme debauchery" in Paris and was ultimately confined in an insane asylum, presumably a syphilitic. Sir Willian Orpen (1878–1931), British portrait and genre painter, is described by Dickson Wright as having brought both gonorrhea and syphilis back from his early Bohemian days in Paris. He was treated for urethral stricture and developed general paresis, which is said to have influenced his later pictures; these have a "modern" character which is of a kind that later came to be attributed to the madness of the world rather than of the painter.

15. VD and Not VD

183. On gonorrhea in children, see Branch; on gonococcal ophthal-mia, see Schofield; J. A. Smith.

184-85. *Granuloma inguinale.* See Goldberg; Hanna.

Lymphogranuloma venereum. Evidence is appearing that the bac-teria-like agents found in LGV form a continuous series with those found in trachoma and other diseases which are certainly not vene-real. The suggestion has been made that the term "LGV" be limited to a clinical condition rather than to a specific microbe. It seems possible that further study may remove LGV from the venereal category to-gether with granuloma. This would leave only three members of the exclusive set. If this should happen, somebody may think of taking a closer look at the third member, chancroid, which, even though we can trace it back to Celsus, is still not well enough understood to let us be complacent about it. On LGV see Abrams; Ford; Schachter.

187. On *Phthirus pubis*, see Fisher; Robertson.

191. *The father on his "cold sores."* See Sheward.

192. On the general question of viruses, cancer, and VD, see Josey; Rawls.

uncircumcised men. This is one of many references to the alleged benefits of circumcision which have been called in question in recent years as, at best, unsupported. E. Noel Preston has reviewed the literature favoring the practice, among which is the suggestion that it may prevent VD as well as cancer of the uterine cervix. Preston argues that circumcision is rarely done for medical reasons (it has been called "ritualistic" surgery), and that, all things considered, its risks, although generally small, may outweigh its benefits.

16. Fruits of the Germ Theory

194. Documentation for Chapter 16 and the following technical chapters has been severely limited to avoid overloading the bibliography. Only a few key references are given, with emphasis on recent ones which give earlier references in their bibliographies. See Alford; Coblenz; Förström; Harris; Kellogg, Lee; Lind; Lochmannová; Mackey; Mamunes; Reyn (1969a); Scotti; Sepetjian (a); Thin.

17. Cure and Curability

214. For the story of Thomas Dover, see Morton (1968).
217. *a German report.* See Schubert.
allergic reactions have never been common. See Idsöe (1968).
222. On the persistence of spirochetes after treatment of late syphilis, in addition to Collart, see Rice; Turner; Yobs.
223. *A group of workers at Johns Hopkins.* See Hardy.
224. For penicillin resistance of gonococci, see Hatos; Maurer; Molin; Reyn (1969b); Schroeter; Willcox (1968b).
225. *penicillin is still . . . the best.* One virtue of penicillin that is sometimes overlooked is that in the dosages now required for treatment of gonorrhea it is also effective against syphilis, which may be present when gonorrhea is first seen but still inapparent because of its longer incubation period. Physicians are being encouraged (in part by drug manufacturers) to use other antibiotics as first choice for gonorrhea, drugs which may have no effect on syphilis. This is hardly an important reason for the recent increase of syphilis, but it may be one among many.

18. The Dimensions of VD

231. *The second study.* See Fleming (1970).
232. *the VD "iceberg."* The emphasis given to this term by Dr.

Brown (1970) is somewhat different and is worth looking at both for this reason and for the contribution his paper makes to this general discussion. Although the title of the paper refers specifically to gonorrhea, the context includes syphilis, and there is little reason to distinguish the two diseases on this basis. Dr. Brown's principal point is that whereas it has been assumed in the past that the submerged part of the "iceberg"—the unseen or unreported cases of VD—tend to be in the middle rather than in the lower class, and white rather than black, several studies made during recent years fail to support this assumption. The hidden portion seems to be similar in composition to the visible portion.

These and other considerations, including the statistics mentioned in the text and those for states given in the note below to pp. 234-35, having the further implication that the bulk of VD, including both syphilis and gonorrhea, and both the visible and invisible portions of the iceberg, is still to be found in the poor of the U.S., especially in industrial areas and in the southern states. The factors of poverty, ignorance, and fear, associated with inadequate or simply unavailable medical facilities and with repellent conditions in the facilities that do exist, emerge as of first importance in the overall pattern of VD control. If this is true, this aspect of the VD control problem deserves much greater emphasis than I have seen given to it anywhere.

thirty years old as I write. We have reason to believe that VD has always been a military problem. Case rates reported for the Prussian army in 1866, during the Austrian war, were as high as 2970 per 100,000 for undifferentiated VD, and as high as 970 for syphilis alone in 1881. The British army at home, in figures considered more reliable, include one rate—for primary and secondary syphilis in 1890—of no less than 10,180, or *10.1 per cent.* A pair of curves comparing the neutral Dutch army with the fighting French during World War I shows a peak above 1000 (per 100,000) for primary syphilis among the latter as compared with some 70 for all early syphilis among the Dutch. Yet syphilis is said to have declined in incidence among the armies of Western countries during the years 1860–1913, even without effective measures for treatment or other means of control.

In the U.S. Army the rates for syphilis per 100,000 during the period 1821–1946 showed peaks roughly coinciding with the Mexican war of 1846 (4620 in 1851), the Civil War (7000 and above in 1861–1866), and an interval between the Spanish-American war and World War I (a peak of 2510 in 1911). The lowest point, 590, appeared in 1941, just before the United States entered World War II.

The earliest figures I know for civilian populations are given in terms of acquired syphilis for two Scandinavian capitals between 1883 and 1942–1945. For each city the earliest figures, for 1883–1885, are the highest: 720 for Copenhagen and 430 for Oslo. The general trend is downward, with peaks in 1886–1900 (490; 410), during World War I in 1911–1919 (550; 350), and during World War II in 1942–1945 (250–290). During the peaceful interval 1933–1939, when the Scandinavian countries were giving the world lessons in VD control, the figures fell to 40 for Copenhagen, 30 for Oslo and 15 for Stockholm. (See Fleming.)

233. *The number of cases* (of gonorrhea). The principal members of the list led by gonorrhea, given for the calendar year 1969 (hence different from those in the text, which are for fiscal 1969 and 1970), are given as total numbers reported in the United States in decreasing order as follows:

gonorrhea	534,872
streptococcal sore throat and scarlet fever	450,008
syphilis	92,162
mumps	90,918
rubella (German measles)	57,686
infectious hepatitis	48,416
tuberculosis	38,650
measles	25,826

(Measles, which had fallen sharply since 1965 after introduction of an effective vaccine, increased in 1970.)

234-35. In fiscal 1969, according to the U.S. Public Health Service, cases of early syphilis came to examination in the following proportions, given as percentages:

	AS VOLUNTEERS	BY BLOOD TESTING	BY CASE TRACING
Primary syphilis	58	11	31
Secondary syphilis	44	23	33
Early latent syphilis (under 1 year)	15	40	45

Rates per 100,000 population for primary and secondary syphilis and for gonorrhea, reported to the U.S. Public Health Service in fiscal 1969 and 1970 by states, are given in the following table:

RATES PER 100,000 POPULATION

	PRIMARY AND SECONDARY SYPHILIS		GONORRHEA	
	1969	1970	1969	1970
U.S. average	9.3	10.0	245.9	285.2
Alabama	10.0	4.9	154.1	196.8
Alaska	2.1	5.2	539.1	888.0
Arizona	12.0	15.4	224.3	230.7
Arkansas	7.0	13.3	305.3	338.8
California	8.8	10.5	410.7	500.3
Colorado	1.9	2.1	147.3	176.9
Connecticut	3.0	4.3	173.2	199.2
Delaware	8.2	17.1	342.7	236.2
Florida	23.6	20.6	263.3	327.9
Georgia	21.8	27.9	500.8	527.6
Hawaii	1.0	1.1	88.1	132.3
Idaho	0.9	0.8	145.8	177.4
Illinois	10.5	10.5	413.2	485.3
Indiana	7.0	9.1	126.7	156.2
Iowa	1.7	1.2	146.2	178.4
Kansas	1.6	3.5	188.0	226.8
Kentucky	4.9	4.5	131.2	135.8
Louisiana	19.8	20.0	219.8	275.1
Maine	0.3	1.5	75.5	96.4
Maryland	12.2	10.8	297.0	353.8
Massachusetts	3.9	4.8	127.3	138.1
Michigan	7.7	6.6	209.3	227.1
Minnesota	1.5	2.5	96.1	107.2
Mississippi	13.9	9.3	258.8	295.8
Missouri	4.1	5.6	284.1	296.3
Montana	1.2	0.4	72.6	76.0
Nebraska	1.6	2.4	162.1	179.7
Nevada	9.5	24.6	300.2	357.3
New Hampshire	1.3	1.0	56.0	64.1
New Jersey	6.9	10.5	125.2	132.6
New Mexico	21.9	20.5	196.8	249.9
New York	15.7	18.8	255.1	271.4
North Carolina	9.2	10.0	244.6	287.7
North Dakota	0.7	2.0	72.1	64.1

	PRIMARY AND SECONDARY SYPHILIS		GONORRHEA	
	1969	1970	1969	1970
Ohio	3.8	3.8	186.0	225.5
Oklahoma	3.2	3.8	176.5	192.2
Oregon	2.1	1.7	218.2	328.0
Pennsylvania	3.4	3.0	137.3	139.5
Rhode Island	3.4	6.7	105.0	93.7
South Carolina	20.3	17.1	365.7	434.3
South Dakota	2.5	4.4	120.7	167.7
Tennessee	7.3	5.7	335.4	373.0
Texas	24.2	23.0	323.6	378.2
Utah	0.8	1.4	99.4	84.1
Vermont	0.2	0.5	85.1	98.4
Virginia	5.8	6.0	271.3	310.3
Washington	1.5	1.7	229.0	250.7
West Virginia	1.1	1.3	78.7	83.7
Wisconsin	0.5	1.7	119.2	158.1
Wyoming	2.2	1.6	51.3	66.2

236. *A Swedish study.* See Gisslèn.

237. *a report from . . . Los Angeles.* See Branch.

239. The papers on Greenland are cited by Willcox (1967).

240. For the two reports on syphilis in the U.S.S.R. see Idsöe (1967); Bohnstedt.

20. After Penicillin: Failure

267. *exposure to VD does not necessarily lead to infection.* Willcox, who has presented some of the material of his long UN paper in two briefer ones (*British Journal of Preventive and Social Medicine* 15:42–47, 1961; and *British Journal of Venereal Diseases* 38:37–42, 1962), reviews the extensive but contradictory data on the effects of medical examination of brothels and other attempts at control of VD among prostitutes or their clients. There are figures available which can be used to support or to undermine any preconception. Nobody doubts that prostitution is important in the dissemination of VD, but it seems virtually impossible to know *how* important it is under any given set of conditions, perhaps excepting such simple ones as certain military situations in which nearly all the VD in the male population

can be traced to female prostitutes. Willcox's papers come closer to a scientific study of this matter than anything else I have seen. His UN paper has 174 references, not all of which deal with prostitution; the bibliography of the UN report as a whole contains 867 items.

Mass eradication of the treponematoses. See Idsöe and Guthe.

270. *by the Atlanta group.* See Schmale.

Studies . . . from Denmark. See Reyn (1969a).

A blood test for the gonococcus. See Norins.

21. The Social Diseases

279. *to limit crews to married couples.* I would not have expected this idea to be original, and since I set it down evidence has turned up that something like it, at least, has been thought of, although not in a context of VD. The *New York Times* for March 12, 1970, had a small item in the business section referring to a ruling by Theodore E. Kheel, acting as arbitrator in a case involving alleged discrimination in the hiring of female seagoing personnel by two United States steamship lines. An official of one of these lines asserted that his company's objection to hiring female seamen was not that they would make for danger to the safety of the vessel in emergencies at sea but rather that Coast Guard regulations requiring private bath and toilet facilities for such women could not be met on freighters.

282. On male prostitutes and homosexuals in relation to VD, see Deisher, Gandy, Neser.

22. The Chance for Vaccines

298. *a group at the Walter Reed . . .* See Artenstein.

301-302. On pinta in chimpanzees, see Kuhn; for some background of syphilis vaccine studies, see Norins.

a separate discussion. See Thatcher.

23. Beyond Technology

308. *laws governing VD.* See Moerloose.

309. *paramedical personnel* ("feldshers"). See Troupin. Other information on VD control in the U.S.S.R., except as noted in the text, is from Willcox (1964).

Conclusion

323. *a vaccine . . . developed . . . in Ottawa.* See Greenberg.

Bibliography

Abrams, A. J. Lymphogranuloma venereum. *Journal of the American Medical Association* 205:199–202, 1968.

Alford, C. A., and others. γ M-fluorescent treponemal antibody in the diagnosis of congenital syphilis. *New England Journal of Medicine* 280:1086–1091, 1969.

Anonymous. *Syphilis, a Symposium.* U.S. Public Health Service Publication No. 1660, 1968.

Artenstein, M. S., and others. Prevention of meningococcal disease by group C polysaccharide vaccine. *New England Journal of Medicine* 282:417–420, 1970.

Astruc, J. *A Treatise of Venereal Disease.* London: Innys, Richardson, Davis, Clarke, Manby and Cox, 1754.

Ball, R. W. Outbreak of infectious syphilis in South Carolina. *Journal of the American Medical Association* 193:13–16, 1965.

Barrett-Connor, E. Infection and pregnancy: a review. *Southern Medical Journal* 62:275–284, 1969.

Bauer, T. J. Half a century of international control of the venereal diseases. *Public Health Reports* 68:779–787, 1953.

Baumgartner, L., and Fulton, J. F. *A Bibliography of the Poem Syphilis Sive Morbus Gallicus by Girolamo Fracastoro of Verona.* New Haven: Yale University Press, 1935.

Baylet, R., and others. Spontaneous treponematosis of the monkey *Papio papio* in Casamance. *WHO/VDT/RES/70.212,* 1970.

Bernfeld, W. K. Iatrogenic venereological complaints. *British Journal of Venereal Diseases* 44:82, 1968.

343

Bittner, J. B., and Horne, G. O. The male gonorrhea "carrier." *Ibid.* 31:155–159, 1955.

Bohnstedt, R. M. (From the dermatological literature of the U.S.S.R.) *Hautarzt* 17:481–484, 1966.

Branch, G., and Paxton, R. A study of gonococcal infections among infants and children. *Public Health Reports* 80:347–352, 1965.

Brown, W. J. Gonorrhoea and the iceberg phenomenon. *British Journal of Venereal Diseases* 46:118–121, 1970.

Brubacker, M. L., and others. Occurrence of leprosy in U.S. veterans after service in endemic areas abroad. *Public Health Reports* 84:1051–1058, 1969.

Bulloch, W. *The History of Bacteriology.* London: Oxford University Press, 1938.

Buret, F. *Syphilis in Ancient and Prehistoric Times,* translated by A. H. Ohmann-Dumesnil. Philadelphia: F. A. Davis Co., 1891 (vol. I); 1895 (vol. II).

Butler, W. P. Cuba's revolutionary medicine. *Ramparts,* May, 1969.

Cannefax G. R. Immunity in syphilis. *British Journal of Venereal Diseases* 41:260–274, 1965.

Clark, E. G., and Danbolt, N. The Oslo study of the natural course of untreated syphilis. *Medical Clinics of North America* 48:613–623, 1964.

Coblenz, D. R., and others. Roentgenographic diagnosis of congenital syphilis in the newborn. *Journal of the American Medical Association* 212:1061–1064, 1970.

Collart, P., and others. Significance of spiral organisms found, after treatment, in late human and experimental syphilis. *British Journal of Venereal Diseases* 40:81–89, 1964.

Collart P., and Dunoyer, F. Résultats d'inoculation aux lapins de biopsies de lésions syphilitiques primo-secondaires prélevées sur des malades non traités. *Annales de Dermatologie et de Syphilographie* 95:285–292, 1968.

Crabtree, E. G., 1934, cited by Buchbinder, L. *Gonococcal infections.* In Gay, F. P., and others. Agents of Disease and Host Resistance, Springfield, Illinois: C. C Thomas, 1935, pp. 575–588.

Curtis, A. C. National survey of venereal disease treatment. *Journal of the American Medical Association* 186:46–49, 1963.

Deisher, R. W., and others. The young male prostitute. *Pediatrics* 43:936–941, 1969.

Deschin, C. S. *The Teenager and VD: A Social Symptom of Our Times.* New York: Richards Rosen Press, 1969.

Downing, J. G. Syphilis in industry. *Journal of the American Medical Association* 158:468–472, 1955.

Farrow, J. *Damien the Leper.* New York: Sheed & Ward, 1937.

Fisher, I., and Morton, R. S. *Phthirus pubis* infestation. *British Journal of Venereal Diseases* 46:326–329, 1970.

Fiumara, N. J., and others. Venereal diseases today. *New England Journal of Medicine* 260:863–868, 1959.

Fiumara, N. J., and Lessell, S. Manifestations of late congenital syphilis. *Archives of Dermatology* 102:78–83, 1970.

Fleming, W. L. Syphilis through the ages. *Medical Clinics of North America* 48:587–612, 1964.

——and others. National survey of venereal disease treated by physicians in 1968. *Journal of the American Medical Association* 211:1827–1830, 1970.

Ford, D. K., and McCandlish, L. Isolation of TRIC agents from the human genital tract. *British Journal of Venereal Diseases* 45:44–46, 1969.

Förström, L., and Lassus, A. The fluorescent treponemal antibody-absorption test (FTA–ABS) in treated latent and late syphilis. *Acta dermato-venereologica* 49:326–331, 1969.

Fracastor, G. *Contagion,* translated by W. C. Wright. New York: G. P. Putnam's Sons, 1930.

Gandy, P., and Deisher, R. W. Young male prostitutes. The physician's role in social rehabilitation. *Journal of the American Medical Association* 212:1661–1666, 1970.

Garson, W., and Barton, G. D. Problems in the diagnosis and treatment of gonorrhea. *Public Health Reports* 75:119–123, 1960.

Gisslén, H., and others. Incidence, age distribution and complications of gonorrhoea in Sweden. *Bulletin of the World Health Organization* 24:367–371, 1961.

Goldberg, J. Studies on granuloma inguinale: V. Isolation of a bacterium resembling *Donovania granulomatis* from the faeces of a patient with granuloma inguinale. *British Journal of Venereal Diseases* 38:99–102, 1962.

——Studies on granuloma inguinale: VII. *Ibid.* 40:140–145, 1964.

Greenberg, L., and others. A gonococcal vaccine for the prevention of gonorrhea. *WHO/VDT/RES/GON/70.42,* 1970.

Greene, F. *China, the Country Americans Are Not Allowed to Know.* New York: Ballantine Books, 1962.

Guthe, T. Failure to control gonorrhoea. *Bulletin of the World Health Organization* 24:297–306, 1961.

Guthe, T., and Grab, B. Surveillance of yaws. WHO/VDT/68.233, 1968.

Guthe, T., and others. Untoward penicillin reactions. *Bulletin of the World Health Organization* 19:427–501, 1956.

Hackett, C. J. On the origin of the human treponematoses. *Ibid.* 29:7–41, 1963.

Hanna, C. B., and Pratt-Thomas, H. R. Extragenital granuloma venereum. *Southern Medical Journal* 41:776–782, 1948.

Hardy, J. B., and others. Failure of penicillin in a newborn with congenital syphilis. *Journal of the American Medical Association* 212:1345–1349, 1970.

Harris, W. D. M. and Andrei, J. Serologic tests for syphilis among narcotic addicts. *New York Journal of Medicine* 67:2967–2974, 1967.

Hatos, G. Treatment of gonorrhoea by penicillin and a renal blocking agent (probenecid). *Medical Journal of Australia* 1:1096–1099, 1970.

Heiser, V. *An American Doctor's Odyssey: Adventures in Forty-Five Countries.* New York: W. W. Norton & Co., 1936.

Holcomb, R. C. The antiquity of congenital syphilis. *Bulletin of the History of Medicine* 10:148–177, 1941.

Horn, J. S. *"Away with All Pests . . ." An English Surgeon in People's China.* London: Paul Hamlyn, 1969.

Hudson, C. L. What the American Medical Association is doing about syphilis. *Medical Clinics of North America* 48:583–585, 1965.

Hudson, E. H. *Treponematosis.* New York: Oxford University Press, 1946.

——— Historical approach to the terminology of syphilis. *Archives of Dermatology* 84:546–562, 1961.

——— Treponematosis and anthropology. *Annals of Internal Medicine* 58:1037–1048, 1963.

Hutfield, D. C. Herpes genitalis. *British Journal of Venereal Diseases* 44:241–250, 1968.

Idsöe, O., and Guthe, T. The rise and fall of the treponematoses. *Ibid.* 43:227–243, 1967.

Idsöe, O., and others. Nature and extent of penicillin side-reactions, with particular reference to fatalities from anaphylactic shock. *Bulletin of the World Health Organization* 38:158–188, 1968.

Josey, W. E., and others. Viral infections of the female genital tract. *New York State Journal of Medicine* 69:1397–1400, 1969.

Kellogg, D. S. The detection of *Treponema pallidum* by a rapid, direct fluorescent antibody darkfield (DFATP) procedure. *WHO/VDT/RES/70.189,* 1970.

—— and Mothershed, S. M. Immunofluorescent detection of *Treponema pallidum. Journal of the American Medical Association* 207:938–941, 1969.

Klein, J. E. Curability of syphilis. *Archives of Dermatology and Syphilology* 33:1055–1059, 1936.

Knipping, H. W., and Kenter, H. *Heilkunst und Kunstwerk. Probleme zwischen Kunst und Medizin aus ärztlicher Sicht.* Stuttgart: Friedrich-Karl Schattauer-Verlag, 1961.

Kuhn, U. S. G., and others. Experimental pinta in the chimpanzee. *Journal of the American Medical Association* 206:829, 1968.

—— Inoculation pinta in chimpanzees. *British Journal of Venereal Diseases* 46:311–312, 1970.

Kurth, W. (editor) *The Complete Woodcuts of Albrecht Dürer.* New York: Dover Publications, 1963.

Lancereaux, E. *A Treatise on Syphilis.* London: New Sydenham Society, 1868.

Lee, L. and Schmale, J. H. Identification of a gonococcal antigen important in the human immune response. *Infection and Immunity* 1:207–208, 1970.

Lind, I. Combined use of fluorescent antibody technique and culture on selective medium for the identification of *Neisseria gonorrhoeae. Acta pathologica et microbiologica scandinavica* 76:279–287, 1969.

Lochmannová, J., and Bartůněk, J. The utility of Reiter's complement fixation test in the prognosis of treated syphilis. *Dermatologica* 139:115–122, 1969.

Mackey, D. M., and others. Specificity of the FTA–ABS test for syphilis. *Journal of the American Medical Association* 207:1683–1685, 1969.

Mamunes, P., and others. Early diagnosis of neonatal syphilis. *American Journal of Diseases of Children* 120:17–21, 1970.

Martin, S. C. *Fracastor's Syphilis, or the French Disease.* Reprinted in Clendening, L. *Source Book of Medical History.* New York: Dover Publications, 1960.

Maurer, L. H. and Schneider, T. J. Gonococcal urethritis in males in Vietnam. *Journal of the American Medical Association* 207:946–948, 1969.

Michelet, J. *Satanism and Witchcraft. A Study in Medieval Superstition*. New York: Citadel Press, 1939.

Miller J. N. Immunity in experimental syphilis. *WHO/VDT /RES/70.195*, 1970.

—— and others. The immunologic response of goats to normal and syphilitic rabbit testicular tissue. *Journal of Immunology* 97:184–188, 1966.

Moerloose, J. de, and Rahm, H. A survey of venereal disease legislation in Europe. *Acta dermato-venereologica* 44:146–163, 1964.

Molin, L. Gonorrhoea in 1968. *Ibid.* 50:157–160, 1970.

Moore, M. Syphilis and public opinion (Spirochaeta pallida, Homo sapiens, and Mrs. Grundy). *Archives of Dermatology and Syphilology* 39:836–845, 1939.

Morton, R. S. *Venereal Diseases*. Baltimore: Penguin Books, 1966.

—— Dr. Thomas ("Quicksilver") Dover, 1660–1742. *British Journal of Venereal Diseases* 44:342–346, 1968.

Neser, W. B., and Parrish, H. M. Importance of homosexuals and bisexuals in the epidemiology of syphilis. *Southern Medical Journal* 62:177–180, 1969.

Nicol, C. S. The recrudescence of venereal diseases. *British Medical Journal* 1:445–447, 1961.

Norins, L. C. Selected aspects of syphilis and gonorrhea research in the United States, 1967. *British Journal of the Venereal Diseases* 44:103–108, 1968.

Ober, W. B. Boswell's Clap. *Journal of the American Medical Association* 212:91–95, 1970.

Osler, W. Fracastorius. In *An Alabama Student and Other Biographical Essays*. New York: Oxford University Press, 1909.

Pariser, H. Infectious syphilis. *Medical Clinics of North America* 48:625–636, 1964.

Parran, T. *Shadow on the Land: Syphilis*. New York: American Social Hygiene Association (Reynal & Hitchcock), 1937.

Partridge E. *Shakespeare's Bawdy*. New York: E. P. Dutton & Co., 1960.

Pereyra, A. J., and Voller, R. L. A graphic guide for clinical management of latent syphilis. *California Medicine* 112:13–18, 1970.

Preston, E. N. Whither the foreskin? A consideration of routine neonatal circumcision. *Journal of the American Medical Association* 213:1853–1859, 1970.

Pusey, W. E. *The History and Epidemiology of Syphilis*. Springfield, Illinois: C. C. Thomas, 1933.

Rawls, W. E., and others. The association of herpesvirus type 2 and carcinoma of the uterine cervix. *American Journal of Epidemiology* 89:547–554, 1969.

Reyn, A. Laboratory diagnosis of gonococcal infections. *Bulletin of the World Health Organization* 32:449–469, 1965.

—— Recent developments in the laboratory diagnosis of gonococcal infections. *Ibid.* 40:245–255, 1969 (a).

—— Antibiotic sensitivity of gonococcal strains isolated in the Southeast Asia and Western Pacific regions in 1961–68. *Ibid.* 40:257–262, 1969 (b).

Rice, N. S. C., and others. Demonstration of treponeme-like forms in cases of treated and untreated late syphilis and of treated early syphilis. *British Journal of Venereal Diseases* 46:1–9, 1970.

Roberts, R. S. The first venereologists. *Ibid.* 45:58–60, 1969.

Robertson, D. H. H., and George, G. Medical and legal problems in the treatment of delinquent girls in Scotland: II. Sexually transmitted disease in girls in custodial institutions. *Ibid.* 46:46–53, 1970.

Robinson, V. *The Story of Medicine.* New York: Tudor Publishing Co., 1931.

Rousselot, J. (editor). *Medicine in Art, a Cultural History.* New York: McGraw-Hill Book Co., 1967.

Schachter, J., and others. Lymphogranuloma venereum: I. Comparison of the Frei test, complement fixation test, and isolation of the agent. *Journal of Infectious Diseases* 120:372–375, 1969.

Schacter J., and Meyer, K. F. Lymphogranuloma venereum: II. Characterization of some recently isolated strains. *Journal of Bacteriology* 99:636–738, 1969.

Schmale, J. D., and others. Observations on the culture diagnosis of gonorrhea in women. *Journal of the American Medical Association* 210:312–314, 1969.

Schofield, C. B. S. The medico-social background to gonococcal ophthalmia neonatorum. *WHO/VDT/69.362,* 1969.

Schroeter, A. L., and Pazin, G. J. Gonorrhea. *Annals of Internal Medicine* 72:553–559, 1970.

Schubert, W. von. Penicillin treatment in neurosyphilis. *Medizinische Klinik* 63:806–810, 1968.

Schwartz, W. F. *Excerpts from Teacher's Handbook on Venereal Disease Education:* Washington, D. C.: National Education Association, 1966.

Scotti, A. T., and others. Syphilis and biologic false positive reactors among leprosy patients. *Archives of Dermatology* 101:328–330, 1970.

Sepetjian, M., and others. Contribution to the study of a specific anti-IgM test in congenital syphilis of the newborn. *WHO/VDT/RES/69.180,* 1969 (a).

—— Contribution à l'étude du tréponème isolé du singe par A. Fribourg-Blanc. *Bulletin of the World Health Organization* 40:141–151, 1969 (b).

Shafer, J. K. Applied epidemiology in venereal disease control. *American Journal of Public Health* 44:355–359, 1954.

Sheward, J. H. Perianal herpes simplex. *Lancet* 1:315–316, 1961.

Sigerist, H. E. *A History of Medicine,* vol. I. New York: Oxford University Press, 1951.

Simpson, R. R. *Shakespeare and Medicine.* Edinburgh: E. & S. Livingstone, 1959.

Smith, J. A. Ophthalmia neonatorum in Glasgow. *Scottish Medical Journal* 14:272–276, 1969.

Smith. W. H. Y., and Hill, T. J. Domestic eradication of syphilis in Alabama. *Journal of the Medical Association of the State of Alabama* 37:1364–1369, 1968.

Snow, E. *The Other Side of the River: Red China Today.* New York: Random House, 1962.

Stevens, K. M., and Hemenway, W. G. Beethoven's deafness. *Journal of the American Medical Association* 213:434–437, 1970.

Thatcher, R. W. The search for a vaccine for syphilis. *British Journal of Venereal Diseases* 45:10–12, 1969.

Thayer, J. D., and Garson, W. *The Gonococcus.* In Dubos, R. J. and Hirsch, J. G., *Bacterial and Mycotic Infections of Man.* Philadelphia: J. B. Lippincott Co., 1965.

Thayer, J. D., and Martin, J. E. Improved medium selective for cultivation of *N. gonorrhoeae* and *N. meningitidis. Public Health Reports* 81:559–562, 1966.

Thayer, J. D., and Moore, M. B. Gonorrhea: present knowledge, research and control efforts. *Medical Clinics of North America* 48:755–765, 1964.

Thin, R. N. T. Immunofluorescent method for diagnosis of gonorrhea in women. *British Journal of Venereal Diseases* 46:27–30, 1970.

Thomas, E. W. *Syphilis: Its Course and Management.* New York: Macmillan, 1949.

Timken-Zinkann, R. F. Some aspects of epidemics and German art about 1500. *Medical History* 13:355–362, 1969.

Troupin, J. L. Medical care and public health in Finland, Soviet Union, Czechoslovakia, Yugoslavia. *American Journal of Public Health* 59:705–710, 1969.

Turner, T. B., and others. Infectivity tests in syphilis. *British Journal of Venereal Diseases* 45:183–196, 1969.

Villon, F. *The Complete Works of François Villon.* (Original and translation by A. Bonner.) New York: Bantam Books, 1960.

—— *The Complete Works of François Villon, Including the Poems Long Attributed to Him.* Translated by J. U. Nicholson. New York: Covici-Friede, 1931.

White, A. D. *A History of the Warfare of Science with Theology in Christendom,* vol. 2. New York: D. Appleton & Co., 1897.

Willcox, R. R. Venereal disease in the Bible. *British Journal of Venereal Diseases* 25:28–33, 1949.

—— The non-venereal treponematoses. *Journal of Obstetrics and Gynaecology of the British Empire* 62:853–862, 1955.

—— Montine vaccinia. *British Journal of Clinical Practice* 11:925, 1957.

—— Prostitution and venereal disease. *International Review of Criminal Policy* (United Nations) 13:67–97, 1958.

—— Influence of penicillin allergic reactions on venereal disease control programs. *British Journal of Venereal Diseases* 40:200–209, 1964.

—— Venereal and skin diseases in the USSR. *WHO Chronicle* 18:48–60, 1964.

—— Perspectives in venereology—1966. *Bulletin of Hygiene* 42:1169–1200, 1967.

—— Perspectives in venereology—1967. *Abstracts on Hygiene* 43:1185–1213, 1968.

—— Problems in the treatment of gonorrhea with particular reference to East Asia. *WHO/VDT/68.353,* 1968.

Wilson, J. F. The nonvenereal diseases of the genitals. *Medical Clinics of North America* 48:787–809, 1964.

Yobs, A. R., and others. Further observations on the persistence of *Treponema pallidum* after treatment in rabbits and humans. *British Journal of Venereal Diseases* 44:116–130, 1968.

Index

77   Oslo study — studied untreated
      patients 28% seemed to totally
      recover.   30 – 40% serious difficult

82   Back Bay   midwestern
       — Maybe

100 –   Deuteronomy quote
   101   Moab
104   Flat nose, barred from temple
        children's teeth

104-5   Chinese

110   *   Shakespeare
117   Ex from Shakespeare